WHEN LIFE
AND
BELIEFS COLLIDE

HOW KNOWING GOD MAKES A DIFFERENCE

CAROLYN CUSTIS JAMES

GRAND RAPIDS, MICHIGAN 49530 USA

ZONDERVAN.COM/
AUTHORTRACKER

 ZONDERVAN®

When Life and Beliefs Collide
Copyright © 2001 by Carolyn C. James

Requests for information should be addressed to:

Zondervan, *Grand Rapids, Michigan* 49530

Library of Congress Cataloging-in-Publication Data

James, Carolyn Custis, 1948 –
    When life and beliefs collide : how knowing God makes a difference /
Carolyn Custis James.
        p.   cm.
    Includes bibliographical references.
    ISBN 978- 0-310-25014-2
    1. Christian women — Religious life. I. Title.
  BV4527 .J353 2001
  248.8'43 — dc21   00-069311

Interior design by Melissa Elenbaas

Printed in the United States of America

---

08 09 10 11 12 13 • 26 25 24 23 22 21 20 19 18 17 16 15 14 13 12

With love to my parents,
Dwight and Lucille Custis,
two of my favorite theologians,
who have loved, supported, and prayed me
through the living and writing of this book

CONTENTS

FOREWORD

A FEW YEARS AGO, MY EDITOR AT ZONDERVAN, JACK KUHATSCHEK, told me, "There's a woman I want you to meet. She's writing a serious and thought-provoking book about women and theology, and I think the two of you will hit it off." He was so right! My heart connected instantly with Carolyn's as I read portions of her manuscript. I was struck by her assertion that all of us—men and women; those who are seminary trained and the people in the pews—are already theologians. The question is, What kind of a theologian are you? And are you a good one?

I thought of all the times my children had peppered me with tough questions when they were small: "Mommy, why is the sky blue? Why did God make ants? Will there be candy in heaven?" And the much tougher questions that came later: "Why doesn't my friend like me anymore? When will I have a boyfriend? Why did God make the world when he knew we would mess it up? Why did Grandpa have to suffer and die? Does God *really* listen when I talk to him?" As a woman, I *did* theology every day! I still do.

This is a concept not to be afraid of but to rejoice in! Far too many women have been steered away from the serious pursuit of deeply knowing God, and our homes, our families, our churches, and even our world are suffering as a result. Without a passionate, knowledgeable relationship with God, our troubles, sorrows, grief, struggles, and disappointments can become unbearable. But knowing God changes everything. Our difficulties don't automatically cease—this is earth, not heaven—but Carolyn skillfully argues that a woman who knows and loves God can become a powerful friend, wife, mother, employee, neighbor, colaborer for the gospel, and ambassador for Jesus Christ.

This book is a call for all Christian women everywhere to come back and sit once again at the feet of Jesus. Read it yourself—then give it to your daughter!

—Kay Warren

PREFACE

AFTER MONTHS OF WORK, THE LAST CHAPTER WAS FINALLY ON ITS way to my editor. But instead of stopping to savor my relief, I tossed my clothes into a suitcase and headed for the Orlando International Airport to catch a plane bound for Oregon. My mother was facing her third major surgery since I started writing, and I wanted to be with her and my dad.

We were barely into her ordeal when my husband phoned from Orlando to tell me the stress test he had just taken had reported an abnormality. The cardiologist was 90 percent certain an artery was blocked and had scheduled him for a heart catheterization. There was a very real prospect of bypass surgery to follow.

There is no way to write a book like this from the safety and serenity of an ivory tower. It takes only a phone call to remind us that we are all in the fray and that trusting God is the hardest thing we will ever do. In these moments of spiritual vertigo, only the vision of God's character has the power to restore a sense of order and help us regain a steady footing. Much as I hope my work will challenge other women (and men) to get serious about their theology, in my heart of hearts, I know I need to know God better too. And so I have written not as one who has everything figured out but as someone who is still learning, still has a long way to go, and who still suffers the same old struggle to trust God in the here and now.

Some have been quick to point out that I am describing a Christian struggle and not a struggle that is unique to women. More than once I have been asked to defend my choice to write a book about the importance of theology for women. "Don't men need to know God just as much as women? Don't they suffer the same tendency to avoid theology as women? Besides, isn't theology for everyone?" The answer, of course, in each case is yes. Certainly the core of what I have written here is not so much about what it means to be a Christian woman as it is about what it means to be a Christian. Theology is not gender specific, and the content of this book applies as much to men as it does to women.

Having said that, I still believe it is crucial to raise the issue directly with women. Many books have been written on the importance of theology to Christians and of the high price we are paying in the church for neglecting it. But for whatever reason— culture, tradition, personality differences, misconceptions, phobia, or plain disinterest—the message seems to bypass a lot of women. The consequences of avoiding theology in my own life have been painful, and I regularly hear from other women that avoiding theology has been costly for them too.

I would hope that rather than dismissing my efforts as superfluous, others will realize the urgency of this message and will write books advocating the importance of theology for men, teenagers, seniors, Generation Xers, singles, athletes, musicians, and any other category of humanity that comes to mind. The issues which I raise in this book are so significant, so pivotal to what it means to be a Christian, so vital to the health of the church, we ought to come at this question from every angle imaginable.

Although writing is a solitary occupation, I have been pleasantly surprised in writing this book to discover I am not alone. Through every chapter, friends have been there for me—cheering me on, making sure I was okay, talking through issues, sharing their own perspectives and ideas, praying and encouraging. It has been a rich experience of how God works through his people to build each other up, and I am deeply grateful for their support.

From the inception of the idea to the completion of the final chapter, an army of women stood with me and, in a very real sense, took ownership of this book. Without their impassioned letters to Zondervan to advocate the need for such a book, there probably would not have been a contract in the first place. Many offered insight and suggestions in the search for an appropriate title. A quartet of women—Susan Anders, Dixie Fraley, Sara Jane Timmerman, and Marcia Yount—read every word the minute it came rolling off my printer and gave me invaluable early feedback. Dayle Seneff organized a lively focus group of women—Laura Grace Alexander, Sharon J. Anderson, Dixie Fraley, Denise Habicht, Marjean Ingram, Jandra Leonard, Becky Martinez, Lori Pedonti, and Crosland Stuart—who read the manuscript and met twice over lunch at the CNL Group headquarters in Orlando to brainstorm ideas and to discuss the complicated issues facing Christian women today and how the book addresses them. Dozens of women shared their stories with me and made sure I wrote with real women and real struggles in mind. Several graciously gave permission for their stories to be included here. To all of these women, I extend my heartfelt thanks.

I cannot imagine what this project would have been like without the constant support of my mother. Not only did she encourage me with her words, she put *my* words to the test as she endured one of the fiercest battles of her life. I cannot imagine a stronger argument for the importance of theology to women than seeing the difference it made for her. Her courage and determination to trust God through one medical setback after another, regardless of whether the pain subsided or persisted, provided powerful evidence that knowing God does indeed make a difference in how we face life's adversities. She has been an inspiration to me, and her influence runs like a deep current through every chapter of this book.

My teenage daughter, Allison, joined in the ups and downs of writing a book, celebrating one moment and lending moral support the next. Things ran smoother at home because she pitched in to help. Her hugs and prayers helped me overcome moments of discouragement. Her support has meant the world to me. But having a daughter helped me remember that it is not enough to write for my own generation. My daughter's generation is already waiting in the wings. Our task is not simply to know God more deeply ourselves but to lead our daughters to pursue a deeper relationship with him too. Allison is reason enough for me to write a book like this.

It may surprise some that a book intended for women should have so many men behind it. But I am deeply indebted to men—five in particular. My dad, a man of the Word and a man of prayer, had enormous influence on this project. Early in my life, his passion for Scripture rubbed off on me and left me with an appetite to study, think, and learn. What a legacy for a father to pass on to his daughter! And I am absolutely convinced a relationship exists between the energy and strength I have found to persevere and the hours he has spent on his knees on my behalf.

Dr. S. Lewis Johnson Jr. was the first person to tell me that I am a theologian and that I need to be a good one. It was a watershed moment in my life, and I will be forever grateful. Theology wasn't cerebral with him, and I had the privilege of seeing him and his wife live out their theology when she was dying of cancer. Even in their suffering, they mentored me and showed me the vital connection between theology and life. It is a lesson I will never forget.

This book would not exist without the support and efforts of two men at Zondervan. Stan Gundry believed in the idea from the start and offered wise counsel along the way to a first-time writer who needed his expertise and godly wisdom. By taking the time to listen, Jack Kuhatschek overcame his initial hesitations and became a self-proclaimed champion for this book. His advocacy was not simply for me but for all Christian women.

Those who know my husband, Frank, will nod with understanding when I say this book could not have been written without his involvement. His passion for the message fueled this project and energized me every step of the way. His love and optimism kept me going through many a rough patch. And who could count the hours we spent batting ideas around and thinking through the issues? His students will know what I mean when I say this is a better book because of his rigorous standards, honest criticism, skillful coaching, and moral support. He is a constant reminder of God's goodness to me, and I am more thankful than I can say that his medical crisis was a false alarm.

Special thanks to Dr. Pamela Reeve, who listened to my ideas and first encouraged me to write; to Carol Arnold, Mike Beates, Steve Brown, Sharon Denney, Mike Horton, and Cristi Mansfield, who went to bat to help me get endorsements; to Mike and Barb Malone, my pastor and his wife, for their thoughtful interaction and support; to my friends at St. Paul's Presbyterian Church who prayed, supported, and always wanted to know how I was progressing; and to Reformed Theological Seminary, Orlando, for encouraging and supporting my work and for the use of library resources for my research.

I am indebted to scholars who reviewed all or part of my work and offered suggestions—Dr. Ellen T. Charry, Dr. Tremper Longman, Dr. Richard Pratt, and Dr. Bruce K. Waltke. Although I accept full responsibility for what I have written, I am grateful for their comments and suggestions.

Above all, I am grateful to God for giving me such an incredible opportunity. Throughout the entire process, many doors have swung open for me, many people have offered support. I know these things would never have happened on their own. My prayer is that he will honor his own name through my work and that his church will grow stronger because of women who seek to know him better.

INTRODUCTION

"No Great Women Theologians"

ONCE IN A WHILE, WORDS SPOKEN IN CASUAL CONVERSATION STICK to you like glue. No matter how hard you try, you can't shake them off. When I was a seminary student, something one of my professors said to me proved to have just that kind of extraordinary sticking power and bothers me to this day.

After generations as an all-male institution, a large evangelical seminary expanded its borders to include women students. Five of us enrolled in the first class. It was a new day for the seminary and for us, but not everyone was comfortable with its dawning. Happily for us, most men carried on with business as usual, some openly expressing the opinion that the change was long overdue. Others seemed hesitant about our presence, and a few stalwarts occasionally lobbed a condescending remark our way. One theology professor, who was not above stirring the pot a little, had an uncanny ability to say things that would shake me up and at the same time challenge me to think. During one conversation, his words hit their mark with unexpected force. With more than a hint of mischief in his eyes, he said, "You know, there have never been any *great* women theologians."

I still wince whenever I recall his words, but for different reasons than I did back then. It was one of those miserable encounters when the right response doesn't come to you until long after the conversation is over. At first the seminary setting distracted me, so that I saw this as a historical issue, one that affected only the very few women in seminaries and religious professions. I knew enough church history to realize there had been few professional theologians before the twentieth century who were women. At least part of the problem was not so much a supposed lack of theological instinct among women as the simple fact that women had not enjoyed the same opportunities as men to pursue theological studies. Having only recently been allowed to attend seminary myself, I saw plenty of irony in his remark. Here, it seemed, was a problem to which this very seminary had contributed for decades.

GETTING TO THE HEART OF THE MATTER

ONLY AFTER MULLING OVER my professor's comment a while longer did I begin to realize the wider implications for all Christian women. The real issue is not primarily one of opportunity for women (although this is surely an issue) but rather that he had defined theology too narrowly. Although this definition served the purpose of rankling me, it also represented a common misunderstanding that removes theology from the heart of life, where it rightfully belongs. In a world of security passwords and childproof lids, theology is one more item that has been put safely out of reach. Theology, most of us would agree, should be left to professionals and experts—those with the credentials and know-how to handle it safely and correctly, who will make sure the rest of us don't get into trouble with it. This thinking reminds me of the reluctance of the Medieval church to allow ordinary people direct access to the Scriptures. Strangely, the difference between the inaccessibility of Scripture then and the inaccessibility of theology in our day is that we condemn the former and heartily endorse the latter, though both are harmful to us. But the more I considered what theology is all about, the more appalling it seemed to keep it under lock and key. Theology, I discovered, is much more accessible than I had thought and is full of everyday practical value. It is really a matter of knowing God, something women have always done and still do today. In time this fuller and indeed better definition would help me see that theology is far more than a professional affair or an abstract system of ideas. Inadvertently, my professor had exposed a problem of enormous seriousness for *all* Christian women, myself included.

Once the initial sting subsided, I might have forgotten the whole episode except for two further developments, which stamped my professor's words indelibly on my mind. The first was my discovery that whether or not we realize it, *all* Christian women are theologians. Since theology is really about knowing God, then anyone who believes anything about God is a theologian of sorts. The second was a growing realization that not only am I a theologian but it truly *does* matter whether I'm a good one. This became painfully clear to me as I began to suffer the consequences of my own neglect of theology, not in the seminary classroom but in my personal life.

When he linked women and theology, my professor started me on a personal journey that would lead me to discover my true heritage as a Christian woman, a heritage of which a whole generation of evangelical women seems unaware and which I believe we desperately need to reclaim. Through a great deal of research, I discovered that the Bible, not to mention church history, records the stories of countless women whose theology led them to make significant contributions at home, in the community, and in the church. Properly defined, the idea of a "woman theologian" is not as revolutionary as it sounds. Indeed, I found that theology lies at the very heart of what it means to be a woman, a discovery that marked a major turning point in my life. Little did I realize on that hot summer afternoon what an enormous favor my theology professor had done for me when he dropped that zinger. As one woman put it, "Metaphorically speaking, men still open doors for women."[1] He had just opened one for me.

This book is the result of the journey that commenced when I walked through that door. I started out in search of great women theologians and ended up discovering I needed to become one myself. It has not been an easy process, for like most worthwhile experiences, it forced me to take an honest look at myself and admit I was far more interested in what God would do for me than I was in knowing him. I have been driven not so much by curiosity and the desire to disprove my professor's assertion (although these motivated me too) as by my need to know God better. The results have been truly eye opening. But before I launch into what I am learning, we need to bring a serious matter into the open.

A SERIOUS DILEMMA FOR WOMEN

MY GREATEST FEAR in writing this book is that many women will read no further than this. I am well aware that by mentioning the word *theology* I have triggered all sorts of negative reactions in some women's minds. Survey any group of Christian women on their favorite topics, and theology, if even mentioned, will rank near the bottom of the list. I could have easily avoided this problem by using less objectionable terminology. But that would be less than honest, and frankly, the women with whom I have discussed my concerns, even those who express the greatest reluctance, appreciate straight talk. They don't wish to be coddled, particularly when it comes to an issue of such gravity to them. However, they also want their valid concerns about theology to be heard.

In my ministry to women, I encounter a wide spectrum of negative attitudes toward theology, from indifference to hostility. A few women here and there may find theology fascinating, may even devote a lot of time to study it, but they are exceptional and, in the opinion of some, a little peculiar. Most women cannot be bothered. As I listen to the reasons behind these negative attitudes, I hear troubling accounts of how theology has been misused in hurtful ways in women's lives. One young wife, whose husband's passion for theology left her out in the cold, pointed to the vast collection of theology books that lined his study and remarked, "These books intimidate me." Another woman lamented the loss of close friendships, casualties of a church fight over some fine point of theology. Others spoke of the arrogance of some self-described theologians and the injuries they inflict with their cavalier assertions. Little wonder women hold negative views of theology and put as much distance as possible between themselves and the dreaded T-word.

But perhaps even more serious an obstacle is the way Christian women have come to view themselves. We have split into two camps—the Marys and the Marthas. These two beloved sisters have unwittingly become a vehicle for categorizing ourselves as either "women who think" or "women who serve." On the one hand, those who call themselves Marthas prefer acts of service to intellectual pursuits. Of a decidedly practical bent, these women care passionately and actively for the needy hurting people around them. They invest time and energy providing invaluable ministry to these pressing and very real needs. They also suspect theology is over their heads and frankly are not all that interested. Marys, on the other hand, are most at home in the world of ideas. They relish an intellectual discussion and the mental challenge of a perplexing argument but feel awkward and out of place in the kitchen.

This distinction is unfortunate, for it leads women to conclude that these two spheres of life are disconnected and incompatible instead of inseparably intertwined and that theology has no part in the living of our lives. We are convinced that deep thinking about God is only for individuals with the disposition and aptitude for it.

This mindset, which is almost second nature to us, is reinforced when theology is presented in ways that strip it of any usefulness or relevance in the real world. Doctrinal statements may keep us orthodox, but they don't seem to matter much when our families are falling apart and we feel hopeless. Women's lives are far too busy, and their problems too serious, to fritter away valuable time on something that is purely academic and offers no relief.

With such formidable obstacles in our path, some might wonder why I would want to tackle writing a book that champions the importance of theology for women. But the seriousness of the matter leaves me little choice. To walk away from the subject without at least trying is to settle for a status quo that ultimately is hurtful to women. Actually, I have been surprised at how quickly these barriers come down when women, even the most stubborn resisters, begin to see how these misunderstandings, distortions, and abuses of theology actually obscure the real danger—the danger that women will neglect theology.

Two things make my task easier and help women overcome their hesitancies and warm to the subject. First, women already are feeling the consequences of their neglect of theology. As a result, they are quite willing to listen when someone talks about something that already troubles them. Second, the biblical evidence for the importance of theology in women's lives is overwhelmingly in my favor.

My own reluctance toward theology quickly evaporated when I felt the impact of my faulty views of God. I may have come at this whole question through the back door, but in hindsight it seems to me that life's struggles are the shortest route to a deep appreciation of our need to know God better.

The encounter with my professor could not have been more timely. I was in the middle of a personal crisis over what God was doing (perhaps *not doing* is more accurate) in my life. My hopes had always been domestic in nature. Yet here I was, single and in seminary, heading for an uncertain future that seemed to be taking me further away from what I wanted most, marriage and motherhood. God's apparent indifference to my disappointment and my prayers caught me by surprise. This was not what I expected, and frankly I found it confusing. At the time, I thought my struggle was over my circumstances when in reality this was a theological struggle, and my theology, which led me to believe God would behave in certain predictable ways, was falling apart.

My ministry to women has brought me into contact with many women whose stories, while different from and often significantly more distressing than mine, invariably led them into the same theological crisis in which they struggled to trust a God they were convinced had betrayed them and let them down. One woman, after a decade of marriage, was devastated to realize she had married an emotionally abusive man just like her father. It was the very thing she had vowed and prayed she would never do. Her words voice the despair so many women are feeling: "How can I ever trust God when he failed me like this?"

Many Christian women are awakening to the bitter reality that their lives have collapsed around them. A failed marriage, the death of a child, financial worries, a self-destructive past, or simply the tedium of a disappointing life has left them wondering where God was when things fell apart. Bewildered and hurt by God's apparent disinterest, they doubt his goodness and love toward them.

For me the turning point came when I realized that my poor theology, my superficial and inaccurate understanding of God, was making things worse instead of bringing the comfort and hope I needed. I did not know God nearly as well as I thought I did. Dr. J. I. Packer stated it more eloquently when he wrote, "Knowing about God is crucially important for the living of our lives. . . . We are cruel to ourselves if we try to live in this world without knowing about the God whose world it is and who runs it. The world becomes a strange, mad, painful place, and life in it a disappointing and unpleasant business, for those who do not know about God. Disregard the study of God, and you sentence yourself to stumble and blunder through life, blindfold, as it were, with no sense of direction and no understanding of what surrounds you. This way you can waste your life and lose your soul."[2]

Since 1993 I have presented this message to a diverse audience of women all over the country. These women represent all ages, life situations, educational, social, and economic backgrounds, and a variety of denominations. Everywhere the response is the same. Women are relieved to be taken seriously and freely admit that their inadequate and faulty views of God exacerbate their problems and make it harder to trust him. When the going gets rough, as it inevitably does, a fluffy spiritual diet simply doesn't sustain them. We all suffer from this. What I and so many others are finding is that a growing understanding of God gives our faith something solid to cling to when life becomes chaotic and nothing seems to make sense.

When I took my search for a great woman theologian to the Bible, I was amazed to find that the Bible presents women as theologians and that there was not merely one but a significant number of great women theologians. These women knew God deeply and drew strength from this knowledge to trust him in their darkest hours and to face life's greatest challenges with extraordinary wisdom and boldness. When I discovered that the Bible views women as theologians, I began to study their lives with renewed interest. The stories of women with whom we are so familiar— Sarah, Hagar, Tamar, Rahab, Ruth, Naomi, Hannah, the Marys of the New Testament, and many, many others—take on deeper meaning when examined in light of how their knowledge of God informed their choices and actions.

ABOUT THIS BOOK

THIS BOOK IS a long overdue call for Christian women to reclaim their theological heritage. We have lived too long with a false dichotomy where we must choose between Mary and Martha. Jesus flatly rejected these categories. He calls us to be a composite of the two: women who take time to know him better and whose theology informs and emboldens their ministries to others.

The purpose of this book is to reunite these two identities and help women begin the process of becoming better theologians. There is no trick to this, no quick and easy method for deepening our relationship with God. It takes time, something in short supply for most women. But anything worthwhile takes time, and what could be more worthwhile than knowing our Creator? My hope is that this book will set a new direction for women and provide us with some useful tools to facilitate a lifetime of deeper spiritual growth.

In part 1 of this book, our journey begins where Mary's began—at the feet of Jesus. Here we will learn with her to listen, to struggle to understand, and to expand our understanding of God's character. Then after taking a closer look at some of the reasons women avoid theology, we will roll up our sleeves and do some theology ourselves by taking up a subject that touches every woman's life. All too often our lives appear to be wildly off course, and we expend considerable time and energy struggling to get back on track or grieving over the futility of even trying. Nothing defeats us more soundly than believing we have missed God's will for our lives and can never recover what we have forfeited through our foolish mistakes, the hurtful actions of others, or simply an unfortunate twist of fate. We will examine how God's sovereignty and Fatherly love change that picture for us. We will ask hard questions, such as, Is God really good? and more to the point, Is he good to *me* in *this* situation?

In part 2 we will join Mary in the trenches, where theology and life collide and real theologians are made. Thinking about God's sovereignty is one thing. Connecting it with a painful personal crisis is quite a different matter. Everything Mary learned from Jesus came under fire when she faced the untimely death of her brother. Her anguish was heightened by her belief that Jesus had let her down. It is in the trenches that we learn it is never enough to know about God in our heads. We must know him in our hearts. That happens when we are forced to trust God in perplexing circumstances. God's sovereignty is far more than a fascinating idea. It is a truth that transforms a woman's life.

In part 3 we will explore how a woman's knowledge of God affects her ministries to others. Mary's theology opened a door for ministry to Christ that she never would have noticed otherwise, and our theology will do the same for us. As our relationship with

God deepens, our closest relationships will be the first to benefit. We will, like Mary, find new ways to minister to those in our families, at work, within the church, and in the wider community.

A WORD TO THE MEN

ALTHOUGH THIS BOOK IS written primarily for women, I hope men will read it too. Women are not the only ones who have problems with theology. Many men experience the same damaging aversion to theology. Others are oblivious to their own incomplete application of theology. They congratulate themselves on their theological expertise when really they distort true theology, injuring themselves and others in the process, because they haven't taken to heart and lived out the truth they affirm. The ability to articulate and debate theological ideas, even from a pulpit, doesn't prove you are a theologian any more than spouting facts about the United States president means you are his personal friend. Real theologians (and history has witnessed plenty of them, both men and women) are those whose hearts are captivated by God himself, who cling to the truth in life, who humbly kneel to adore him, and whose lives are transformed by what they have learned. Theology makes a difference in all of us.

THE LAST WORD

IN AN ARGUMENT NOTHING is sweeter than having the last word. And for me nothing has quite equaled the satisfaction of finding the first of many great women theologians and seeing my professor's bold assertion against women fall apart. Hopefully, by the time you finish reading this book, you will be as convinced as I am that he was sadly mistaken.

Any inclination I might have to gloat is dampened by the sobering thought that while great women theologians have always been around, they could become an endangered species in our generation. My prayer is that God might use this book to dispel our reluctance and stir our hearts to pursue him earnestly. May our generation see a rise in the numbers of great women theologians.

PART ONE

OUR NEED TO KNOW GOD

PART ONE

OUR NEED TO KNOW GOD

1

IN THE SCHOOL OF RABBI JESUS

Mary Learns at Jesus' Feet

LUKE 10:38–42

THE DIFFICULTY THAT CONFRONTED ME FROM THE OUTSET IN MY search to find a great woman theologian was that I wasn't exactly sure what I was looking for. I found myself in the same predicament as people in airports who hold placards bearing the names of individuals they've never met. They scan the sea of faces streaming off the plane, looking for the passenger who with a single look will identify themselves as the owner of the name. In the meantime, expectations run unchecked and hope and dread alternate until one traveler steps forward to end all speculation.

At first I had all sorts of mental images of what a great woman theologian would be like, images drawn from my misconceptions of what it means to be a theologian. For starters, I confined my search to the realm of the professional academic. Undoubtedly, a great woman theologian would be a scholar, intelligent, highly educated, and slightly intimidating with her deep knowledge.

Although she would probably never be shortlisted for the Ten Most Admired Women of the Year award, she would nevertheless be admired—not because women would ever want to be like her but because of her impressive academic pedigree. My hope was that in time, theology, just like other fields now open to women, would see women rise to the top and stand shoulder to shoulder with theological giants like John Calvin and Martin Luther. What I didn't realize was that it had already happened, not just once but countless times, and that far from being nonexistent, great women theologians were actually quite common.

The women I was about to discover would change my view of what it means to be a theologian. Contrary to my expectations, they would not be academics or scholars but ordinary women—wives, mothers, singles, young and old, and from every walk of life. Their legacies are not bound in thick volumes of systematic theologies or hidden in the tattered remains of lecture notes they have left behind but are wrapped in the simple stories of their lives.

These women taught me what *true* theology is all about. They fearlessly employed their minds to pursue a deeper understanding of God's character and ways. The results of their efforts were visible in both the everyday and extraordinary moments of their lives. Their hearts were strong for God, and they drew courage, wisdom, and determination in the face of overwhelming adversity from the certainty that God is on his throne and that he is good. Most of their words have been lost or long forgotten. But among the few that survive are some of the most eloquent and profound statements ever spoken concerning God's unfailing love for his people. Their stories supply convincing evidence that there have always been and still are great women theologians. What is more, these women not only measured up to the high standard set by great male theologians; many times they surpassed it.

But for me one woman stands out from all the rest. I have learned more about what it means to be a theologian from her than from any other theologian, male or female. For those of us who are visual learners, her story is particularly useful because she shows us how theology looks in a woman's life from the earliest stages to the moment when she emerges as a mature theologian. She was a thinking woman, to be sure, who hungered for God and didn't give up even when knowing him wasn't all that easy. The effect of theology on her life raised a stir back then and still has people talking about it today. For me, her story demonstrated, in terms I could understand, how knowing God benefits a woman's life and opened my eyes to new possibilities of ministry. Somehow our need for theology makes more sense when we see the difference it makes for someone else. What is more, the physical presence of Jesus in her story exposes us to his perspective on the subject of women and theology and underscores the seriousness of the matter for all of us. But to be honest, what intrigued me most about her and influenced my preference for her over all the others was the fact that she was not simply one of many great women theologians. As I studied her life to understand what kind of theologian she was, I was stunned and not a little gratified to realize I had not simply discovered yet another great woman theologian. She was, I am firmly convinced, also the *first* great New Testament theologian. We know her as Mary of Bethany.

Mary's Story

NO MATTER HOW MANY times we hear Mary's story, we never seem to tire of it. Its universal appeal to women enables it to withstand the familiarity that causes other stories to wear thin. Even women who do not identify with Mary, feeling more akin to her sister, Martha, are drawn to her and admire her pluck for seizing the opportunity to sit and listen to Jesus. At that one moment in her life, any of us would happily trade places with her. Although she was far from perfect, Mary was a good listener, a thinker, a learner, and above all, a friend of Jesus. We remember her best for skipping out on kitchen duty and getting away with it. We relish the sweet moment of vindication when Jesus refused to send her back to the kitchen, where Martha insisted she belonged. In many ways we are the direct beneficiaries of her actions. When Mary stepped forward to sit at Jesus' feet and later knelt to anoint him, a barrier crumbled, freeing us to join her at his feet to listen and learn without fear of rebuke or the suggestion that we are out of place.

Her story, which gospel writers capture in three emotionally charged scenes, is the stuff of life—high drama in which every episode is marked by controversy centering on the interaction between Jesus and Mary. Each scene works as a stand-alone story—compact, complete, and meaningful. But when I placed the three events side by side and examined them in sequence, a single story emerged, revealing a depth in Mary's relationship to Christ I had never noticed before. Also, I saw striking similarities among the three and a powerful momentum that builds from one episode to the next.

Each time, Mary is at the feet of Jesus: first to listen, learn, and reflect; second, in grief and confusion over her brother's premature death; and in the last, to anoint him for his burial. Always she is in trouble, twice for actions which others judge irresponsible and inappropriate, and once because she is disappointed with Jesus. Although her words are few, she is always thinking. She struggles to understand his teachings and to grasp who he is. She tries to connect the dots between his words and his bewildering actions. Ultimately she searches for ways to live out what she has learned.

Onlookers (her sister, neighbors and friends, and finally Judas and the other disciples) are drawn into the action by their growing sense of disapproval as they observe Jesus and Mary. When they can no longer contain their frustration, they blurt out words of criticism and disappointment aimed primarily at Jesus.

Their words make us uncomfortable, but Jesus remains unflappable. On the surface, he appears to react to the awkward situations their words create instead of initiating the action. But he is fully in charge and carefully employs each situation to help his followers know him better. No one is ever prepared for what Jesus will do. His words and actions invariably inject a surprise element and unsettle onlookers as he staunchly defends Mary's unorthodox actions and releases her brother from the terrible clutches of death.

In every case, Jesus, in his refusal to be governed by onlookers' expectations or limited by their false sense of propriety, steers a firm course in keeping with his mission. With each successive encounter, Jesus draws Mary (and others if they will come) deeper into relationship with himself. In the process, Mary's understanding of Jesus—her theology—is challenged, refined, deepened, and lived out. Her faith grows stronger as she learns more about him. Though Mary's story applies to every Christian, it contains a clear message for women concerning our most pressing need—the need to know God better. Mary's story is the perfect place for us to begin our pursuit of a deeper relationship with God.

JUST A BEGINNER

LUKE GIVES US OUR first glimpse of Mary in the small Judean village of Bethany, where she is at home with her sister, Martha, and their brother, Lazarus. It is a bustling scene. Jesus and his disciples have just arrived in town and received a hearty welcome at the home of the three beloved siblings. Hospitality is the all-consuming order of business, and Martha, along with Mary, has thrown herself into the rare privilege of hosting Jesus and his disciples for a meal. In the face of such a daunting challenge, not even Martha Stewart could outdo her ancient counterpart, who has spared no effort to honor Jesus and ensure his comfort while he remains a guest under her roof. In his coming, Martha sees an extraordinary opportunity to minister to her Lord. Mary sees something quite different.

Somewhere in the flurry of activity, an unexpected change occurs that momentarily escapes Martha's notice. Her dependable assistant quietly retreats from the hubbub of the kitchen and exchanges her apron for the opportunity to hear and learn from Jesus. This is where we find her—listening quietly at his feet, deeply absorbed in thought. The clatter and aromas from the kitchen where her sister is industriously preparing dinner are powerless to distract her from Jesus. Mary is unaware of the gathering storm.

Of the three snapshots we possess of Mary, this is the frame in which most people spot the theologian in her. Here is the quintessential thinking woman. So much is going on inside her head, and after all, isn't that what theology is all about? What we often fail to realize is that if taken alone, this episode leaves a stunted impression of what it means to be a theologian—all head and no heart. Nothing could be further from the truth, as Mary will soon show us. Not a word Jesus speaks will be wasted, but everything she learns will prove useful, indeed indispensable, when the conversation is over and she resumes her ordinary activities. Furthermore, we do Mary a terrible injustice if we conclude she appears as a thinking woman only in this scene. To the contrary, every time she surfaces in the Gospels she is a thinking woman, a true theologian in action.

But she is not a full-fledged theologian here. This encounter with Jesus marks only the beginning. We have caught Mary at the earliest stage of her development, at the moment when she begins to take this relationship seriously and to pursue a greater understanding of Jesus. She will gain much from this first meeting. But she will not reach maturity until she has had plenty of time to wrestle with what she hears now, has put his words to the test through the fires of personal tragedy, and has learned he is worthy of her trust. For now, though, it is enough to lay aside other pressing matters and listen thoughtfully to him.

THEOLOGY IS A RELATIONSHIP

SOME MAY THINK it is going too far to claim Jesus is teaching Mary "theology." Surely nothing quite so dull and heavy as theology is being discussed here. Our mental images of Mary eagerly drinking in every word and seeming to enjoy the process argue against such a notion. Besides, she was just a woman. She would never rise to the level of an apostle or a great teacher, so why on earth would she need theology? To answer this question, we must turn to the central figure in the story.

Although we are not told what Jesus said to Mary, no one mistakes this for ordinary conversation or small talk. Jesus was a rabbi, a religious teacher. Seated at his feet, Mary assumed the posture of a disciple, a student, ready to receive his teachings and to learn. But Jesus was no ordinary rabbi. He was God in the flesh. He embodied the message he presented. He was God's last and best word to the world. When Mary sat down, she came face to face with her Creator, the giver and definer of life, the only true link between God and herself. Apart from Jesus she would never know or understand God, nor could she truly know herself. Furthermore, when we look at other conversations in which Jesus' words are recorded, we quickly discover that Jesus always talked theology. More than anything, he wanted his followers to know his Father, and by far the shortest route to knowing the Father is to know his Son.

Strange as it sounds, Jesus was talking about himself. Jesus was the subject of his teaching. Just as he taught his male disciples, he was teaching Mary who he was, what he had come to do, and about the one who had sent him. She listened, not simply to become informed on the latest hot topics being bandied about Judea but to know Jesus. He already knew her fully, better than she knew herself. This was a golden opportunity for her to know him. Their conversation signaled the beginning of a relationship, which Jesus welcomed and Mary desperately needed. It reminds us of the often forgotten fact that *theology is a relationship*—our relationship with God.

Somewhere along the way, we have forgotten *who* theology is all about. From Mary's vantage point, this was harder to do, for she had a face to associate with the words. It was impossible for her to detach the ideas from the person. For Christians today, it is easier to forget that the focus of all theology is a person. If we are not careful, God can easily become eclipsed by the mountain of ponderous ideas and heady concepts we call theology. Technical definitions, which describe theology as "the study of God,"[1] "the science of God," or the "queen of sciences," can contribute to this problem. Sometimes these lifeless definitions make God seem like information to store in a database or an object to inspect under a microscope. In contrast the picture of theology that Mary and Jesus give us is taken from life itself and reflects the compelling warmth of a relationship.

Interestingly enough, the word often used for theology in the Bible is the relational word *know*. Moses used it to express his longing for an intimate relationship with God when he prayed, "If you are pleased with me, teach me your ways so I may *know* you and continue to find favor with you" (Ex. 33:13, emphasis added). David described the benefits of such a relationship when he sang, "Those who *know* your name [or your character] will trust in you" (Ps. 9:10a, emphasis added). The Hebrew word used in each case is the same word used elsewhere to describe the tender intimate relationship between a husband and wife. For example, Adam was said to *know* his wife Eve, implying both knowledge and intimacy.

Jesus' greatest passion for his followers, both men and women, was that they would enjoy this kind of intimate relationship with God. It is not overstating things to say that Jesus' mission was to make great theologians out of all of us. He stated as much when he said, "I have come that they may have life, and have it to the full" (John 10:10b), for as he later explained, "This is eternal life: *that they may know you,* the only true God, and Jesus Christ, whom you have sent" (John 17:3, emphasis added).

As if this were not enough, the language of relationship permeates theology. Theological words like grace, mercy, faith, love, hope, and joy are essentially relational. Their true meaning cannot be understood outside the context of a personal relationship with God. It is only within this relationship that we discover the ultimate purpose for which we were created, "the meeting and marriage between ourselves and God ... the highest and holiest and happiest hope of the human heart, the thing we were all born hungering for, hunting for, longing for."[2]

A POWERFUL ADVOCATE FOR WOMEN

I OFTEN WONDER HOW Mary managed to get to Jesus. It was no small feat to get out of the kitchen and into the place of a disciple. All sorts of pressures and customs stood in her way. Did he make it easier by inviting her to suspend kitchen duties and come? Or was this an involuntary act on her part, where her curiosity got the best of her and, before she realized what was happening, she had left her work behind and crossed the line? Perhaps it was a self-conscious overt choice that moved her—the stunning moment when she finally tuned in to her heart's hunger to know and listen to Jesus like her brother was so free to do. We do not know what prompted her or what thoughts passed through her head as she moved out of her comfort zone. When we arrive, the deed is done, and we are left to wonder how it had happened.

An Indian woman I met in England gave me a fresh appreciation for what Mary had done. Fatemah and her husband were fundamentalist Muslims who had come to Oxford for his doctoral studies at the university. I soon discovered there were two sides to Fatemah. Around other women, she was lively and outgoing, even something of an extrovert. But in mixed company, she became withdrawn and guarded. There was a physical dimension to her withdrawal. Whenever she stepped outside, even for something so routine as calling her children in from play, she was cloaked from head to toe to shield herself from the improper gaze of masculine eyes. She rearranged their student flat so she and her two small children could remain secluded in the living area whenever her husband hosted other male graduate students and colleagues in a side room. While the men conversed, she was permitted to serve them food and drink in silence but afterward was expected to return promptly to her quarters. She knew her place, and it would have been unthinkably brash and required enormous courage to sit down among the men, if only to listen. She never did.

Mary was different. Her need to know Jesus overcame the knot in her stomach and the paralyzing fear of what others might think or say. She could no longer be satisfied with bits and pieces she overheard as she moved about her duties or with secondhand information pried from her brother and others who knew him personally. She must know Jesus herself.

Happily, Mary's fears were soon forgotten, at least for the moment. To her great relief, no one uttered a word of rebuke or attempted to push her away. Even Jesus, whose reprimand would have pained her most, was neither cold nor dismissive but warmly engaging, suggesting she was not out of place but precisely where she belonged. Luke, the meticulous historian who would be unlikely to overlook a misstep, records the event without a flicker of disapproval as though this was the most natural and proper thing in the world for her to do.

It is a moment of staggering importance for women. No longer relegated to the kitchen, we are encouraged, by none other than Jesus himself, openly and actively to study and learn more about him. The apostle Paul continues the theme when he urges, "A woman *should learn* in quietness and full submission" (1 Tim. 2:11, emphasis added), a clear call for us to follow Mary's bold lead. No less important, Jesus affirms our rightful place among his disciples. Is it any wonder we love to hear Mary's story again and again?

A CALL TO ALL WOMEN

IF THE STORY ENDED HERE, we might easily assume that Jesus had opened the door for Mary and women like her to pursue higher learning, if they have the inclination. A welcome option for women, right? At least for some. But when Martha appears on the scene to challenge her sister's actions, the significance of Jesus' words will move beyond Mary to include her distracted sister as well.

It is ironic that a woman should be the one who finally speaks out against what is happening. In fairness to Martha, we should note she doesn't criticize Mary for learning. Rather she complains that her sister suffers from misplaced priorities and has unfairly left her to prepare the meal by herself. Anyone who has hosted a dinner for prominent guests can understand Martha's irritation. It is unreasonable to think she could pull off this dinner without Mary's help. But with Martha's complaint, the issues become more complicated and women, despite our universal admiration for

Mary, begin polarizing into two groups represented by the divided sisters. Those who share Mary's love of learning applaud her actions and cannot imagine forsaking this newfound privilege to return to the kitchen, while others empathize with Martha's frustration and embrace her commitment to ministry. We are miles apart, guided by our temperaments and inclinations—oil and water, unlike elements that do not mix.

This dichotomy is unacceptable to Jesus, who with a few firm but gentle words bridges the gulf and calls us back to a common purpose. Both groups of women have something important to learn from him here, for both can fall into the trap of divorcing theology from life. Jesus was calling Martha's attention to that mistake. But if Mary thought for a second that he was exempting her from serving or from involving herself in the lives of others, she was sadly mistaken. His words were intended for the women who love theology every bit as much as for those who hate it.

One might expect that because they were discussing his dinner, Jesus would side with Martha. Yet he takes a very different view of the matter. Neither sister could have anticipated his response. Instead of sending Mary scurrying back to the kitchen, Jesus defends her and gently hints that Martha should join her sister and listen to him a while. Dinner can wait. For the moment, neither woman belongs in the kitchen. They have more important concerns to attend.

Jesus was not merely mediating a conflict between sisters. Nor can we reduce this discussion to differences of personality types and temperaments. What is at stake even transcends such vital concerns as female literacy or the place of women among the disciples, which Jesus strongly advocates by his actions here. Something far more serious underlies Jesus' comment. We look at the situation and see only one promising theologian. But Jesus sees two. By defending Mary, Jesus sends both women a clear message ultimately intended for our ears, not that dinner is canceled or that Martha's efforts in the kitchen do not matter but that both women share a profound need to know him better. This need supersedes everything else that demands their attention and carries enormous practical implications, as they would soon discover. More than simply granting women permission to learn as his disciples, Jesus calls Mary, Martha, and the rest of us to make knowing God our highest priority.

This call is in keeping with Jesus' well-established practice of challenging women to think more deeply about God. His ministry to women dispels the notion that women and theology do not mix. He wanted women to know God as well as the men did and took extraordinary measures to ensure that women heard and understood theology. His actions should give us second thoughts when we dismiss theology as irrelevant to and useless in a woman's life. He not only taught where women might conveniently and discreetly overhear; he decisively broke with the conventions of his day that excluded women from receiving instruction on the Law and taught them openly and individually on the same profound matters he taught his male disciples.[3]

When Jesus taught the multitudes, he employed metaphors from a woman's experience to draw their interest. He visited places where women commonly gathered. Beside a well, he engaged the Samaritan woman in serious theological conversation about living water. And here, in the house at Bethany, he spoke at length with Mary, despite her unfinished domestic duties and pressure from her sister. With each new encounter between Jesus and the women of his day, it becomes clearer that "the foundation-stone of Jesus' attitude toward women was his vision of them as *persons* to whom and for whom he had come. He did not perceive them primarily in terms of their sex, age or marital status; he seems to have considered them in terms of their relation (or lack of one) to God."[4]

I find it instructive to probe further and ask *why* Jesus felt so strongly about this. Why did he take such deliberate steps to include women? The simplest answer to the question, one that squares with everything else he did, is that Jesus taught women theology because he knew they needed it.

Mary and Martha would soon discover how utterly practical Jesus was to call them away from everything else to focus their attention on knowing him. In the very near future, two deaths would rock their ordered world and shake them to the core. Their brother, Lazarus, would unexpectedly succumb to an illness after Jesus' shocking failure to arrive in time to help. Shortly afterward Jesus would suffer a brutal death at the hands of his enemies. These deaths would cast a dark shadow over Jesus' character. He knew that a superficial knowledge of him would leave them ill-prepared for such a devastating blast. To stand firm, they needed to know him well.

Interestingly enough, Jesus' concern is similar to the concern we express when we warn our children about strangers. Our intent is to teach children not that all strangers are evil and will harm you but that you cannot trust someone you do not know. We are called to trust a God we cannot see and often do not understand, which is infinitely more difficult to do when we are content with what we already know about him or if our understanding of his character is faulty and superficial. Mary and Martha might forgo the opportunity to become thinking women here in the calm before the storm. But once the crisis hits, there will be no choice.

It is that way for all of us. Whether we think of ourselves as Marys or as Marthas, when some unexpected crisis rips the rug out from under us and sends us sprawling, we all become thinking women. We can't stop thinking. Our brains are flooded with disturbing theological questions that won't leave us alone: Is God good? Does he really care about me? If he does, then why is he allowing this to happen to me? Why won't he do something to make it stop?

All of us have had such thoughts at one time or another. Soon Mary and Martha would have them too. The time they spent learning more about Jesus now would fortify them against the difficult days ahead. Knowledge of his character would place in their hands a reliable compass when the storm hit and life dissolved into a disorienting blur. Nothing would spare them the confusion and anguish of the ordeal that awaited. But they would weather the storm differently if they knew the one who was taking them through it.

OVERCOMING OUR RELUCTANCE

WE FACE THE SAME CHOICE that confronted Martha. We can dismiss the implications of Jesus' words for us, especially when our time is limited and we are juggling so many other demands. Or we can face our need and begin working to know God better. Whatever we decide, we must not forget *who* puts this challenge before us and the depth of his concern. The real choice is not whether we will become thinkers *or* doers. We are called to be both. But we will be better at both if we heed Christ's call to dig deeply into the heart of God. This never means stepping out of life to devote ourselves to something abstract and useless; rather it means to plunge into the very essence of life. We were made for this, and it is only as we grow in our understanding of God that we will satisfy the deepest longings of our hearts and find the meaning we ache for.

But even more, we *need* to know him. Mary and Martha learned the hard way, and we do too. If my own struggles have taught me anything, it is that my greatest need is to know God better, and I am not alone. To be blunt, life is simply too demanding and overwhelming at times to think I can manage without knowing the one who rules the winds and waves that batter my little vessel. We ask too much of ourselves to try to trust a stranger. Neglecting our need to know him better is, as Dr. Packer so wisely warns, "to sentence ourselves to stumble and blunder through life, blindfold, as it were, with no sense of direction and no understanding of what surrounds you."[5] We hurt ourselves if we shrug our shoulders and walk away.

It is time we started. There is much to do and more to learn. Not even a lifetime will be enough to know God completely. But our smallest efforts will be richly rewarded, for "the time it takes to dig deep into the heart of God is often repaid by striking a vein of gold or an oil gusher. The effort is repaid with joy and power beyond all expectation."[6]

If you are dragging your feet or you still shudder at the prospect of doing theology, the next chapter should help. There we will enter into an honest discussion of the serious objections women often raise against theology and why they should not deter us any longer.

2

THE DREADED T-WORD
AND WHY WOMEN AVOID IT

SOME OF THE BEST THEOLOGY LESSONS I EVER HAD CAME FROM A
woman who was dying of breast cancer. She was my mother's life-
long friend, so I heard a lot about this energetic no-nonsense
woman long before I met her. I didn't have an opportunity to
know her myself until I was in my twenties and moved to Texas.
She promised my mom she would keep an eye on me, and true to
her word, as soon as I arrived in town, she took me under her wing
and treated me like a daughter. She was always ready with a listening ear, down-to-earth advice, good food, and lots of fun. It
was wonderful to have a homey place to go for a study break
whenever I felt the inclination. Little did I realize, when I began
to wear a path between my apartment and her house, how much
theology I would learn from her.

This happy arrangement changed abruptly with the ominous
news that her cancer was back. She had already survived a
mastectomy and radiation treatments a few years earlier and, to
everyone's relief, had seemed to win the battle. Now with this new
diagnosis, she entered the final stretch of her race. She would run

the last lap ensconced in an overstuffed red chair whose arms and cushions empathetically sagged and grew worn as the cancer raged on and she neared the finish line. While she sat in that chair, we talked about God—his plan for our lives, his unfailing goodness, the prospects of death, his sovereign right to do as he pleased with her, and her resolve to trust him to the very end. Scholars would label our conversation "theology proper" because it centered on God's character and nature. To me it seemed more like "Life 101," for the same questions about God confronting her under the heading of "cancer" were hitting me in the uncertainties of the single life.

It was my first up-close view of how theology looks in a woman's life, and I could see how it was helping her. From the pulpit, her husband spoke of God's character and ways with a depth and passion that stirred my heart and made me long for more. The rest of the week, I watched her practice what he preached. This wife, grandmother, friend, and cancer patient was also a wonderful theologian. I saw her cling to God when life wasn't going the way she wanted. She didn't sail through her ordeal without flinching. She felt blasted by the pain, the loss, the disappointment of being cut short. The grief of parting with her husband and her children swamped her at times, and it saddened her to know she would miss seeing her grandchildren grow up. Hands that once were never idle, forever flying away on a project for a friend, now grew still and clenched with pain.

Through the worst of her struggle, her theology sustained her. She didn't know how it would all turn out, but she knew the one who was taking her through these rough waters. Her faith held firm because it was buoyed by her knowledge of his character. Sometimes the only thing that kept her from sinking was the certainty that God is good and can be trusted, even when his ways made little sense to her. She knew she could trust him, and she did. It was the last time I would ever wonder if theology is important for women.

In the midst of the crisis, something she said threw me a curve and put me right in the center of the dilemma women face over theology. She told me that in her younger days she had taught numerous women's Bible classes but stopped because she was concerned that some women were beginning to get ahead of their husbands. Ironically, and despite her own well-developed and heavily used theology, she believed a woman with too much knowledge might upset the spiritual balance at home.

This incongruity left me suspended in midair—caught between needing, wanting, and being called to know more about God, and a warning (from someone I respected precisely because of her theology) that getting too serious about theology might not be the best idea for me. I couldn't connect this warning with the powerful scene I was witnessing or with my own growing hunger to know God better. Since then I have heard the same logic voiced in similar warnings and seen it played out in countless decisions women have made to maintain a healthy distance between themselves and theology. I have heard it from institutions, well-known preachers, and Christian leaders (both men and women), as well as from individuals I love and admire and who have my best interests at heart. A glance around Christian circles seems to indicate how well women have heeded these warnings.

When I began working on this book, I had already assembled a list of reasons why women avoid theology—some taken from my own history, some from private conversations with women over the past few years. To round out my list, I conducted an informal survey of a group of women on the internet, asking them about their attitudes toward theology and why they believe so many women are inclined to avoid it. Overnight my in-box was flooded with mail. Clearly I had struck a nerve. Their responses contribute much to what follows.

As we prepare to examine these reasons, let me reiterate that the avoidance of theology is a churchwide problem, affecting men as well as women. Other authors have addressed this issue from a general perspective of the church at large. I am focusing more narrowly on the influences that uniquely affect women.

THEOLOGY IS FOR MEN

ONE OF THE STRONGEST deterrents to women pursuing theology is the belief that theology is for men. Rarely does anyone come right out and say it. It comes across in more subtle ways—in hints that the woman who pursues theology has crossed the line, that women are "not responsible" for such concerns, and even in the suggestion that women may not be equal to the challenge. Women hear it all the time. I heard it in my friend's decision to withdraw from teaching women. It surfaced recently in a young graduate student's encounter with a clerk in a Christian bookstore. When she inquired about theology books, the clerk looked up with surprise and replied, "We have books for *men*." Later when she attempted to make her purchase, he cautioned her that the content of her theology book might be "too deep" for her. In effect he was saying, "Theology is not for women; it's for men." I heard it again when a young man asserted flatly, "It wouldn't be *natural* for a woman to be interested in theology. God didn't wire women that way."

Two ideas seem to bolster the notion that theology is for men and not women. The first is the belief that God did not equip women for theological pursuits. According to this thinking, women are more relational and practical, and their role centers on being a wife and mother rather than on theological reflection. The presupposition is that God designed a world in which womanhood and theology are incompatible. The second is the conviction that deep knowledge conflicts with the biblical idea of wifely submission; a thinking woman will find it difficult to submit to her husband and to church leaders. Consequently, the safest and most sensible path, according to some, is for women to leave theology to the men.

The first idea, that there are limits to what a woman can or should know about God, has a long history, which makes it doubly hard to shake. Evangelical scholars confirm that in ancient synagogues, women were permitted to listen to the exposition of Scripture, but only the men were expected to think and learn.[1] Most first-century rabbis believed teaching women was a ridiculous waste of time and did not hesitate to say as much. Jesus was undoubtedly counteracting this notion when he affirmed the necessity of teaching Mary.

There is an ancient story of a Jewish woman who boldly asked a theological question in the synagogue. The indignant rabbi in charge refused to answer. Instead Rabbi Eliezer replied scornfully, "There is no wisdom in woman except with the distaff [spindle]."[2] In other words, "Stick to your knitting, honey." But the story does not end there. Her question so roused the curiosity of the men that as soon as she was out of earshot, they pressed the rabbi for the answer to her question. This woman's experience illumines for us the attitude that has prevailed and influenced so many of us through the centuries.

Even more disheartening is the tendency of some women to marginalize themselves. Surprisingly, men are not the only ones to advance the idea that theology is inappropriate for women. Women are among the strongest advocates of this view. To such women, theology is just another incomprehensible male obsession like boxing, auto mechanics, and chewing tobacco and seems equally uninteresting and irrelevant in the real world. A young architect, with an eye trained to distinguish the practical from the extraneous, told her Sunday school teacher she thought the class theology textbook would make a good doorstop. To his credit, he did not laugh. But when women believe theology is useless and embrace an exclusively masculine image of theology, the shortage of great women theologians becomes about as disturbing as the absence of female sumo wrestlers. It explains why some women, rather than working through their own theology, have been known to ask their husbands or pastors to *tell* them what they believe.

If we are not careful, we will post a "men only" sign over theology without stopping to realize that what lies beyond is for every Christian. The whole issue comes into focus when we remember that theology is knowing God. This is not a gender issue. It is not a matter of aptitude, instinct, or intelligence. It is about what it means to be a Christian. In one sense, it is fair to say no one—man or woman—is wired to know God. All of us are blinded by our sin, and the task of knowing our Creator dwarfs every Christian's abilities. Yet it is also true that God never leaves us to our own resources. He sent his Son to remove the only real barrier that prevents us from knowing him—our sin—and to help us on our way with a flesh and blood picture of what God is like. His Holy Spirit opens our minds and works in our hearts so we will understand and embrace him.

Oddly enough, the very qualities presumed to weaken our ability to know God can actually help us become better theologians. The theology I heard coming from the red chair was deep and profound, but there was nothing abstract or theoretical about it. She was a thinking woman, but she wasn't simply wrestling with ideas. She was wrestling with God. The struggle centered on her relationship with him. Is he good? Can I trust him with this? You can't get more practical than that. Maybe the fact that so many women have withdrawn from the conversation partially explains why theology has become such a cerebral endeavor in the church. Theology is never an end in itself. We cannot truly understand it until, as Protestant reformer Martin Luther urged, we take it *pro me* (for me). Rather than being detriments, I tend to think our instincts for relationship and practical matters are assets in understanding theology, because they compel us to take our theology to heart— to explore how knowing God makes a difference in our lives.

The second idea which tends to limit theology to men, the perceived conflict between biblical submission and theological pursuits, has led some to conclude that a woman who persists in pursuing theology may, in the long run, diminish her femininity, jeopardize her relationships with men, and upset the balance of things at home and in the church. She may lose respect for her husband and make him feel he is less of a man if she knows as much as or more than he does. Besides this, her knowledge may cause her to become too independent and less inclined to follow her husband's spiritual leadership. In sum, theology in a woman weakens male headship and impairs her ability to be a good wife.

None of these warnings is lost on us. Women care deeply about marriage and the church. Hearing we are about to embark on something that might threaten these two God-given institutions is enough to slow most of us down. A young single friend admitted avoiding theology after her mother cautioned, "Men are not attracted to women who know too much." It is admirable to be sincere about your faith and active at church and in Bible studies. Getting serious about theology is a different matter. Do the latter and you risk sitting home alone on Friday evenings. Little wonder women make themselves scarce when the topic turns to theology.

Men suffer from these fears as well. Consequently many Christian men seek wives who know far less than they do or who have little interest in theology. The assumption is that a woman who knows less will make a better wife. Her ignorance will be an asset to the relationship, or as another woman put it, "The less a woman has in her head, the lighter she is for carrying."[3] This assumption leads women to conclude that the godly thing to do is hold back for his sake. And so the age-old game carries on—a woman keeps herself in check to make a man look good. It happens all the time.

How differently the Bible portrays women. There they are admired for their depth of theological wisdom and their strong convictions. Women in the Bible did not need anyone to carry them. Their theology strengthened them to get under the burden along with the men and contribute in significant ways to the task at hand. Contrary to current fears, these wise women did not demean, weaken, or overthrow the men. They empowered, strengthened, and urged them on to greater faithfulness and were better equipped to do so because of their grasp of God's character and ways. Consider Deborah,[4] who judged Israel and accompanied and encouraged Barak in the heat of battle (Judges 4, 5); Abigail,[5] whose godly intervention saved lives and prevented David from dishonoring God by taking rash and ungodly action (1 Samuel 25); and Ruth,[6] whose boldness mobilized Boaz to go beyond the letter of the law to fulfill its spirit (Ruth 3, 4). These theologically informed women were valued, praised, and pursued for their wisdom.[7]

The ideal woman of Proverbs 31—a great theologian in her own right—is not known for holding back. She freely and joyfully invested all her energies and resources for the good of her husband, her family, and the community, as well as for her own fulfillment. She was a woman of action, whose mind was deeply engaged in the ways of God. "She speaks with wisdom, and faithful instruction is on her tongue" (v. 26). Her husband was the first to benefit. Far from being a threat or a problem, she "brings him good, not harm, all the days of her life" (v. 12). He stood taller in the community because he had such a wife.

The common belief is that biblical submission entails passivity and that therefore a godly wife ought to leave theology to her husband. But such a notion is surely misguided. Christian submission, which finds its ultimate example in Christ, is an act of strength, understanding, and determination. Jesus modeled not a mindless limp compliance but a thoughtful vigorous resolve. His actions did not result from a power struggle with his father but expressed their union. Jesus was not defeated; he was determined to fulfill his father's will: "No one takes [my life] from me, but I lay it down" (John 10:18).

Likewise, the believer's call to submission—in the church, in the home, in the workplace, or to government officials—is never to a blind or unthinking submission. It carries a heavy responsibility to know, approve, and pursue what is pleasing to God. Passivity and ignorance render us incapable of distinguishing when to move forward and when to resist, as Peter and John did when they asserted, "We must obey God rather than men!" (Acts 5:29). Unthinking submission is risky business, both for the one who submits and the one who leads. Such blind submission cost Sapphira her life (Acts 5:1–11).[8] Theology reminds us that God alone is the center of the universe and that we are here for his glory. It gives us a reference point for our decisions and actions and enables us to live out the ancient truth that "two are better than one" (Eccl. 4:9–12). How much better when two minds and hearts are together on the alert, actively engaged in seeking the will of the

Lord and helping each other to understand and do it, than when one faces the challenge alone and must carry (or drag) the other along too.

New Testament writers add much to our discussion. You will find no hint in their writings that when it comes to knowing God, less is better. The apostles encouraged men and women to pursue theology—wholeheartedly, freely, and together. They compared knowing God to milk and meat (1 Peter 2:2; Heb. 5:14)—essential nutrition for every believer—and urged us on to heftier portions (Eph. 1:16–19a, 4:14–15; 2 Peter 1:5–8). According to apostolic thinking, an enlightened mind results in a transformed life (Rom. 12:2). In contrast, the pagan's problems were attributed not simply to dark passions but to darkened minds and ignorance of God (Eph. 4:17–19). Paul's instruction for women to ask questions of their husbands at home (1 Cor. 14:35) was designed not to shut women down but to open up a rich theological conversation at home. You can't read far into the New Testament before you begin to wonder if our modern theological timidity would raise a few apostolic eyebrows.

Far from diminishing her appeal, a woman's interest in theology ought to be the first thing to catch a man's eye. A wife's theology should be what a husband prizes most about her. He may always enjoy her cooking and cherish her gentle ways, but in the intensity of battle, when adversity flattens him or he faces an insurmountable challenge, she is the soldier nearest him, and it is her theology that he will hear. A woman's theology suddenly matters when a man is facing a crisis and she is the only one around to offer encouragement.

So long as we believe that theology is not for us—that it is for men or that we are not wired for it—we will, without the slightest hesitation, settle into complacency. The world will go on spinning and life will carry on as usual if we never give theology another thought. Why bother? But another deterrent leads to something stronger than complacency; it makes us want to run from theology.

THEOLOGY IS BAD FOR THE SOUL

YEARS AGO I MET a woman who is without question what some people would call a Martha. She thrives on giving hospitality and is always thinking up ways to reach out to newcomers and outsiders. First in line when someone ill needs a meal or a friendly visit, she is often at the local nursing home, taking time away from her busy schedule to brighten the lives of elderly women others have forgotten. If you are new to her church, she will be among the first to greet you, and before long, you are sure to put your feet under her dinner table for a meal straight out of *Southern Living*. But her warmth and outgoing demeanor evaporate whenever anyone mentions theology. She pales and beats a hasty retreat. If Sunday school electives include a class on theology, she will choose anything else (even volunteer to work in the nursery) just to stay away.

What drives her fierce aversion is her uneasiness about what theology will do to her. She has seen what it has done to some of her friends. She has watched theology drain their hearts of compassion, gentleness, and a willingness to serve others. She has been hurt by disapproving looks when her own words didn't quite measure up to someone's standard of theological correctness. She has endured sermon after sermon on lofty theological concepts that never seemed to touch down in people's lives. She feels close to God and doesn't want her love for him or her passion for others to shrivel up for the sake of a few oversized religious words. Small wonder this Martha heads for cover whenever the conversation turns to theology. Her impression of theology is a far cry from what I observed as my friend clung to God and reached out to me in her private war against cancer.

Decades earlier and half a world away, a gifted Oxford University student expressed similar concerns when his college chaplain advised him to pursue theological studies. The young scholar (better known to us as Dr. J. I. Packer, one of the strongest advocates for theology today) had seen enough arrogance, rancor, and bickering in theological circles not to want any part of it. "Theology," he argued staunchly, "is bad for one's soul."[9]

Many women share this grim conclusion. Arrogance and pride are the pitfalls that concern us—individuals who know a lot, grow puffed up, and look down their noses at Christians who know less. Most of us have felt humiliated by some theological gaffe we have made or have felt bewildered by someone's technical dissection of some truth we hold dear. Some encounters with theologians— professional or lay, male or female—cannot be brief enough and leave us with a bitter metallic taste in our mouths.

Other times we are troubled when ideas seem more important than people. It is sad enough to observe; it can be excruciating to experience. One woman in an abusive marriage was devastated when church elders seemed more concerned about fine-tuning abstract ideas than in understanding her predicament and protecting her. Instead of offering help and safety, they sent her back into the danger zone to try to be a more submissive wife. Another woman, after nearly two decades of membership in a large metropolitan church, was dismayed to realize that her pastor, a man widely regarded for his theological knowledge, didn't even know her name. How can it be that a person can know God and care so little for his people? Yet instead of intensifying our compassion and involvement in each other's lives, theology seems to create distance, insensitivity, and isolation within the church. It is a tragic distortion of theology.

Sometimes theology drives a wedge into relationships. The woman who marries a self-described theologian can be shattered to realize his books and heady concepts are dearer to him than she is. As the wife of a seminary professor, I have encountered more than one distraught student wife who has discovered theology is her husband's mistress. She returns home after working long hours to support his seminary education and finds him submerged in his books. Like a groundhog about to see his shadow, he surfaces momentarily from behind his computer and pile of beloved books to offer her a disinterested peck before blissfully vanishing once again into his studies. Instead of drawing them together, theology affords him the perfect excuse to be dysfunctional and leaves her feeling abandoned and hurt by his preference for theology over her. Many a seminary student or pastor's wife has been thoroughly soured on theology because of her inability to compete with such a captivating rival.

But to reject theology because others misuse it is to throw out the baby with the bathwater. Looking back over his "dark suspicions" of theology, Dr. Packer now believes he was talking "twaddle." The problem, as he later discovered, was not so much with theology as with the hearts of those who misused it. "But this," he added, "only shows how a good thing can be spoiled." [10]

It also shows how easy it is to pay lip service to ideas. Women do this as readily as men. Ideas can fascinate us without penetrating our hearts and making a difference. Jesus didn't invite Mary into the kind of theology in which she could bring her mind along but leave her heart behind. He had no interest in filling her head, or anyone else's for that matter, with a bunch of amazing facts about himself. So far as Jesus is concerned, mental assent is never enough. He wanted Mary to use her mind, but he also was after her heart, indeed her whole life.

Knowing God is not like sitting on the couch in front of the television, passively absorbing information. We are not spectators but participants in a relationship. As Mary listened to Jesus, she became part of the story too. Over time, she would learn that everything he said about himself and his Father also had to do with her. The process would not produce arrogance in her, for she would learn how far off the mark she was both about him and about herself, and how much she needed him.

Women are wise to be disturbed by some of the actions carried out in the name of theology. We must guard ourselves against a knowledge that fascinates our minds but fails to invade our hearts and stir our love for others. We must use our long-established ability to distinguish the baby from the bathwater, to discard what is worthless and come away with what is precious. Women who embrace theology, instead of walking away when others misuse it, enrich their lives enormously. What is more, these women also benefit the church.

THEOLOGY IS FOR PROFESSIONALS

LAST BUT NOT LEAST, the church has also played a part in discouraging women from getting serious about theology, sometimes in ways that discourage men too. A big problem for both sexes is the assumption that theology is only for professionals and church leaders. One man mused, "How can we tell women theology is important and encourage them to think and, at the same time, deny them access to positions of leadership in which theology is critical?" It is as though some religious glass ceiling makes it pointless for women (or men) to pursue a deeper knowledge of God if they will never be pastors or elders. This leaves the vast majority of Christians without an incentive to know God at the deepest level. Women's ordination may be a much debated subject; the question of a woman's need for theology should never be debated.

However, restricting theology to church leadership also permits the church to turn a blind eye when women get stuck on a milk diet and never advance to solid foods. We would be deeply troubled if our children could digest only milk; no one seems to notice when that's all women can digest. Consequently the church often does not take women's ministries seriously but instead winks knowingly over "women's doings," satisfied if the women are busy with their meetings and activities but taking little or no interest in the content of their gatherings.

Conversely, the thought of women studying theology can cause alarm. The implicit fear, as we have already noted, is that women who get serious about theology will become restless and start an insurrection at home and in the church. And so women are not encouraged to overcome their aversions to theology. One woman even recalled hearing several pastors preach against women studying theology. It is a line of thinking that weakens the overall health of the church and runs counter to our biblical calling as Christians *and* as women. In subsequent chapters we will explore why knowing God is good for women, good for their relationships, and also good for the church. But a few remarks are appropriate here.

Women need theology for themselves. As I have been writing this book, an elderly woman I know has been devastated by the death of her husband and a bitter conflict with his children over his meager estate. Grief and loneliness have swallowed her up. It is hard for her to carry on alone—so many decisions, so many details to attend. Her sense of abandonment is so overwhelming, even small irritations make her crumble. Her eyes are often rimmed in red from hours of crying. As this older woman's life seems to be collapsing, a younger woman is facing the biggest challenge of her educational career as she packs boxes of books and clothes to ship to England, where she will spend the next few years of her life studying for a doctoral degree. For the moment, her elation over being accepted in a doctoral program is overshadowed by the prospects of being an ocean away from family and friends, adjusting to a new culture, and spending hours in solitude to research her thesis. Worry that this time she may have bitten off too much gnaws at her.

Life comes to women in stiff doses. When it does, and we are crushed or shattered or stretched beyond our limits, we need to surround ourselves with good theologians—husbands, pastors, and steadfast friends in fraying red chairs—who will encourage and help us. But at the end of the day, it won't be *their* theology we will lean on, no matter how good it is. We will lean on our own. Adversity and adventures have a way of exposing the state of our theology. We may have heard a lot about God. In the thick of things, we will discover what we really believe about him. We ask too much of ourselves to wade into these deep waters with so little to keep our faith afloat.

Women need theology for each other. Years ago I read an article in a magazine for Christian women that listed ways to cope with depression. One suggestion was to paint your nails. Perhaps a manicure, a trip to the mall, or a good laugh may serve to distract some from their pain for a moment. But in the end this trivializes our problems and leaves us right where we started. If that's the best we can do, we are in a sorry state for sure.

During the past year and a half, doctors performed four major surgeries on my mother. A fifth looms in the near future. Between surgeries she received radiation treatments, battled fierce sciatic pain from the removal of a tumor in her hip, and strained through countless hours of physical therapy to regain the use of her left leg. When the surgeries commenced, a young woman in her church picked up her pen and began writing letters—one a week—filled not with chatty warm thoughts but with rich theology to encourage my mother and herself. I have read some of those letters. They are much needed reminders that although all else may change, God never changes and can be trusted.

Women need theology for their children. Many Christian leaders today would echo John Wesley's words: "I learned more about Christianity from my mother than from all the theologians of England." One of the biggest and most significant tasks facing the church today is to raise the next generation of strong believers. Is there a more pressing task than for us to leave behind an army of theologians—our own daughters and sons—stronger than we proved to be? It is a task to which every woman and man in the church is called and which demands the best from us. Some of the toughest theological questions are asked between supper and bedtime. The most perplexing problems we will ever face come to us from a teenager caught between the allure of the world and the claims of Christ on her heart. Children and young people need adults—parents, friends, and mentors—who have something real to offer them. They don't need just to hear it from us; they need to see it—when we trust God in our own struggles and hold each other up in the rough places.

Women need theology for men. Questions of leadership and teaching aside, women often have unique opportunities to minister to the deepest needs of men. Have you ever noticed that almost every man in a position of leadership in the church returns home, discouraged and frustrated after hours of wrestling with church problems, to a woman? A wife knows better than anyone the depth and intensity of her husband's struggles. If her theology is weak or superficial, she will be ill equipped to come alongside with strength, encouragement, and godly counsel that she alone can give. One Christian leader stopped discussing his problems with his wife because it was too upsetting for her. Instead of getting under the burden with him, she would fall to pieces. Her weak theology left her defeated and ill equipped to stand with him when he needed her support.

My father, who has been a pastor for over fifty years, identifies a woman as one of the greatest influences on his ministry. Edith Nanz Willies was an elderly widow when he first met her. She was retired from foreign missionary activity but vigorous in ministry to anyone who got near her. She was also a great theologian; as he often says, "She knew God and his ways." Her theology gave her the rare opportunity of pastoring the pastor. He will never forget the fresh strength and hope in God that pulsed through him when she entered into his struggles and spoke words of truth to him.

Well-known Christian author and speaker Jerry Bridges calls Grace Peterson his "Moses on the top of the hill" and draws courage to persevere in his work from her faithful prayers and words of encouragement. Far from being detriments or threats, women with good theology enrich men's lives and become their most valued fellow soldiers.

Women need theology for the church. By likening the church to a physical body, the apostle Paul shows the folly of neglecting theology. Weakness in any part of the body, no matter how small or insignificant, is a burden to the whole. "If one part suffers, every part suffers with it" (1 Cor. 12:26). Just think how self-absorbed we can be over flabby stomach muscles, the need for reading glasses, thinning hair, or a sore toe—nothing life threatening, but serious matters when they affect your body. Yet in the church, we do not simply tolerate weakness; we actually promote it. The consequences have been devastating. Atrophy and malnutrition are rampant in the body of Christ, and we have grown comfortable with them.

God calls women, along with men, to be runners (Heb. 12:1–2), warriors (Eph. 6:10–18), ambassadors (2 Cor. 5:20), body builders (Eph. 4:16), teachers, and encouragers (Col. 3:16; Heb. 3:13; 12:12–13). These callings stand in hopeless conflict with so-called feminine virtues of ignorance, passivity, and neediness. Each demands high levels of strength, courage, and activity—impossible for the spiritually malnourished.

When it comes to helping women become better theologians, the church should be first in line. The church is not threatened if we do. It is endangered if we don't. Where there is weakness in the church, we are all vulnerable. When women are not included in the conversation, there are blind spots in the church's ministry— overlooked needs and issues, places where our theology is underdeveloped and detached. In Christ's body, every member needs all the others—not simply to be there but to contribute.

THEOLOGY IN A DRESS

NEARLY TWO MILLENNIA AGO, a woman shouldered her water jug, took a deep breath, and stepped cautiously out of the shadows of her doorway and into the bright light of the street.[11] It was midday, and she had timed her errand carefully to avoid the piercing eyes and cruel tongues of her neighbors, who had been out and about earlier. A Samaritan, she had suffered the scorn and derision of Jewish citizens who abhorred their "half-breed" cousins. Her personal life, a subject of unspeakable pain to her, was tabloid fodder for her neighbors. The saga of her five failed marriages had long been public knowledge in her village. Her longings for love and relationship held her captive and led her to form yet another illicit relationship that still had people talking. And so she commenced her solitary journey to the well at a time she was sure no one else would be there.

By the time she saw him, it was too late to turn back. The stranger sitting beside the well represented her worst fears: he was Jewish, he was a man, and he was in her path. Instinct told her she was about to suffer the very abuse she had tried so hard to avoid. Imagine her astonishment when, instead of spewing words of derision and bigotry, Jesus began to talk theology.

This was not the village gossip normally overheard at the well. Any passerby would have thought it an odd and abstract conversation. It was not. Jesus knew her heart and spoke to her deepest needs—for forgiveness, for love, and to belong—with an understanding and power that caught her by surprise. He gave her lessons in grace by offering friendship when she expected humiliation, ridicule, and scorn. His strange comments about living water raised her hopes for an end to these secretive treks to the well, then turned her thoughts to the deeper thirst that was driving her desperate choices and destroying her life. At length they spoke of modes and places of worship, and she learned to her amazement that there was a place for her among the Father's worshipers. Jesus spoke with unsettling awareness of the intimacies of her life. His omniscience (complete knowledge) assured her that no new revelations about her private life would ever change his mind about her. He already knew all. By the time the conversation was over, she was a different woman—not covered with shame but dressed in her theology. The change in her led to changes in her actions. Without a moment's hesitation, she left her empty water jug behind and ran to seek the neighbors she had been avoiding. She wanted them to know him and taste the water that had satisfied her. In the end, her efforts would bring revival to her town. In one brief conversation, Jesus said it all: Theology is for women. It is practical. It nurtures, transforms, and shapes a woman's life and her ministry to others.

Ellen Charry, wife, mother, and professor of systematic theology at Princeton Theological Seminary, used similar language to describe her first moments as a theologian. "I lifted my arms up and I put [theology] over me like a dress. I tried it on myself. It wasn't just words. I tried it on like a dress and I just fell over." For her, theology was that personal, that feminine, that transforming, that everyday.

My views of theology began to change when someone took the time to tell me I was a theologian. I'm sure I never would have thought of it on my own. But in reality, *theologian* is just another word for Christian. It sounded radical at the time. I have heard it so many times since, I have stopped puzzling over it. Now I'm more concerned about what kind of theologian I am becoming.

The value of theology for women is growing clearer all the time. Women are tired of "stumbling and blundering" and riding an emotional roller coaster. We want to know the one who made us, who defines who we are and how we should live, and who holds our lives in the palms of his hands. We are ready to lift our arms, put on our theology, and wear it into the trenches where we need it most—where tight schedules, traffic congestion, runny noses and dirty knees, difficult relationships, bad news, discouragement, fatigue, and sagging red chairs throw us off balance and expose our need for God. Our goal is to bring knowing God out of the ivory tower and into the ordinary moments of our lives.

3

COLLIDING WITH GOD

IT WAS A SUMMER DAY TO MAKE NORTHWESTERNERS FORGET THE endless months of winter rain and inspire beach-bound Californians to migrate north. When sunny skies and cool breezes coincide with the weekend, you don't need any further excuse to abandon yard work and household chores to head for the country, the berry fields, the mountains, and the rivers. On this particular day, one of my former high school friends and her husband packed a picnic lunch, scooped up their one-year-old son, and headed for Sandy River Park in Oregon, along with another young couple. They had every expectation of a day filled with fresh air, relaxed fun, and pleasure together. No one dreamed that a day that began with such promise would end in tragedy.

Sometime after the couples' arrival, the two men went wading with the baby. Meanwhile the wives finished setting out the food for lunch, glancing from time to time at the happy scene in the river. The water wasn't all that deep, so there was no cause for concern. Everything seemed picture perfect until my friend's husband, who was holding the baby, stepped into a hole in the riverbed and suddenly lost his footing. As he fell, he tried to spare the baby from a sudden dunking by pushing him toward his friend, who, in the confusion of the moment, missed. And my horrified friend watched helplessly from shore as her baby vanished into the swift waters of the river.

It took rescue teams twenty-four hours to recover the baby's body. But there would be no recovery for the young mother who lost her baby that day. In one shattering instant, her life was changed forever and she entered the darkest struggle of her life.

Moments like this bring out the theologian in all of us. Regardless of our opinion of theology or how carefully we try to avoid it, when we slam into it as my friend did that summer, there's no escape. The moment the word *why* crosses our lips, we are doing theology. Although none of us were there the day of the accident, we know precisely what questions went charging through my friend's mind the instant the enormity of her loss began to sink in. We know because we have asked the same questions about our own circumstances. No matter what went wrong or how others may have contributed to our suffering, ultimately our struggles lead to God's doorstep.

Giving Ourselves Permission to Ask Hard Questions about God

We take a crucial step toward becoming better theologians when we give ourselves permission to ask the hard questions, such as my friend's agonized, "Where was God when my baby drowned?" And Joni Eareckson Tada's pointed, "Do you think God had anything to do with my breaking my neck?"[1] And our own, "Why won't God step in and do something?" These are theological questions. Tribulation, pain, and anger have a way of jarring us out of polite religious conversation with God and our habit of handing him his daily to-do list. Rabbi Kushner's questions were driven by his anguish over his son's terrible death and the sufferings he witnessed among his congregants.[2] He wanted to know how God could be both powerful and good at the same time. Our questions draw us out of ourselves, beyond our circumstances and into serious dialogue with God. Some of the most intense and productive exchanges between God and his people occur in moments when we are most bewildered by him. An honest reading of the Bible uncovers plenty of anger and frustration. Read the Psalms if you want a taste of it. "How long, O LORD? Will you forget me forever? How long will you hide your face from me? How long must I wrestle with my thoughts and every day have sorrow in my heart?" (Ps. 13:1–2). Like the psalmist, we are frustrated by our lack of control over our lives and reluctant to trust a God who does not comply with our desires.[3] In every case, for the psalmist and for us, anger is a symptom not of how wrong God has gotten things but of our need to know him better.

Every woman has her story. Some of us, like this grieving mother, have been hit all at once—a late night phone call bringing unwanted news, a dreaded diagnosis, the resurfacing of a carefully suppressed memory, deaths, accidents, failures, things broken that can never be fixed, losses we will never recover. I listened over coffee as a woman in her late thirties spilled out her heartache over a last-minute broken engagement. She was in the midst of canceling wedding arrangements and explaining to friends and family that the marriage was off. After our conversation, she headed home to box up the wedding dress she had dreamed of wearing and stuff it, along with her heart, up on the closet shelf. A young college graduate fought a grueling battle with cancer. Medical treatments saved her life but destroyed her hopes of ever bearing children. Another woman's world was shattered, along with her tidy ideas of God, when her grandparents were brutally murdered. Most of us are familiar with Joni's story and how a diving accident in 1967 left her paralyzed in body but invigorated in mind and heart as she wrestled to reconcile her devastating tragedy with a loving and good God.[4] Sooner or later, one way or another, theology finds us. Few of us get through life without colliding with it.

Not every woman's story makes the headlines. Some of us take a slower route into theology, but we get there just the same. Cyclical disappointments of infertility, loneliness (both inside and outside of marriage), a life that always seems to fall short of expectations, and a host of everyday pressures join forces, inching us to the edge where we begin to wonder about God.

While my friend was reeling from the initial shock of her loss and wrestling with what it implied about God, similar questions surfaced in my life under different circumstances. My ideas of God began to unravel during a decade-long stretch of singleness, when I ached for guidance and a sense of direction. Yet year after year dragged by without a clue as to where I was headed. The same questions returned with increasing frequency in the early years of my marriage, when my plans to quit work, put down roots, and start a family were thwarted by a series of career changes for both of us, nine moves over five states and two continents, and a battery of medical problems that landed me on the operating table more times than I care to remember. No matter how much prayer and personal diligence or how many convincing arguments I brought to the table, God could not be persuaded to advance my plans.

TAKING A CLOSER LOOK AT GOD

THE STRUGGLES of a woman's life inevitably lead us to take a closer look at God. Certainly my struggles did. I was already out of seminary and working on staff at a church in Texas when I first began to realize my theology was lacking. The symptoms were hard to ignore. I felt defeated and dragged down. My life was at a standstill, and there was no sign of change on the horizon. Not only did my theology undermine my ability to deal with what was happening to me, it led to serious failure in my relationships with others. Instead of going to my grieving friend when I first heard of her baby's death, to enter into her grief and struggle to trust God *with* her, I stayed away. My confusion over God's silence in my life convinced me I had nothing to say.

I knew basic ideas about God, but I had never concentrated my attention on him, never given his character much thought or taken time to study his attributes. My efforts to study and read the Bible tended to be self-focused. I wanted encouragement and nourishment for myself. I wanted to see God's hand at work in my life and my prayers answered. Terrible as it sounds to me now, I wasn't looking for God. I was looking for ways to make life better for me. I felt derailed and wanted to know if and when he was going to help me get back on track. I was discouraged about the present and apprehensive about the future. Like a lot of women, I suppressed my unhappy thoughts about God for years, until I just couldn't do it any longer. I needed to find out more about the God who held my life in his hands.

The questions about God that seem to surface most often in conversations I have with women center on God's sovereignty and character. Is God really in control, or does sovereignty change hands from moment to moment, shifting between God, the devil, and pure chance? Does God care only about the major events and choices of my life, or does he also rule over the details? What kind of God would allow such painful things to happen to us? Do I really matter to God, or am I less important than others who seem more entitled to his attentions? These questions about God (which weighed heavily on my own heart) send us back to read the Scriptures again, this time with theological eyes, searching for God. It can be a mind-expanding experience, for theology inevitably enlarges our vision of God. As one startled woman admitted, "God is a lot bigger than I thought." When God is big, everything begins to look different.

GOD IS ON HIS THRONE

SOVEREIGNTY IS A DOCTRINE the church has prized throughout her history. Most of us firmly believe God is king over his creation.

Exactly what we mean when we say that is another question and has been a subject of debate among Christians through the centuries. The conclusions we draw on this issue, however, have serious ramifications for how we see ourselves and our circumstances. To understand sovereignty, we must leave behind our democratic ideals and enter the world of the monarch—a world uncluttered by popular elections, the Bill of Rights, and delicate systems of checks and balances.

We find one of the most impressive examples of human sovereignty in ancient King Nebuchadnezzar, who from 605 to 562 B.C. held the reins of power over the vast Babylonian Empire. Neighboring nations trembled at the mention of his name, and many of them fell when his armies laid siege against their city walls. We remember him for terrorizing God's people and leveling Jerusalem. When all attempts to appease him failed, this invincible tyrant destroyed Solomon's temple, overthrew Judah, and dragged her nobles off in chains to Babylon. Nebuchadnezzar seemed unstoppable. He could issue a royal decree without consulting a soul and see it ruthlessly enforced to the letter. People were tortured, executed, or had their lives radically reconfigured at his word. Others gained enormous wealth and rode to heights of power on his coattails. He possessed power and the sovereign's divine right to exercise it any way he chose.

But King Nebuchadnezzar collided with the only true sovereign, the King of Heaven (Daniel 4). At the height of Nebuchadnezzar's pride, God plucked him from the pinnacle of human sovereignty, took away his authority, drove him from his people, and set him down for a time to graze mindlessly among beasts of the field. When his ordeal was over and the old king was reinstated, his perspective had changed. The staggering dimensions of God's sovereignty had cut Nebuchadnezzar's massive world empire down to size. No longer self-sufficient or enamored with his own powers, the king knelt to acknowledge the Most High God who was sovereign over him.

There is no mistaking the sharp contrast between Nebuchadnezzar's powers and God's sovereignty. The Babylonian Empire looms large in history books but seems shabby and frail next to God's almighty reign. A human kingdom, bounded by time, geography, and the life span of a mortal, shrinks before the eternal kingdom of heaven and earth. God's realm has no borders but ranges from the farthest reaches of the universe to the minute details of human lives. His dominion encompasses the "powers of heaven and the peoples of the earth" (v. 35). The devil and his hordes are under God's thumb, and God reigns supreme over human beings too—not just people of consequence and power but ordinary men, women, and children. Nebuchadnezzar's reign was suspended by his own mental breakdown and corrupted by the selfishness and evil of his own heart. Eventually Babylon was overthrown by the rising Medes and Persians. But God's kingdom marches on, unbroken and undiminished "from generation to generation." No flaws, weaknesses, or rival powers threaten God's collapse or hinder him from achieving his purposes. He is God. "He does as he pleases with the powers of heaven and the peoples of the earth. No one can hold back his hand or say to him: 'What have you done?'" (vv. 34–35).

It is terrifying to contemplate such power and freedom. If we were in other hands, we would have reason to tremble, but not so with God. Even God has his system of checks and balances—one that will never fail and that secures our well-being, for God is governed by his own heart. Which explains Nebuchadnezzar's confident assertion that "everything [God] does is right and all his ways are just" (v. 37).

This is a completely different picture of God's sovereignty than I had in mind. Here is a purposing, planning, active, accomplishing God. There is nothing passive, hesitant, or indecisive about him. Nebuchadnezzar's God doesn't just step in from time to time when conditions seem favorable to his intervention or we reach the end of our ability to manage without him. He isn't waiting to see how things will turn out before taking action. He doesn't need our invitation to get involved or our advice to know what to do next. He is continuously, actively running things here and now.

Nebuchadnezzar's sober reflections are backed by God's description of himself: "I am God, and there is no other; I am God, and there is none like me. I make known the end from the beginning, from ancient times, what is still to come. I say: My purpose will stand, and I will do all that I please" (Isa. 46:9–10).

It may be reassuring to think God has King Nebuchadnezzar and his evil empire under control, and comforting to know God directs events of history to fulfill his plans for creation. But how far are we to go with this? How does God's sovereignty relate to me and my life?

When we go back to the Scriptures with these questions, God's sovereignty narrows its focus and, in short order, we are caught in the beam of his headlights. Although at times it unsettles us, the Bible sets our lives squarely within the parameters of God's reign. We are called to run the race God has "marked out for us" (Heb. 12:1–2). David boils it down when he writes, "All the *days* ordained for me were written in your book before one of them came to be" (Ps. 139:16, emphasis added).

As difficult as this might seem at first glance, it is hard to avoid concluding that the details of women's lives are part of God's great plan. Even King David, with all the terrible tragedies and mistakes of his life, strongly believed that long before we are born, God plans the details of our birth, the moment of our death, and all the days between. The implications are astonishing. Our lives are not haphazard journeys that evolve as we go along, depending on what we do or what happens next. Each of us is running the race God has marked out for her. This race is not determined by the good or evil actions of others, no matter who they are or how much power they hold over us. Neither do we run wherever we please. God has planned our race, and he is carrying out his plan—a plan that guarantees our good and his glory. Nothing—not principalities or powers, not the devil himself, not even we—can throw God off his plan or prevent him from accomplishing his good purposes for us. We run a planned race.

Most women don't see their lives in such bold terms. A lot of women live with a subterranean sense that God doesn't have a plan for them. If there is a plan at all, it is only temporary and quickly discarded when "someone" comes along with a real plan.

Single women with this point of view are waiting for the plan to commence. Until a husband arrives on the scene, they are on hold or must default to a second-class plan that is not nearly as good or meaningful as that of a married woman. Singleness is perceived by many in the church (including some singles) as a woman's private purgatory—a suspended state of uncertain duration useful only as a bridge to marriage. What single woman hasn't cringed at the question, Why aren't you married? This question implies that she has broken rank or somehow failed to live up to God's plan for her. The mistaken assumption that God uses the same plan for all women—to marry, conceive children, raise a family, and move on to grandmothering—is painful for women who fail to fit the profile at any given point. In the meantime, there is an unspoken consensus among Christians that what a single woman does with her life is an interim or makeshift plan—a way to mark time until she marries and the real plan begins. Such notions can lead to some rather half-hearted living.

A married woman faces a different problem when she believes the plan she's on belongs to her husband. Her plan seems eclipsed by God's plan for him. I'm afraid it's true that many evangelical men see their wives as merely a supporting actress in his story or as a spectator, alternately cheering him on or biting her nails as she waits to see where God will lead him next. But wives also buy into this one-sided view. She braces herself for his next big decision and the adjustments she will have to make. She invests herself in her children's lives and watches them move on in God's plan for them, but she doesn't have a plan of her own. When someone asks a married woman why she moved to town, nine times out of ten she will say it is because God brought her husband to such and such a job, and plenty of seminary wives and women on the mission field justify their presence by saying, "God led my husband here." I understand what they mean, but it troubles me that so few women have any inkling that God relocated them because it was his plan for her. It's hard to have a clear sense of purpose or calling if you're convinced you are only tagging along.

Women who live on the other side of marriage because of death or divorce suffer from thinking the plan is over. Their grief over the termination of their marriage is compounded by the deadening sense that unless they remarry, any plan God had for their lives is spoiled for good.

God's sovereignty puts women back on the map of life. It reminds us that God has a unique plan for each woman. We are called not to sit on the sidelines but to be players, active contributors, to run the race he has marked out for us. If God is sovereign, then every day of our lives has meaning and purpose because God has planned it. We are not left in the wake of God's plan for someone else. No matter how intertwined our lives become with the lives of husbands, friends, and family members, God's plan for us is individual and personal. Each Christian is on a personal journey with God.

Those who believe that God has a plan for them sometimes encounter another problem—the conviction that they have lost God's best plan for them. They believe that they have missed or fallen off the plan, or that something has happened to destroy it. I know a young woman whose husband thought *she* was plan B. Earlier he had been engaged to the girl of his dreams, but everything fell apart when his fiance broke their engagement and walked out of his life for good, taking plan A with her.

We know the feeling. Somewhere along the line, we zigged when we should have zagged, and now we're hopelessly stuck with plan B. It only takes a foolish youthful decision, a missed opportunity, the interference of someone else in our lives, or our sinfulness, and plan A is gone forever.

But if God is sovereign, then plan B is a myth. No matter how dark things look to us, or how big the mess we're in, we're in plan A. God's plan for us is intact, proceeding exactly as he intended, neither behind nor ahead but right on schedule. Nothing—not our sins, failures, disappointments, bad decisions, nor the sins of others against us—can deter a sovereign God from accomplishing his purposes.

God does not wait for perfect conditions to advance his purposes. If the realities of a fallen world and the failings of sinful hearts can obstruct God's progress, then there is little hope for any of us. If we think about it, we will admit God always accomplishes his plan in spite of us. Our obedience is always flawed; our best efforts are never enough. Nebuchadnezzar and Isaiah seem to suggest God accomplishes his good purposes in and through the mess. Instead of despairing over the demise of God's plan, we find comfort in knowing that a good God is working out his good plans in everything that happens in his world and in the lives of his children.

There is deep mystery here, to be sure. God's sovereignty doesn't answer all of our questions. But it gives women a framework from which to view their lives. It enables us to see life at its worst and know God is still on his throne. There's a net below us. Suddenly, the "strange, mad, painful world" Dr. Packer warns us of becomes safe, ordered, purposeful, and full of meaning with God at the helm. But our comfort rests not on sovereignty alone but on other aspects of God's character, for the king's character will inevitably determine how he governs.

GOD'S CHARACTER MATTERS

I FEAR THAT SOME zealots for the doctrine of God's sovereignty miss the mark when they isolate sovereignty from the rest of God. Even Nebuchadnezzar couldn't speak of God's rule without mentioning his justice and goodness. God's character is crucial, for there are moments in life when God's goodness and love seem to come under a blackout. No matter how we strain our eyes, we cannot see any good, not a trace of God's love. These moments—and we all have them—remind us of the urgency of becoming better theologians. When faith cannot find something tangible to grasp, we are compelled to fly back to the ark of God's unchanging, unfailing character. But faith will not find much of a foothold here if God is a stranger to us. Faith, in the final analysis, is trusting someone you know, even when you don't always understand what he is doing.

God's character is revealed on every page of the Scriptures. But there is one place where we see him with unequaled clarity—the cross. "To stand beneath the cross is to stand at the one place where the character of God burns brightest."[5] Here on the grand stage of human history, God bares his heart and spreads his goodness before us. Here love, sovereignty, goodness, and glory meet with cataclysmic force. It is at the cross that God defines himself and we come to know him. John Stott was right when he said, "Just as human beings disclose their character in their actions, so God has showed himself to us in the death of his Son."[6]

We are not the first women to stand here. When the horrific event was taking place, a small group of women, including Jesus' mother,[7] stood nearby, appalled as they watched their hopes destroyed, battling through their own set of questions, trying to reconcile all they had heard from him with what they were seeing now. We follow their gaze to the agonized form suspended between heaven and earth—Jesus, the only Son of God, dying in our place. We have known him since he was a baby and followed his footsteps to this place. We know his history and his character—the love that brought him here, his compassion and tenderness for the downtrodden and the outcast.

But Jesus and his mother were not the only ones at the cross. If we look honestly, we see the Father here too. He is in the rumble of thunder and in Jesus' desperate cry, "My God, my God, why have you forsaken me?" (Matt. 27:46). Listen carefully to Jesus' words. He wasn't wrestling with the devil or Roman authorities. He was wrestling with his Father. Although the forces of evil were at work, ultimately Jesus was not crucified because of Satan's efforts, dark plots of Jewish religious leaders, wild passions of the mob, or the unscrupulous powers of Rome. He was here according to his Father's plan and by his own choice. The apostle Peter (who didn't see it at the time himself) later draws back the veil to reveal the truth. "This man [Jesus of Nazareth] was *handed over to you by God's set purpose and foreknowledge;* and you, with the help of wicked men, put him to death by nailing him to the cross" (Acts 2:23, emphasis added).

At the cross, God is not making the best of a bad situation. He is not reacting to events that have spun out of control. *He* is in control. This was God's plan for Jesus and for us. In one terrible episode, God's plan, through Christ's suffering, accomplished infinite good for us and blinding glory for God. This was not an hour of shame and defeat for the Godhead. It was an hour of glory—an hour when God's unveiled character was displayed before the world. Jesus knew what the cross held for him, and yet he spoke of it in terms of glory: "*Now* is the Son of Man glorified and God is glorified in him" (John 13:31, emphasis added). Glory is the uncovering of God's character—the disclosure of who God is.[8] Not even Moses' vision of God's glory on the mountain,[9] when God had to shield him because the sight was so overpowering, compares to this hour of glory.

In the cross, we see God's sovereignty and God's glory. But we also see his heart. The Son's love and passion for us are abundantly obvious. But we must look closer to see the Father's heart. Our maternal instincts help us see the depths of his love, the lengths he is willing to go for our good. Agonies that throbbed in the breast of Jesus' mother as she watched her son die are multiplied by infinity in his Father. What she watched, he inflicted. When Jesus' body was nailed to the cross for our sakes, the Father's heart was nailed there too. The inconsolable cries and empty arms of a mother on the banks of a swiftly flowing river give us a glimpse of what the Father felt when the cross severed him from his child. The cross defines the dimensions of God's love for us. "He who did not spare his own Son, but gave him up for us all—how will he not also, along with him, graciously give us all things?" (Rom. 8:32).

This is why it is so crucial for us to develop and test our theology within earshot of the dying cries of Jesus. At the foot of the cross, we begin to understand that God's plan, shaped and propelled by his love and goodness, includes pain and tragedy—for Jesus and for us. Strange as it seems, God's goodness and love become more vivid in the tragedy itself. In God's mysterious wisdom, pain and suffering become vehicles for his glory to be displayed to us and through us. And can we not see this played out in our own lives? Our sufferings take us into deeper realms of God's character and enlarge our vision of him. I can't count the times I have heard women say after a time of painful struggle, "I wouldn't go through that again for anything. But I wouldn't trade what I have learned about God for the world." How often are those who speak most warmly of God's love and goodness to them the same ones we have watched endure unspeakable sufferings? They have seen more of God's glory in their pain than others can imagine in their comfort. Knowing God is the ultimate end toward which we all are moving.

THE FATHER AND HIS DAUGHTERS

THE CROSS BRINGS everything together—sovereignty, goodness, and glory. But the cross also tells us that sovereignty, goodness, and glory are family matters. Our lives weren't planned by a disinterested sovereign in heaven but by an involved Father whose heart is bound up in the lives of his children. He is raising his daughters. Every inch of the way, our Father is working to accomplish his purposes—to deepen our relationship with him and cultivate the family resemblance in us.

But it is when we speak of God as a father that a lot of women turn away. Their experiences with their own fathers cloud their ability to think of God this way. You can see it in their eyes the moment the subject of fathers comes up. Their stories cover the spectrum—from kind but distant fathers to alcoholic, violent, and abusive fathers. One daughter, whose father had filled her early years with cruel abuse, could not recall a single pleasant childhood memory. It's hard to think of God as Father when memories of your own father stir up so much pain.

But our Father in heaven is the antithesis of these human fathers. Even the best human fathers are only dim shadows of what our heavenly Father is like. God is the perfect Father. He defines what *father* means, and his parenting leaves nothing to be desired.

He wrote the book when it comes to healthy relationships and nurturing. Our understanding of God's plan for us takes on new dimensions when we understand that it comes from our Father's hand.

First, our lives are purposeful. We are not being flung about by chaos or chance. God's good purposes are in place for each of us, moving forward exactly as he has planned. His parental hand is mightily at work behind the scenes at all times and in every detail. Every second counts. He never loses interest or takes his eyes off us for a moment. Each experience and situation serves his good purposes for us. He wants us to know him and to be close to him. He is steadily restoring his image in us so that we will be able to enjoy him fully and reflect his likeness in our world.

God's methods are something like our high school science classes, which combine both lecture and lab. We have lecture when we probe the Scriptures in search of God and learn of him from teachers, pastors, and books. But just as theory alone will never produce a great scientist, so sound theological ideas detached from life will not make a good theologian. Our Father will never be content for us to know him in the abstract, and so he conducts labs. He wisely brings us into life situations and circumstances that press the truth into our hearts and help us live out what we have learned of him.

Second, God treats his children as individuals. No two plans are alike. Although he has a multitude of children, he is not like the old woman who lived in a shoe, who had so many children she didn't know what to do. He knows what to do. He does not treat his children en masse or use a cookie cutter to manufacture identical plans. He doesn't assign a plan A to some of his children and leave the rest to cope with inferior plans. He has perfectly and meticulously tailored each plan to accomplish his good purposes for his daughters.

In a way God treats each of us as though we were his only child. At any given point, we could turn the camera on one of God's children and say, "God runs his universe just for her." Historical events, the world economy, political developments, patterns in the weather, natural disasters, births, deaths, relationships, actions and movements of other people, and everything else are orchestrated and perfectly timed to serve his purposes for you. No other plan takes precedence over the one he has planned for you. Your story isn't a spin-off of what God is doing in someone else's life. He runs the world as if you were his only concern. It works that way for all of us.

I realized this for the first time after we moved to England. My three-year-old daughter and I crossed the Atlantic so my husband could pursue doctoral studies at Oxford University. It was a difficult move for all of us, and I thought we were there because of God's plan for Frank. But as time passed, I began to realize there were other equally valid ways of seeing the same set of circumstances. From my point of view, it was fair to say that God worked through my husband's academic career to fulfill the English phase of his plan for me. It was a pivotal time in my life. Shortly after our arrival, I started my own business as a software developer. Through that venture, friendships I forged, and the experience of living so far away from home, I received an education of my own. I learned so much about God's ways and about myself that it was easy to think this chapter of family history had been written just for me. But there was a third equally significant plan being carried out in our family. The parents of a little preschooler packed up and moved overseas to study and start a business because God had planned her earliest memories to come from friendships and experiences she would encounter in England.

Plan A reminds us that no matter how our lives mingle with the lives of others, God has a fully formed plan for each of us. His plan for you and for me always remains intact, always is purposeful, always proceeds at the rate he intended, always remains a priority with him. It encompasses all the days of our lives. No matter our marital status, our age, our history, or our prospects, God is powerfully at work right now, accomplishing his good purposes in and through us.

The third aspect of God's plan is something no one wants to hear. Christians may be in denial over this, but the race God has marked out for each of us involves struggle. The difficulty for us is in understanding how these troubles fit into plan A. No doubt most of us think of plan A in ideal terms. Plan A is what we all thought Lady Diana Spencer was getting—beauty, wealth, fame, and marriage to a prince with a Happily Ever After banner floating along behind. The assumption that plan A means warm winds and smooth sailing doesn't match up with what we experience or with God's promise that we will have struggles in this life. God's goal isn't to make us comfortable here but to help us know him and to intensify our longings for him. Our troubles are not signs of abandonment but are evidence that he is mightily at work. He uses trouble to draw us closer and open our eyes to see more of him (see Heb. 12:5–11).

Last, the Father's glory—his reputation—is on the line in our race. God's glory cannot be separated from what he does, from his plan for you and for me. God cannot be glorified if his goodness breaks down along the way. If he fails to be good for a split second, or if even one runner crosses the finish line with a negative report of his faithfulness, then shame will displace glory. The promise of God's glory is the guarantee that no story will put God to shame; they all will only add to the mounting evidence of his great goodness.

Epilogue

LONG AFTER THAT TRAGIC summer, I saw my friend again. Her eyes brimmed with tears as she pulled out a well-worn photo of her little one, and we talked again of her unspeakable loss and all she had learned. There is no way to measure the agony she suffered as she tried to piece her life back together and struggled to understand God. She told me it was only as she came to understand God's character better that she finally found peace.

We will never have answers to all of our questions. Some aches will never go away. But there is comfort in this: God is on his throne and he is good. He has marked out our race, and his plan is perfectly consistent with his character.

But we have other questions about God's sovereignty that we must consider before exploring how theology looks in a woman's life and what it means to run this race God has marked out for us.

4

SURVIVING THE WAR
ZONES OF LIFE

WHEN U.S. TROOPS WITHDREW FROM SOUTH VIETNAM IN 1975, vivid images of the collapse of the small Southeast Asian country invaded American living rooms through the window of television. A sea of frantic Vietnamese flooded the streets of Saigon, some laden with bundles, others clutching their children, fleeing for their lives with no place to go. It is hard to erase the memory of terror on their faces and the bolted gates of the American Embassy, which refused to yield to the onslaught of humanity as the enemy closed in. It is the kind of terror most of us meet only in dreams in which running takes you nowhere and the thing you dread pursues relentlessly without any impediment to slow it down. It was a shocking disruption to our day, a news snippet of horrors taking place on the far side of the globe. We didn't want to think about it for long. How easy it was to turn away from such desperate scenes to more manageable problems at home—a point made too well by an aspirin commercial that interrupted the news to pose the question, "How does America handle a headache?"

The problems of life cannot be remedied by a pill, even if we wish it were so. Life has a way of crashing down on us without warning. Whether we like it or not, sooner or later all of us end up in the war zone, where life ceases to be tidy and the pain threshold goes off the charts. Women are not spared this kind of active combat, which makes it all the more urgent for us to think through our theology so our views of God will sustain us when the battle begins to rage. Otherwise we will sink in despair instead of standing firm and fighting with courage, determination, and confidence in God.

Recently I was reminded just how terrible life is for many women. Christian psychologist and author Dr. Diane Langberg told a gathering of four thousand evangelical women that by the age of eighteen, one in three American women has been sexually abused and that one in four women has suffered at least one incident of physical violence in her marriage.[1] Statistics like these do not stop at the church door but march right on in. Listening to Dr. Langberg brought to mind a woman I met several years ago at a conference where I was speaking. When this young woman approached me, her face was clouded with burdens I wasn't sure I wanted to hear. She reached into her past to help me comprehend the full weight of her question—back to a childhood shattered by abuse at the hands of those who should have protected her. When she was a teenager, she turned to alcohol and promiscuity to fill the void and dull the pain of her home life, and by early adulthood, she was caught in a downward spiral that led to addiction, an unwanted pregnancy, and an abortion. Now, as a Christian, not only was she dragging the past around with her, she had new problems—a disappointing marriage to a husband who didn't understand her and a guilt-laden battle with infertility. She asked me point-blank, "Can this be God's plan?"

It was a fair question, and no doubt it speaks for many of us. Our stories may not be as tragic as hers, but all of us have looked at our own lives and wondered the same thing. How do God's sovereignty and goodness stack up when life sinks to such lows? Can

God's plan for me withstand the devastation that comes from living in a fallen world? If our ideas of God are only helpful for headaches, only make sense in the safety of a living room, only comfort women living cozy lives behind white picket fences with adoring husbands and model children but leaves other women out in the cold, something is terribly wrong. How can any of us trust God if he occasionally vacates his throne or if there are places beyond the reach of his goodness?

The war zones of life force us to take our theology seriously, to see if our beliefs about God hold up when the tragedies and perplexities of life press down upon them. Our theology, if it is true, must apply to all of us and include all points on the Richter scale of human suffering. If God's goodness cannot penetrate the darkness of a woman's world or breaks up under the weight of such wretchedness, if there are pockets of our lives beyond God's reach, then none of us can really count on him. Our hope in God is no better than a placebo if his plan doesn't encompass all of life—the dark side as well as the bright.

But to say that God's plan is comprehensive doesn't make it any easier to swallow. All of us have moments when things become so chaotic or painful that we lose sight of God's plan. It seems to make sense everywhere but here and now. That's how I felt when my mother was hospitalized a year ago for surgery to remove an abdominal tumor. It was one of four major surgeries she would have that year. The tumor, it turned out, was benign, but it was attached to the nerve that runs the length of her leg. Instead of relieving the pain she had been experiencing, the surgery ignited a fierce nerve pain that shot down her leg like a bolt of electricity and wouldn't relent. Days and nights were filled with frantic moments trying to bring her agony under control. It was sheer madness—the voltage of the pain, our helplessness to stop it, and the absence of a miracle to bring her relief. Could God stop that pain? We all knew he could. Yet for some reason, he didn't. The only miracle we got came from a prescription of narcotics, a lot of trial and error to determine the right dosage, and long months of imperceptible healing that never fully stopped the pain. It looked to me as though God, instead of stepping in, had stepped away. How could such agony be part of God's plan?

Even after hearing from King Nebuchadnezzar that nothing can interfere with God's plan for us, we have lingering doubts. His words make sense on paper. But paper theories go up in smoke in the war zone. There are too many places where God seems to drop out of sight or evil looms so large that God's plan seems irreparably destroyed.

If we were to name the biggest threats to God's plan for us, most of us would list three. The most obvious threat comes from Satan and his evil forces. We have read enough about him to know he has dark plans of his own. Sometimes it seems he has succeeded and God's plan has failed. And what about people? How many times have people's actions, both unintentional and deliberate, redirected our lives or put some tender hope forever beyond our reach? But perhaps the biggest threat to God's plan comes when we're the problem. God's plan may survive everything else, but, it seems, it will never recover from the damage we have done ourselves.

Our theology must confront these formidable foes and the threat they pose to our confidence in God. Our purpose is not to fine-tune our theology for the sake of being right but to find out what is true about God. When the darkness of life is so thick we can feel it, it matters whether God is still on his throne or we are simply at the mercy of the devil, a human interloper, or the darkness of our own hearts.

Before we address these challenges to God's plan, we need to make a distinction. Frequently Christians refer to God's plan as his will. The Bible and theologians speak of two different aspects of God's will—the revealed (or moral) will of God and the hidden will of God (or God's providential government of all things). God's *revealed* will is contained in the commands and teachings of Scripture, found in the Ten Commandments and New Testament instruction. "God's moral commands are given as descriptions of how we should conduct ourselves if we would act rightly before him."[2] God's *hidden* will is what we have been discussing in the last two chapters—God's plan or his decrees. It refers to God's governing all events of this fallen world to accomplish his purposes for us and bring glory to himself. The Bible itself makes this distinction. Moses spoke of both when he wrote, "*The secret things* belong to the LORD our God, but *the things revealed* belong to us and to our children forever, that we may follow all the words of this law" (Deut. 29:29, emphasis added).

God's revealed will is known to us. His commands are clear, perfect, and holy, and he calls us to live in obedience to them. His hidden will, however, is just that—hidden. We know it only in retrospect. How it works is a great mystery, because it encompasses everything—not just those things that please God but also the things he hates. It is important for us to see how the Bible distinguishes between these two aspects of God's will because this distinction enables us to maintain, on the one hand, that God's will (revealed) is always for us to live holy lives of obedience to his Word and, on the other hand, that God's plan (hidden will) is to accomplish his good purposes for us through everything that happens, even through the evil that takes place in his world. In a fallen world populated by sinners and relentlessly assaulted by the powers of evil, the sphere of God's reign would be minuscule indeed if it extended only to areas where his moral will was being obeyed. If God's hidden plan is contingent on perfect compliance with his revealed will, then his plan has been unraveling ever since the serpent slithered into the Garden of Eden. Even so, it is one of the great mysteries of Scripture that God's plan is so comprehensive. Living with mystery is uncomfortable for us. But faith inevitably takes us into mystery, where we don't—and won't—have all of the answers and where, from time to time, we have to affirm truths that to our finite minds seem to conflict. The paradox we are wrestling with now is that God's good purposes, his hidden will, are preserved and advanced even when the devil takes a hand in our lives, when we fall into the hands of other people, or when we, with our own two hands, pull our lives crashing down around our ears.

One of my struggles in writing this chapter, as well as the previous one, is that I know the things I am saying will be difficult for some women. I know this because they are difficult for me. It is one thing to read about God's hidden will from a detached, objective point of view. It is quite another to read it from within the context of acute personal pain. If you find it hard to digest some of these ideas, you are not alone. One of the most extraordinary things about the Bible is that it tells us truths that we don't want to hear but that are important nevertheless. In my own spiritual journey, I have learned it is worth the struggle to wrestle with hard teachings. For over a decade, I believed God had abandoned me, that I had fallen out of his plan and there was no way to get back on track. Then when I began to grasp something of God's sovereignty over my life and the durability of his plan for me, I felt something solid beneath my feet for the first time. Knowing that God's plan includes the hard times as well as the good was, in a strange way, a comfort to me. This helps explain why I feel it is so urgent for women to become strong theologians. There's no place theology matters more than in the war zone. If you struggle with these ideas (and it will surprise me if you don't), I hope you won't abandon the effort to understand.

The Bible often communicates theology through stories. So I have chosen three familiar stories which I believe powerfully illustrate how God's hidden plan is accomplished despite and even through the intrusion of evil, the injurious ways of other people, and our own sinfulness.

When Evil Forces Are at Work

A lot of Christians see the world as a sort of teeter-totter battle between God and Satan.[3] Sometimes God wins. Sometimes Satan does. You never can tell, from one day to the next, whether good or evil will have the upper hand. Admittedly this is how things sometimes look from our vantage point. Even so, it is unsettling to think that at certain points, Satan is in charge and for the moment God's hands are tied.

Ordinarily, life seems to follow certain laws of cause and effect. People who work hard can put food on the table and pay the bills. Attentive parenting produces responsible young adults. Balanced nutrition and regular exercise generally lead to good health. But for many Christians there are times when this dependable pattern goes awry. Recession, market shifts, and downsizing put good workers on the streets. The child of loving diligent parents experiments with drugs and goes off the deep end. A health-conscious jogger has a heart attack or is diagnosed with cancer. When the formula is disrupted, we are quick to suspect interference from Satan and his minions.

That's what happened to Job. His problems began behind the scenes when Satan questioned his loyalty to God. Satan was convinced Job's faith in God was nothing more than a selfish pragmatism that would evaporate if God ceased to reward him with material blessings. And so to our dismay, God accepts the challenge and grants Satan permission to afflict Job. A series of calamities follows, as disaster rains down on Job. A natural disaster takes the lives of all ten of his children, marauders confiscate his property and murder his servants, and his own body is tormented with painful sores. As if that were not enough, he is divided from his grieving wife and crushed by words from well-meaning but misguided friends.

Despite all this, Satan's scheme backfires. Rather than distancing Job from God as expected, suffering intensifies Job's focus on God. And Satan, after the opening scenes, skulks offstage like an insignificant extra, leaving Job behind to wrestle with God. If we read carefully, the central issue in the story is not what Satan is doing but what God is doing. The plan that falls apart is Satan's, not God's. The book of Job drives home the point that God is the central figure behind even the tragic events in our lives. He is the one who is in charge and who holds us in his hands. Not even the devil can touch us without God's permission, and even then God overrules and works through Satan's schemes to accomplish good for us.

And what is the good God does for us? Most of us would turn to the last chapter of Job's story and point out how his fortunes were doubled and his wife gave birth to ten more children. But we miss the point if we tie up the story with a bow and a happy ending. To be sure, Job's crisis did come to an end, and these physical blessings no doubt brought comfort to him. But Job's story isn't ultimately about happy endings, as any parent who has suffered the loss of a child will tell you. There is pain in the epilogue, for Job would never get over the loss of his children. In a real sense, he would always be a sufferer. It is important for us to see this because so many of our own struggles have pain in the epilogue—there isn't a neat resolution and our fortunes don't take an upward turn.

But God's plan isn't defined by happy endings; neither is it about getting answers to all of our questions. God never explained to Job why all these afflictions had fallen on him. Job would always have unanswered questions, and so will we. God's plan for Job, as for all of us, went much deeper than material blessings or divine explanations. In the furnace of affliction, God was revealing himself to his child. Through the eyes of suffering, Job saw more of God than he would ever see through the eyes of prosperity. God worked through Satan's cruel designs to reveal himself more fully to Job. What Satan intended to destroy and tear down, God used to build up and mature his child. By the end of his life, Job's theology had taken a quantum leap. God had gotten bigger, and his relationship with God had been reinforced with deeper truth.

If we learn anything from Job, it is that the forces of evil cannot upset God's sovereign plan for us. In fact, God always overturns their destructive schemes to advance his good purposes for us. I don't pretend to know the whereabouts of Satan or to be able to spot telltale signs of his involvement in my struggles or anyone else's. What I do know, and draw comfort from, is that a good God is seated upon his throne. Satan may afflict, sift, and try to devour, and when he does, we will feel the fury of his efforts. But no matter what Satan might do, God is there all along, accomplishing his purposes in every detail of our lives. It is a startling truth that God doesn't work around our troubles; he works through them, orchestrating events to ensure that the outcome will benefit the souls of his children and draw us closer to himself.

Sometimes we see God more clearly in the dark, when he has our undistracted attention and we struggle to know if the hand that rules the night is as good and powerful as the hand that rules the day. The river drowning of a one-year-old child, a broken neck from a headfirst plunge into a lake, a life of pain, a miscarriage, a fire, a flood, the loss of family, friends, health, or property—listen to what the sufferers of the church have to say if you want to taste the goodness of God. "God never wastes pain. He always uses it to accomplish his purpose. And his purpose is for his glory and our good."[4] Like Job, some of our best theologians are those who have suffered most. Suffering has stripped away their false notions and given them eyes to see a God who is worthy of their trust.

But what happens to God's plan when people get in the way? Are there points in life when the interference of another person is so disruptive that God's plan falls to pieces?

WHEN PEOPLE GET IN THE WAY

AN OLD TESTAMENT SCHOLAR once surprised me when he described Abraham's family as dysfunctional. But when I looked closely at their history, I could see exactly what he meant. Troubled marriages, weak parenting, favoritism, deceit, jealousy, and fierce sibling rivalry defined the relationships among Abraham's descendants. By the time Jacob's family arrived on the scene, the family was in chaos. Grown-ups were so absorbed in their own conflicts that they didn't notice when they passed their problems on to the next generation. Although the men's stories dominate the narrative, the women suffered greatly under the weight of such fractured relationships. Jacob's wives, Leah and Rachel, were locked in a bitter rivalry for their husband's love and the number of their sons. His only daughter, Dinah, wandered off to visit pagan neighbors and was devastated, first by rape and then by her father's silent indifference to her violation. The widowed Tamar suffered injustice when her father-in-law, Judah, refused to secure a husband for her to preserve the family line. It's not exactly the sort of family you would be glad to see moving in next door.

But what is striking about this dysfunctional family is how God's hand was at work in the midst of these relational disasters. You see, this wasn't merely Jacob's family. This was God's family, a family to whom God had pledged his unfailing love. While it looked like God's plan for them had cracked in a lot of places, the thriving state of his plan was affirmed by the greatest sufferer in the family.

Joseph enjoyed the best of his father's love and indulgence but paid dearly for it with his half brothers' jealousy and hatred. Just the sight of him was a bitter reminder of their father's rejection. Passions exploded when Joseph was only seventeen. His brothers assaulted him and threw him in a pit. Then instead of killing him as planned, they pulled him up and sold him off to Midianite slave traders bound for Egypt. The memory of Joseph's cries would later haunt his brothers, but at the time, they were incapable of pity. A few pieces of silver changed hands, and Joseph's life was completely reformatted.

The psalmist describes Joseph's travail. "They bruised his feet with shackles, his neck was put in irons" (Ps. 105:18). We have to read between the lines to get the rest, but it isn't too difficult to imagine his emotional pain. The rejection, betrayal, and murderous hatred of his brothers and the separation from his father and younger brother pierced his soul. He was dragged off to a land, a people, and a language he did not know and thrown into the stale hopeless air of an Egyptian prison. Joseph knew the meaning of depression. As if this were not enough, the trajectory of subsequent events resembled an unstable electrocardiogram as his hopes rose sharply with opportunity, then dropped abruptly with disappointments. He was always the victim of another person's treachery or forgetfulness. Joseph could have easily believed God's plan had been shattered the instant his brothers seized him and threw him in the pit.

It must be said that God didn't let Joseph's brothers off the hook for the evil they perpetrated against their brother. Sin is never a trivial matter with God, as the cross so vividly reminds us. But when famine reunited Joseph and his pain with his brothers and their guilt, no one was prepared for Joseph's response. Instead of bitterness, resentment, or anger, he spoke of the mystery he had learned in the depths of his misery, which had given him the incentive to make the most of his grim circumstances. The same lips that once begged his brothers to stop, that trembled and sobbed with grief over his loss and ruin, that pressed together in silent disbelief over later betrayals, now spoke with unwavering confidence in God's plan. "You intended to harm me, but God intended it for good" (Gen. 50:20).

Behind the wickedness of his brothers and of others who had injured him, Joseph saw God's hand at work. Despite his suffering, he knew God's purposes were being carried out even through the wrongs done against him. Joseph could well have echoed what one female survivor of sexual and physical abuse wrote: "In those troubled times, in the night watches, God became more and more real to me. He covered me with his outspread wings. My affliction became the cord with which He drew me to Himself."[5]

If we learn anything from Joseph, it is that other people, no matter how injurious they are in our lives, cannot overturn God's plan for us. His plan seems secure and good when loyal friends and allies are active on our behalf. But it is just as secure and good when we fall into the hands of the wicked. In perilous moments like these, a deeper, resilient faith lays hold of God alone. Our God surely presides over ordered and enviable lives. But he also presides over broken lives in which hearts are torn, hope is illusive, and wounds are too deep for words. I can't explain the mystery of God's hidden plan—how he works good for us through such appalling circumstances. I know only that he has given his word that "in *all* things" he *is* at work for our good and that through the ages his people, like Joseph, have said it is so. Even in the worst moments, God's scepter never slips from his hand.

When I'm My Own Worst Enemy

ANOTHER TIME WHEN HOPE and God seem to slip away from us is when we look in the mirror and know, in our heart of hearts, we have only ourselves to blame for the mess we're in. Church pews are filled with deep regrets. A lot of women look back on a single decision they made too hastily or without enough maturity that has shaped the miserable contours of their lives ever since. If only they had known then what they know now, they never would have married him. If only they had known then how they would feel now, they never would have gotten into the back seat of that car or walked into the abortion clinic. Others agonize secretly over a dark time in their lives when they recklessly pursued destructive relationships and lifestyles—what the prophet Joel calls the "years the locusts have eaten" (Joel 2:25). Their wounds are self-inflicted, and it is impossible to get back what they have squandered. Whatever may have influenced them, they will be the first to admit they have no one to blame but themselves. I have met several young women who, despite the cheerful front they manage to maintain at church, feel worthless and inferior around other Christians because of a shameful past. The past looms so large in their thoughts, it dampens any future hopes. They find it hard to imagine that God maintains his plan for such awful people.

Rahab was such a woman. While Israel wasted forty years in the wilderness, complaining against God, Rahab was living in the city of Jericho, wasting herself. She was turning tricks and piling up a mountain of sordid memories that would trouble her the rest of her life. When she looked at her life through the rearview mirror, all she saw were rubble, ruin, and shame. In the years following, Rahab must have wondered at the timing of her rescue and what she might have been spared if God had brought Israel over the Jordan just a few years earlier.[6] Marked forever by her Gentile ancestry and her shameful past, Rahab would never outlive the stigma of her profession. We still think of her as "Rahab the harlot."

How did Rahab feel when the Israelite army escorted her back to the camp of God's people? Worthless? Dirty? Full of shame? She was hardly the crown jewel of Jericho, but Rahab was treasure in God's sight. Who would imagine that with all the prominent people in Jericho—leading citizens, wealthy merchants, people of honorable professions—God would reach out and rescue a prostitute? Far from being worthless, a ruined woman, destined to second-class status among God's people, Rahab was the apple of God's eye, and he was carrying out his plan for her. She did not become a skeleton in Israel's closet. In fact, God put her name in lights as a mother in the royal line of King David and as an ancestor of Jesus, the King of Kings (Matt. 1:5). She is named among the leading lights of God's people, held up for us to admire and emulate as a courageous woman of faith who loved and lived for the God of Israel (Heb. 11:31).

Rahab became a theologian with special expertise in grace. What a contrast her voice must have made among Israelites whose taste for God had gone flat. She understood the depths of her own sin, so she felt his mercy more strongly than those who took his grace for granted. She was the Old Testament counterpart to the sinful New Testament woman who bathed Jesus' feet with tears and kisses and wiped them with her hair (Luke 7:36–50). Rahab "loved much," for her sins were many. God's plan for Rahab included raising a son and instilling in him a tender consciousness of God's grace. We know nothing of her husband, Salmon. But we know plenty about Rahab and her son, Boaz. Perhaps it was his mother's lessons in God's grace that motivated Boaz to display compassion and grace to another foreign woman, Ruth the Moabitess. If Boaz' treatment of Ruth is any indication, Rahab was indeed a gifted mother and theologian.

If we learn anything from Rahab, it is that our own sins, failures, and mistakes cannot destroy God's sovereign plan for us. In fact, he is at work in the midst of our self-destructive actions and the pain we bring upon ourselves to advance his good purposes for us. Rahab's theology was forged by her dark and shameful past. God's plan isn't contingent on a sterling resume or a flawless life, or none of us could ever hope to serve him. Not even our sins can obstruct his plans.

Most everyone feels a pang when they look in the rearview mirror. But once we have felt the warmth of God's grace, new feelings emerge when we look over our shoulders—an overwhelming gratitude to God, a passion for holiness, and a softer heart toward other sinners. We feel an irrepressible urge to worship and to follow the God who redeemed us and who was at work in spite of our prodigality to prosper our souls and draw us to himself.

THE MYSTERY OF CONCURRENCE

WHAT WE ARE REALLY discussing when we say God advances his plan for us even through darkness and sin is the ancient doctrine of *concurrence*. This doctrine helps us understand that God is intimately involved in our lives and mysteriously exercises his will through our wills. Concurrence is when two actions occur simultaneously, or concurrently. It means that God is good and absolutely sovereign over all things, yet at the same time, we are not puppets or robots but have real choices and willingly exercise our wills. Furthermore, we are responsible for our actions and suffer real consequences for them. The Bible teaches all of these ideas repeatedly, emphatically, and concurrently. The challenge for us is to avoid choosing one truth over another and instead to hold them all simultaneously.

The stories of Job, Joseph, and Rahab demonstrate that God has a comprehensive plan—a plan he mysteriously implements through human choices. The doctrine of concurrence describes this mystery but cannot explain it. Our comfort is not in the mystery itself but in the revealed character of our God—a God who moves relentlessly through all that opposes him to secure our good and his glory.

WAR ZONE READINESS

LIFE DOESN'T HOLD STILL. While I have been working on this chapter, reports have been coming in from the war zone. A woman battling breast cancer saw her white blood cell count plummet dangerously low for the second time. A survivor of sexual abuse, who thought she had put that battle behind her, was devastated to learn she has a sexually transmitted disease. Four single women are opening new chapters in their lives, filled with enormous challenges and a lot of uncertainty. A new mother is experiencing the joys (and the sleep deprivation) of caring for a newborn, while another young wife faces yet another month of disappointed hopes for conceiving a child. A college coed lost her father when he died suddenly of a heart attack, a mother ached and prayed as her adult daughter made another self-destructive sinful choice, and doctors scheduled another major surgery for my mother.

Women are called to be soldiers. Readiness for battle is crucial, for we never know when we are going to be called up. Sometimes the battle descends on us without warning. Other times we march into the war zone for someone else—a husband, a friend, or a child. A woman's theology can make all the difference in how well she fights the battles that are part of God's plan for her. Sometimes theology is all we have in the war zone. When faith is stripped to the bone and all our props and crutches are gone, our knowledge of God—that he is good and still on his throne—is the only thing that keeps us going.

Our courage and determination in battle hang on our understanding of God's character. Soft theology won't sustain us on the battlefield. Marching into battle with superficial, false, and flimsy ideas of God is like going to war with a popgun tucked under your arm. When fatigue hits and still the battle rages, it makes all the difference in the world to know that God's plan is in place, even here. The thought that he has temporarily surrendered his sovereignty to someone else undermines our confidence, drains us of courage, and weakens our hope.

None of us can afford a theology that cannot withstand the pressures of the war zone, that fits only within a world of comfort and pleasure, where all our ducks are in neat rows and the pieces fit neatly together. We are called to be soldiers, to enter the war zone, to feel the heat of battle for ourselves and for each other, and to see God more clearly within the context of our struggles.

Mary of Bethany may not have realized she was in boot camp when she sat down at Jesus' feet. She probably had no idea she was heading for the war zone. But very soon she too would feel the heat of battle. In the trenches, she would soon discover the true state of her theology. She would also see Jesus in a different light, and what she would learn of him would steel her for the greatest battle of her life.

PART TWO

KNOWING GOD IN LIFE

5

DISAPPOINTED WITH JESUS

Mary Weeps at Jesus' Feet

JOHN 11

"GRIEF AT THE LOSS OF A LOVED ONE IS AS OLD AS THE HUMAN RACE. Everyone who loves will experience it sooner or later, and the greater the love the greater the grief when the time of loss arrives.... As the enjoyment of another's love invigorates one inside, so the blow of losing someone near and dear drains strength from both mind and body for months and perhaps years. And if the bereavement was unanticipated and not prepared for, grief hits harder and hurts more.... We did not know we could feel so strongly, and words fail us to express our feelings adequately."[1]

These words, from the pen of a modern theologian, fittingly describe the agonies that gripped the soul of Mary of Bethany when death severed her from her beloved brother and her ordered world began to break apart. Sandwiched between her earlier breakthrough encounter with Jesus and her future bold anointing of him on the eve of his own appointment with death, this tragic second scene takes Mary to an all-time low. It is the least well-known of the three short clips we have of her life, the most unflattering snapshot on file. This is the photo that never makes it into the family photo album but gets buried in the bottom of the box of pictures we don't want to look at but can't discard. In my family there are no photographs of events surrounding the sudden deaths of my dad's fifty-year-old brother after a three-week siege with a brain tumor, or of two cousins, a four-year-old who died of cancer and a young adult who took his own life. We don't want to remember how we looked and felt when the pain was so fresh and raw. We do not want these grim reminders mixed in among the happy carefree faces smiling back at us from the pages of the family photo album. Death is not the time to bring out the camera; it is the time to draw the curtains and turn out the lights.

So we tend to avoid this shadowy snapshot of our heroine. Every time I stumble over Mary in an art museum, a book, or a sermon, she is usually at home listening to Jesus or anointing his feet at the feast. Whenever her name crops up (and it seems to happen often), she receives well-deserved accolades for her actions in the familiar first and last episodes. Mary, who made "the better choice," who was "swift to hear and slow to speak."[2] Mary, who had her priorities straight, because she listened intently to Jesus rather than getting caught up with domestic chores that could easily wait. Mary, who displayed a remarkable sense of timing and values by lavishing expensive perfume on Jesus at the right moment instead of cashing it in for other worthy but less urgent causes. The weeping Mary in the middle is largely forgotten except in commentaries, which do not have the luxury of skipping over chapters. Here, in this death scene, she does not come off so well but instead falls flat on her face and appears to miss the point that seems so obvious to the rest of us.

My guess is that one of the reasons we neglect this segment of her story may be that it is hard to reconcile this distraught Mary with the idealized Mary in the other episodes. But this part of her story is crucial to our understanding of Mary as a theologian. It rips away our inclination to define theologians simply in terms of where they studied and what they accomplished, without reference to their personal lives. The merits of theologians seem invariably to rest on their academic pedigree and the number of volumes that bear their names on library shelves. This paradigm fits with how we want to remember Mary. She studied under Rabbi Jesus, and although she never wrote a theology text, she did receive public recognition for the significance of her single contribution by none other than Jesus himself when she anointed him for his burial. "Wherever this gospel is preached throughout the world, what she has done will also be told, in memory of her" (Matt. 26:13).

We will never understand Mary as a great woman theologian, or even what it means to be a theologian in the first place, if we omit this middle phase of her story from our discussion. In fact, our tendency to bypass this chapter is symptomatic of one of the biggest problems we have today with theology. We can talk so easily of theological terms and propositions without ever considering the essential process of *living our theology* that comes between learning and ministry. A logical system of words and ideas from a theologian who has never felt despair and confusion, never wrestled with who God is and what he is doing in this world, can sound hollow and insensitive and can be so disconnected from real life as to seem worthless. True Christian theology does not stand aloof from life but fearlessly gets its hands dirty in our everyday lives.

The shattering crisis over Lazarus' death is the hinge on which Mary's entire history turns. It joins her learning and her service by calling into question everything she believes about Jesus. It transforms her learning into survival training and his anointing into a heroic wartime effort. With her brother's illness, Jesus takes Mary to the edge where she will have to *rely* on what she has learned. It is a crucial stage in Mary's development, for here she learns three important lessons about being a theologian: first, that it isn't easy to be a good one; second, that a true theologian *lives* her theology; and third, that God is not a subject she will ever master.

UNPACKING MARY'S THEOLOGY

THE MOOD IN THE GRACIOUS home at Bethany had grown somber. Lazarus was desperately ill. His devoted sisters attended him with increasing uneasiness as his condition worsened. No doubt they had consulted medical experts and tried every possible cure. Still he continued to decline. Those of us who have sat at the bedside of a loved one and watched them slowly fade away know about the growing tightness in Mary's throat, the sinking feeling in her stomach, and the worried lines on her face.

To make matters worse, Jesus was away—somewhere over the Jordan River ministering with his disciples. Apprehension hung ominously in the air as Lazarus' condition steadily deteriorated. The sisters (no doubt after exhausting local remedies as well as themselves in efforts to revive their brother's health) were desperate. As death closed in, they dispatched an urgent message to Jesus.

It is reasonable to assume Mary had done a lot of thinking since the first time she sat at Jesus' feet. Lazarus' illness came near the end of Jesus' ministry, so by this time all Judea was abuzz with reports of Jesus' activities and teachings. Living in a small village the size of Bethany, especially so near Jerusalem, it would have been next to impossible for Mary to avoid hearing about him. You can be sure that she, with her inquisitive mind, would have been on the lookout for new information about Jesus. She had plenty of time to ponder his words, and as she gathered information, listened, and observed, Mary's ideas of Jesus—her theology—slowly began to take shape.

Mary embraced the common opinion that Jesus was a great healer. The quantity of supporting evidence that was public knowledge made it difficult even for his adversaries to deny his miraculous powers. Thousands walked away with full stomachs and lots to tell after Jesus multiplied a few small loaves and some fish to satisfy their hunger. Everywhere you turned, someone else was describing how Jesus had delivered them or someone they loved from an affliction. Even at Lazarus' tomb, mourners were still talking about Jesus' latest miracle, the healing of a man who was born blind. Reports of his miracles had created such a stir, Jesus could hardly go out without being swarmed by mobs of needy and curious people.

But Mary's views of Jesus went beyond popular opinion, for she also knew him as Rabbi—the teacher who had drawn her, a woman, into his inner circle. Despite the hardened traditions of her culture, and the educational and social restrictions on her sex, she had broken through and secured the right to sit at Jesus' feet and learn. Regardless of how such practices were viewed elsewhere in the culture, Jesus had made it clear that it was both accepted and desirable—more than that, that it was necessary—for women to be this rabbi's disciples. Mary wouldn't take his invitation lightly but doubtless seized every opportunity to enjoy this new-found privilege. Her understanding of Jesus would have grown as a result. His visits to her home, accompanied by his disciples, exposed her to information inaccessible to most Israelites. No doubt she was also privy to accounts of miracles witnessed only by the Twelve, which she heard as the disciples sat and talked about Jesus' stilling the storm, filling their empty nets to the bursting point with fish, and walking on water. These discussions went beyond the sensational to the meaning behind his miracles and the implications for Jesus. She may have heard them repeat his explanations of parables and miracles, given in private after the multitudes dispersed. And who knows how many questions she freely discussed with them? Without a doubt, Mary was well informed and probably knew as much about Jesus as anyone.

In addition, she was an Old Testament Israelite with the rich theological heritage of a daughter of Abraham. She brought to her acquaintance with Jesus a wealth of biblical knowledge that her female contemporaries understood and eloquently articulated.[3] She shared Israel's messianic expectations and felt her own hopes stirred not just by what she observed but by what Jesus told her directly. Surely he was the long-awaited Messiah on whom Israel's hopes depended.

But perhaps the most surprising aspect of Mary's theology was the fact that Jesus was her friend. This second scene reveals a warm and unique intimacy between Jesus and the three siblings who hosted him. Three times, and from three different angles, the narrator confirms Jesus' great love for Mary, Martha, and Lazarus. Both sisters sensed his love and banked their appeal for his help on it (v. 3). After all, how many times had they seen Jesus stop what he was doing to aid a stranger? Would he do less for a beloved friend? The apostle John stated Jesus' love for the three as a known fact when he pondered Jesus' bewildering actions (v. 5). And their friends observed it aloud as Jesus wept openly at the tomb of his beloved friend, "See how he loved him!" (v. 36). This was no passing acquaintance but a deep and ongoing relationship that would strengthen Mary's confidence when she turned to him for help.

From this wealth of information, a clearer picture of Jesus was emerging. To Mary, Jesus was healer, teacher, Messiah, and friend. By this time she probably could have passed a rigorous theological examination. She even might have been able to satisfy a skeptical, demanding seminary professor. But knowing propositions about Jesus, even making profound connections between Old Testament prophecies and him, essential as these truths were to Mary's spiritual development, would never be enough to make her a great theologian. What she was learning had to be lived. She had to try it out, to connect her beliefs about Jesus with what was going on at home where Lazarus was dying, to articulate her theology not simply in words but through her life. Jesus was the only hope for this daughter of Abraham and sister of Lazarus. He alone could reverse the malady that was slowly squeezing the life out of her brother. As she watched Lazarus deteriorate, Mary's beliefs about Jesus converged in a simple but confident call for help. As if to remind Jesus of his ties to Lazarus, she and her sister laced their message in terms of his love for their brother: "Lord, the one you love is sick."

DISAPPOINTED WITH JESUS

IF MARY WAS ANYTHING like the rest of us, long before the messenger shrank to a speck on the eastern horizon and disappeared from sight, she was already calculating the earliest moment it would be reasonable to look for Jesus to appear. From that moment on, the two sisters almost certainly divided their watch between the bedside of their ailing brother and the window where they looked anxiously for the first sign of their friend's approach.

Even in our era of 911 convenience and high-speed vehicles, waiting for help can be hair-raising. Several years ago a friend of mine was preparing for company and decided to air the house. After checking on her two young sons, who were playing contentedly in their bedroom, she opened windows and the sliding glass door that led to the swimming pool to let in the fresh Florida winter air and returned to her work. The day might have passed uneventfully if the dog hadn't bounded out the door and gotten into a ferocious fight with the neighbor's dog. At the sound of vicious snarling and snapping, my friend dropped what she was doing and raced outside to stop the fight. She was gone only a few moments, but that was long enough for her two-year-old to toddle through the open door and tumble into the pool. She didn't realize anything was wrong until she had disentangled her dog and the uproar had subsided. Only then could she hear her older child's cries. In a matter of seconds she was pulling the small motionless body of her child from the water. She rushed to the phone and dialed 911. To her horror, there was silence at the other end. In a panic she dropped the receiver and, still carrying her lifeless child, dashed into the yard, desperate for help. Her eyes darted frantically in search of a neighbor or passerby just as a squad car screeched to a halt in front of the house and officers sprang out in time to revive her little boy. The emergency operator had heard her cries for help, even though she couldn't hear him, and had instantly dispatched the closest rescue team to her doorstep. From the moment her call came through to the screech of brakes in front of her house, only sixty seconds had elapsed.

Mary and Martha's emergency call got through too. But Jesus' response was shockingly unlike that of the officers who revved up their car's engine, put the pedal to the floor, and raced to save a young child's life. Instead of flying straight to Bethany for a dramatic rescue, Jesus calmly remained where he was for forty-eight crucial hours. Meanwhile in Bethany, Mary and Martha continued their vigil with sinking hearts and disbelief until, in one final breath, brother and hope expired together. By the time Jesus arrived, it was too late. Death had claimed its victim, the funeral was over, and Lazarus had been entombed for four days.

Mary couldn't have been less prepared for the wretched turn of events that led to her brother's death. She might have wondered whether the courier would be able to find Jesus or whether their message would reach him in time. Never in her wildest thoughts did she or anyone else imagine that Jesus simply would not respond. When she put together everything she knew about Jesus, it didn't add up to this. Perhaps she made excuses for him at first, but the longer Jesus took to reach Bethany, the harder it was to avoid the awful truth that the problem wasn't with the message, the messenger, or the distance. The problem was with Jesus.

It was a double crisis for Mary. Her devastating grief over Lazarus' death was compounded by her disappointment with Jesus. Nothing she or anyone else could say would soften this stark fact: Jesus was too late. Even John the apostle, who was traveling with Jesus at the time and knew about his delay, seemed perplexed when he wrote, "Jesus *loved* Martha and her sister and Lazarus. Yet when he heard that Lazarus was sick, he *stayed* where he was two more days" (vv. 5–6, emphasis added).

In a way, every grief is two-dimensional—the loss itself along with the nagging thought that it could have been prevented if only God had acted. We all have felt Mary's disappointment. How many crises have we suffered in which the simplest, most obvious solution was for God to step in and provide, heal, or fix— something he was fully capable of doing and a sure route to glory for him? We prayed our hearts out and rallied friends at church and on the internet to pray with us. Yet the clock ticked away, days passed, conditions worsened, and still there was no sign of him— no fire from heaven, no breathtaking miracle, no stilling of stormy waters. Events played out without interference from heaven. In the numbing aftermath we nursed our shattered hopes and tried not to think about God's silence. C. S. Lewis, grieving the death of his beloved wife after a grueling battle with cancer, wrote,

> When you are happy, so happy that you have no sense of needing Him, so happy that you are tempted to feel His claims upon you as an interruption, if you remember yourself and turn to Him with gratitude and praise, you will be—or so it feels—welcomed with open arms. But go to Him when your need is desperate, when all other help is vain, and what do you find? A door slammed in your face, and a sound of bolting and double bolting on the inside. After that, silence. The longer you wait, the more emphatic the silence will become. There are no lights in the windows. It might be an empty house.... Why is He so present a commander in our time of prosperity and so very absent a help in time of trouble?[4]

LOOKING DISAPPOINTMENT IN THE FACE

THE SISTERS' REACTIONS WHEN Jesus finally does arrive are dissimilar only on the surface. Martha, the more direct and outspoken of the two, runs to the outskirts of the village the moment she hears of his approach. There she greets him with the enigma that was tormenting both women: "Lord, if you had been here, my brother would not have died" (v. 21). Meanwhile Mary remains secluded inside the house with a few friends. In part what holds her back may be the "half-numb apathy, frequently alternating with bouts of tears"[5] that sets in after such a devastating loss. The widowed Lewis brooded, "There is a sort of invisible blanket between the world and me. I find it hard to take in what anyone says. Or perhaps, hard to want to take it in. It is so uninteresting. Yet I want the others to be about me. I dread the moments when the house is empty. If only they would talk to one another and not to me."[6] But for Mary there is the added strain of facing Jesus. How can she bear to face the friend she had counted on and who had left her brother to die?

To most people, I suppose the climax of the story comes when Jesus calls forth Lazarus from death. I am inclined to think the climax comes much earlier—when Jesus calls Mary forth from her confusion and despair. This meeting between the student who hungers to understand and the rabbi who is committed to teach her and is himself the subject forms the centerpiece of the story. It is an encounter of pivotal importance to us. Although Jesus comes as friend to friend, he also comes as rabbi. Clearly both sisters see him as their rabbi. Even Martha, when bringing word of his arrival to her despondent sister, simply whispers, "The *Teacher* is here" (v. 28, emphasis added). No other label is needed to identify him to Mary. Once again, the eager student is at her rabbi's feet—still full of questions, this time prompted not by curiosity or a hunger for knowledge but by her aching need to understand him. The classroom has changed; Jesus has taken his student out of the sitting room and into the war zone. So Mary gathers herself and hurries to the edge of the village where he stands waiting for her. At the sight of him, she collapses under the double weight of grief and disappointment, sobbing words he has already heard from Martha, "Lord, if you had been here, my brother would not have died."

It isn't so difficult to understand Mary's confusion, for Jesus never seems to do what we expect. When we look for him to act, he stalls. When we think he would avoid an unsettling encounter with Mary, he seeks her out. And when he is finally with her, instead of giving the counsel and explanation we are waiting to hear, he weeps. Everything he does catches us off-guard and forces us to do what Mary had to do—take a closer look at Jesus.

Thinking over the events which have led up to this moment, it is clear that from the outset, Jesus was firmly resolved to do things his way. In every scene, he moved and acted according to his own agenda, his own time frame, and his own good purposes. It was a costly choice for him, for the crisis over Lazarus precipitated a second crisis that raised questions about his character. Did Jesus really care for his friends or was he indifferent? Did he abandon them in their hour of desperation or was there something more to his perplexing behavior? The answer is summed up in Jesus' calm remark to his distressed disciples upon receiving word of Lazarus' illness. "This sickness will not end in death. No, it is for God's glory so that God's Son may be glorified through it" (v. 4).

Upon first reading, it seems Jesus is more concerned about himself than he is about Lazarus and his sisters. This impression gains strength as the story unfolds and Jesus seems strangely out of touch with the gravity of Lazarus' condition. It is a bit worrying when we think how this might play out in our own lives. But when we look carefully at God's glory, we see that Jesus couldn't have given his disciples a stronger reason to trust him. God's glory is bound up with his reputation, his great name, his honor. God's reputation can never be divorced from what happens to us. "It was God's good pleasure to join you to himself in such a way that his name is at stake in your destiny ... in such a way that what becomes of you reflects upon his name."[7]

God's glory is the governing principle behind everything he does. The rock solid ground of our hope is God's "indomitable delight in the worth of his own reputation" and his determination never to allow it to be tarnished in any way by how he cares for his own.[8] The intermingling of God's glory and our good reminds me of a Reformation story I heard when I was living in England, a story about the mingling of the bones of Catherine Vermigli, wife of reformer Peter Martyr Vermigli, with those of Saint Frideswide, patron saint of Oxford. During the reign of Bloody Mary in England, Vermigli's religious enemies tried to degrade, humiliate, and torment him by exhuming Catherine's bones and throwing them on the city dung heap. Their efforts were permanently undone when friends retrieved her bones and mixed them with the bones of the revered Catholic saint. Now the cohorts of Queen Mary could not remove a bone for fear of tampering with the remains of the wrong woman. God's glory and our good are so intermingled that they can no longer be distinguished. And so for Jesus to assert at the outset that this tragedy would bring him glory was the surest promise that the good of his own had already been secured.

For Jesus to gain glory, he must pursue his own path, even if it means disappointing his dearest friends. Their call was to trust him—easy to say and hard to do when circumstances unravel as they did here. But trusting is on his terms, not theirs. To be ruled by their suggestions and appeals, or to veer to any course other than his Father's sovereign plan, would deprive them of what they needed most—a clearer view of God. "God will go his own way, he will pose and nonplus reason, he will work by improbabilities, he will save in such a way as we think would destroy. Now he acts like himself, like an infinite wonder-working God."⁹ Although Jesus seems to let things go too far with Lazarus, here the gentle rabbi teaches his daughter about faith and frees her from "the incessant need to understand exactly what he is doing before [she places her] confidence in him."¹⁰ And she discovers that he can be trusted in the worst of circumstances, that no matter how chaotic and hopeless things appear, he is good and nothing is beyond his control.

The crisis also achieves the unexpected. Although it breaks Mary's heart and brings her to the edge of her faith, instead of distancing her from Jesus, it draws her closer. Instead of weakening their relationship, it intensifies the bond between them. Instead of undermining her faith, it multiplies her reasons to trust him. This tragic death was part of the race marked out for his glory and her good that he was calling her to run. And so with the message Martha whispers, Mary begins her journey back to Jesus.

WHEN JESUS WEEPS

WHEN THE TENSION of a novel reaches a certain level of intensity, many readers cheat and read the last chapter. Others, unable to bear the suspense, put everything on hold to read through to the end. At night, I have caught my daughter with book and flashlight under the covers, reading the last lines of a plot that was too suspenseful to wait until morning to finish. Going to sleep a little later than usual seemed a good deal better to her than lying awake for hours wondering how it would all turn out. It is hard to linger over this wrenching scene with Jesus and the prostrate Mary, especially when we know what Jesus is about to do. We want to get beyond the pain, to the relief just around the corner. Images of Caroline Kennedy Schlossberg's drawn and ashen face after the plane crash that killed John F. Kennedy Jr. are fresh reminders of how devastating it is to lose a beloved brother. Mary's pain is so fierce, her disappointment so profound, we are eager to move on to the site of the tomb, where Jesus vindicates himself and at last we hear the powerful words that relieve this stress and restore Mary's decaying brother back to life. Turn the page please. There is too much tension here.

But the tension is intentional, and we are supposed to feel it as Mary weeps inconsolably at Jesus' feet. There is much to lose if we pass on quickly and do not pause to probe her disappointment and his role in it. It is particularly important for us because, sooner or later, all of us end up where Mary is—at the end of our rope, thinking God has failed us and feeling confused about him. Our obsession with happy endings and our propensity for tidy formulaic views of God press us to move on and distract us from the benefits this uncomfortable meeting offers. This is the hardest place to be, but it is also the only place anyone can make sense of her struggle.

A grieving C. S. Lewis may not have gotten his wish that his friends would comfort him without words. Mary doesn't have that problem with Jesus. He doesn't try to coax her out of her despondency or chide her for falling apart when she "should have known better." When you study how Jesus treats Mary here, you don't get any sense that he looked askance at her behavior or scored her lower than her more composed sister, like the commentator who wrote, "In piety she [Mary] is, of course, equal to her sister; but in composure and serenity she is inferior."[11] Jesus utters no such criticisms or disparaging remarks about female hormones or a woman's emotions. Nor does her weeping unnerve him, as it would some men. Rabbi Jesus—the man whose theology was impeccable, who knew perfectly well how the story would end, who stood most to be offended by her tears and disappointment in him—treats her collapse with disarming empathy and tenderness. He speaks to her in a language that would penetrate the most grief-numbed soul. His own chest heaves with a sigh that every eye can see, and soon his own eyes stream with tears of grief. (Would that Christian men would come to prize this dimension of true manliness.) Mary's pain is both real and profound, her grief inescapable. Jesus does not stand above or outside of Mary's pain, much less urge her to snap out of it. He is neither philosophical nor patronizing, for he has not come "to redeem the world from imaginary grief or to make grief over death imaginary,"[12] and only he knows just how real her grief truly is. He acknowledges her sorrow and validates her suffering by entering himself into the full measure of her distress without reserve.

Surely Jesus' behavior should prevent us from ever thinking good theology makes us impervious to our pain or indifferent to the suffering of others. Jesus himself suffers here and will agonize again when his own hour of suffering arrives. Good theology—in Jesus and in us—coexists with broken hearts, shattered lives, and unimaginable pain. It produces a reservoir of patience toward ourselves and others who hurt and cannot understand what is happening. Jesus not only gives Mary space and time to sorrow deeply; he sorrows with her.

Why does Jesus weep?[13] It is a question that probably will always fascinate scholars. Surely these cannot be tears of despair, for Jesus soon will raise Lazarus to life and ultimately will conquer death itself. There may be, as some suggest, a cosmic dimension here—a mixture of grief and consternation over the havoc wreaked by the forces of evil and death that have invaded his world and caused such injury to his loved ones. But the simplest explanation (which is almost always the best one) is that Jesus weeps for Mary. He weeps with her over the loss of her brother and his dear friend. He weeps for her because she is confused, and he knows how hard it is for her to understand him. He weeps because she suffers. His tears tell us that our pain is real and that he will never minimize it.

I used to think I had failed miserably as a Christian if I couldn't maintain a stiff upper lip and a light step under the worst of circumstances. I was convinced God expected me to keep my spirits up regardless of what was happening in my life. Recently I heard of a cancer patient who tried to conceal her despondency, because she felt obligated to "be a testimony" for everyone else. It's the old "God won't give you something you can't handle" mentality and the conviction that good Christians are always triumphant. It leaves us berating ourselves and feeling like failures when we fall apart and adds an unnecessary layer of guilt to our suffering, a layer Jesus refuses to pile on Mary. We think we've let him down, that he'll be angry or disappointed if we can't hold ourselves together or if our problems depress us. What a surprise to see how he treats Mary. What I have seen in myself, and believe is happening here to Mary, is that all of us fall flat on our faces a good many times and that, in fact, it is good for us when we do. He brings us here—to feel such pain and through it to know the depths of our need for him. He uses our struggles to help us realize we don't know him nearly as well as we think we do and to draw us closer to him. Difficult as it is to be here, this is where we do our best learning—not theoretical learning but the deeply personal learning to trust our God when he doesn't fit our expectations. He has our attention, and we are no longer blinded by an inflated sense of our own powers and understanding. No, Jesus was not angry with Mary. I don't think he was even disappointed. He orchestrated the circumstances that brought her here so that he could connect with her at a deeper level. And so he weeps with her.

But the story doesn't end with weeping. Jesus is not just the sympathetic Savior. He is our help. He is with us in the sorrow, but he is also working through the sorrow to fulfill his good purposes for us. And so Jesus leads Mary forward—out of despair and on to discover that no matter when he comes, he is never too late.

TRUSTING GOD ALONE

THE BRIDGE BETWEEN the awkward meeting between Jesus and Mary and the moment he weeps at his friend's grave is his simple question, "Where have you laid him?" Those who lead Jesus to the tomb and there observe his grief, ask again the question that boils just beneath the surface of the story, "Could not he who opened the eyes of the blind man have kept this man from dying?" (v. 37).

Jesus approaches the tomb where Lazarus' body is already decomposing. A heavy stone blocks the entrance to the cave, sealing the dead away from the living. Once again Jesus does the unexpected. In a voice which must have jarred his companions, Jesus commands, "Take away the stone" (v. 39). The shock this produces on the small cluster of family and friends would be hard to exaggerate. They are aghast. Mary remains silent, but Martha cannot be so restrained. As the dead man's sister and the family spokesman, she objects: "By this time there is a bad odor, for he has been there four days" (v. 39). Jesus doesn't back down. Several mourners heave the cumbersome stone aside, where it thuds to the ground in a cloud of dust. Jesus speaks again, this time commanding the impossible, "Lazarus, come out!" (v. 43). All eyes fix on the opening. For a second, all is silent. Then to the disbelief of all, faint stirrings sound from deep within the tomb.

I would give anything to have been there, to see the look on Mary's face as she waited and watched, and then as her brother, still bound in burial linens, staggered into the sunlight that splashed against the opening of the tomb, and again as her astonished gaze turned to look at her Lord. It was a watershed moment for Mary. I can only imagine the thoughts and emotions that shot through her. Who is this Jesus? She had been right about him all along. He was the healer, the teacher, Messiah, and friend. And although that was surely enough to command her trust, it only scratched the surface of what there was to know of him. For he is the Lord of life and of death, the one who always moves and acts in perfect concert with his nature and according to his Father's plan and who is sovereign over all.

Surely a new discontentment surged inside of Mary, a discontentment we would all do well to feel—the insatiable hunger to know him better. Although she could and must increase in her understanding of him, she would never master him. He is Master, and he cannot and will not be confined within the narrow wooden boundaries of her expectations. He is God, and he called her to trust him on his own terms, even beyond what she could see and understand.

GRIEF IN THE PRESENT TENSE

LATE SUNDAY EVENING, I switched on the computer to check for e-mail. There was one message—a short note from my friend Dixie Fraley asking how I was coming with my writing. We had seen each other that morning in church but hadn't had a chance to talk. Little did I know when I read her encouraging note how her story would get tangled up with this chapter or how images from real life would get all mixed up with those from Mary's story.

Monday morning Dixie kissed her husband, Robert, good-bye, and he headed for the Orlando airport, where he, along with two close friends, business partner Van Ardan and U.S. Open champion Payne Stewart, boarded a private jet bound for Dallas. By midmorning America was glued to the television as military pilots shadowed the Learjet that had veered from its flight plan. From as close as fifty feet from the iced up windows of the plane, which appeared to be flying on autopilot, the air force pilots reported seeing no signs of life. Initial speculation was that all onboard had lost consciousness after a sudden catastrophic drop in cabin air pressure, which may have happened shortly after takeoff. Military planes tracked and monitored the doomed jet to the end of its fuel supply and its disastrous destination in a South Dakota farm field.

A wave of grief washed over Orlando. As the nation watched, three women, Dixie, Debbie, and Tracey, braved the staggering weight of their losses. Death was no longer simply a word on my computer screen but an enemy capable of inflicting indescribable pain. Television reports and church memorial services were filled with men—professional athletes and colleagues—who wept openly for these women's losses, as well as their own. I will not soon forget hearing Mets pitcher Orel Hershiser sob as he eulogized his beloved friend Robert, or seeing the heaving chest of golfer Paul Azinger as he honored his friend Payne Stewart. It brought to mind the words spoken so long ago, "See how he loved him!"

When the crisis hit, there was no time to sit down with a theology book. No one took these women aside and rehearsed the truths of God's character to help them get through. No one needed to. Instinctively, they did what all of us do. They turned to their theology—to what they knew of God—and clung for dear life. To the amazement of the rest of us, one of them commented, "Even when you hit bottom, there's still a rock to stand on."

Moments like this teach us why theology is so important for women. Suddenly it makes a lot of sense why Jesus defended Mary's right to sit at his feet and what he meant when he said, "Mary has chosen what is better, and it will not be taken away from her" (Luke 10:42). He didn't say this merely to enable women to keep up with men in learning and studying deep truth. It wasn't even simply to prevent the tragic waste of a woman's intellect, much as these objectives mattered to Jesus. No, Jesus wanted Mary to learn because he knew how desperately she and other women would need it—not just for the terrible shock of first grief but for the long road ahead. When the bottom dropped out of her life and she was in a freefall, what she knew of Jesus would be all she had to hold her up. Knowing him wouldn't spare her from pain and suffering, or even from disappointment, confusion, and grief. But it would give her hope in the darkest moments and a pervasive sense of purpose in the most confusing times.

Not every sister's brother is brought back to life after being dead four days. Not every mother's child revives after falling into the pool. Sometimes we live the rest of our lives with an ache that won't go away, a pain that never subsides. It isn't easy to live in a fallen broken world where we hurt and neither God nor life always make a lot of sense. But one thing is sure. Whether we are in pain ourselves, or grieving over the sufferings of others, we all live out our theology. Either we will live under a cloud of despair, believing that God has abandoned us, that for a moment we were out of his hands and in the hands of fate or the devil, that we were mistaken when we thought he loved us, that others are more important than we are, or that his power simply doesn't reach this far. Or we will live with hope, even in the midst of pain, knowing that a good and loving God has marked out the race we are running. He has done it for our good and his glory.

Mary is maturing as a theologian. When the fires heat up for her again, as they soon do, we will see the benefits of her struggle with Jesus, not only in her but in the way she reaches out with hope and encouragement to others. But for now, we will explore what it means for us to live out our theology as we run the race marked out for us.

6

BATTLING OUR UNBELIEF

FEW CITIES HAVE PLAYED A MORE PROMINENT ROLE ON THE WORLD'S stage than the Medieval English city of Oxford. The minute you set foot inside her borders, you sense it. The feeling grows as you wander down her cobbled streets and into St. Mary the Virgin Church or Christ Church Cathedral, as you savor the silence of the Merton College quadrangle and the tolling of ancient bells, or gaze at the spires and towers that pierce the skyline overhead. Oxford is steeped in culture, history, and greatness. Since the Middle Ages this city and her famed university have grown accustomed to the spotlight. She has harbored such influential religious and literary figures as John Wycliffe, Archbishop Thomas Cranmer, the Wesleys, Lewis Carroll, C. S. Lewis, and J. R. R. Tolkien. Many of her sons and daughters have risen to heights of power—England's Margaret Thatcher, Pakistan's Benazir Bhutto, and America's Bill Clinton. And within the university's hallowed walls, scholars are busy pushing the boundaries of human knowledge and perpetuating the legacy—what professor C. S. Lewis once called "the hum of the hive." Oxford is a heady place.

The first time I set foot in Oxford, in 1989, I had more mundane things on my mind—finding the nearest grocery store, purchasing a hair dryer and a toaster wired for UK wattage, checking out St. Clement's Preschool for three-year-old Allison, who was ready for new playmates, figuring out the local bus schedule, and scavenging items to furnish our student flat. We weren't here on holiday but to make Oxford home for the next three and a half years while my husband earned his doctorate in history. At first there were lots of adjustments and deep yearnings for home and family. Over time I would come to love this old city, not simply for her architecture, history, and culture but also for the lessons in theology I would learn during my stay. Although I would not walk away with a degree to show for what I had learned, Oxford would be a seat of learning for me too—the place where I would wrestle again with how to put my beliefs about God together with what was happening in my life.

It is fair to say I wasn't here by choice. Unlike other new arrivals, our coming to Oxford was not the fulfillment of a life-long dream. After years of pouring hard work and thousands of dollars into a master's degree and a Ph.D. in theology, we were bone tired of training and eager to settle down and begin our life's work. But early in the launching of his academic career, my husband had reached a dead end. The academic job market was glutted with scholars in search of teaching appointments. For every opening there were hundreds of applicants, and it was easy to get lost in the shuffle. A two-year teaching appointment in California would be the end of the road for him, unless (as one realistic professor advised) he pursued a second doctorate that would set him apart from the pack. The prospect of several more years of education, expense, and delay was devastating. Yet at the same time, we were beginning to see that God was leading us to start all over again. This was part of the race he had marked out for us—disappointing and costly as it appeared.

Unbeknownst to me, this was another opportunity to know God more deeply and to see how life and theology come together in a woman's life—not just in my life but in the lives of other women I would meet in Oxford. In this great city, theology would become part of the everyday fabric of my life as I began to connect my ideas of God with the day-to-day circumstances of my own life.

BORN TO RUN

EVERY WOMAN STRUGGLES with aspects of God's plan for her. There are points along the way where everything inside us rebels against what is happening. Just when we reach the spot where we thought the grass was greener, something new emerges and our struggle resumes. I recall one friend whose plan to enjoy a perfect summer afternoon in the park was spoiled by the appearance of a swarm of gnats. After her frantic attempts to drive them away only succeeded in making her look silly, she groaned, "Why is there always something?"

That tells the story for all of us. Life isn't perfect, and at almost every stage we can point to something we wish we could change. Sometimes the spoilers are nothing more than gnats, which if they arrived singly, would have little effect on us. But their cumulative effect is wearying and leaves us frustrated and unhappy. Sometimes our problems are more like elephants than gnats—like the death that shattered Mary of Bethany. It is one thing to talk about the race God has marked out. It is quite another to run it.

Sooner or later all of us will ask the question, If this is God's plan for me, how do I move forward? How do I run the race he has marked out when I am disappointed with it and frustrated with him? At least part of the answer lies in the urgent words of the ancient epistle to the Hebrews: "Let us throw off everything that hinders and the sin that so easily entangles. . . . Let us run with perseverance the race marked out for us. . . . Let us fix our eyes on Jesus" (Heb. 12:1–2). These three exhortations show us how to bring our theology to life, to take up what we are learning about God and begin to live as theologians.

Let Us Throw Off Everything That Hinders

The first time I met Hong Kong–born Mee-Yan, I had no idea anything was weighing her down. This exuberant Chinese woman didn't seem to have a care in the world. She lived with her husband (an Oxford don)[1] and their beautiful child and ran her own successful consulting business, providing "Organisation Development Consultancy" services to major British corporations and political parties. She seemed to enjoy the best Oxford had to offer. She was a true entrepreneur, not just when it came to business but also in extending warmhearted hospitality to foreigners in need of friendship, as my family discovered soon after meeting her. Always ready to try something new, she invited us to help her host an American Thanksgiving for some of her local friends. She roasted the turkey, and I brought pumpkin and pecan pies, which they called puddings and ate with spoons.

But what defined her more than anything else was not so much her warm personality or her accomplishments. It was her grief. Underneath a charming and brave exterior, she was in enormous pain. The suicide of her older sister would have been enough to explain it. This sister, who was in full-time Christian ministry, had been Mee-Yan's spiritual mentor, her inspiration. But for Mee-Yan this was only the beginning of sorrows. Not once but twice she had lost babies to SIDS.[2] The heartache she always carried around with her, and the questions it provoked about God, seemed more than anyone should have to bear. I could hardly look at her without aching.

The writer to the Hebrews knew, no doubt from personal experience, that we would be hampered if we tried to carry heavy burdens and run at the same time. Ancient Greek Olympians understood this and were radical about unburdening themselves. They stripped to the skin and ran naked. The exhortation to "throw off everything that hinders and the sin that so easily entangles" calls us to adopt the same ruthless mentality. By speaking so broadly of what hinders, the writer leaves room for us to fill in the blank with anything—sinful or otherwise—that interferes with our running. "Every encumbrance and impediment, everything likely to occasion a fall, must be carefully got rid of."[3]

But when we step back and examine the letter to the Hebrews as a whole, the writer seems to have something more specific in mind. His readers, first-century Jewish Christians, were suffering from persecution. Many had been humiliated, insulted, and imprisoned. Some had even lost their property, and they lived under the constant threat of further trouble.[4] These sufferings were beginning to take a toll, and these Christians were beginning to wonder about God. How could he let their tormentors get away with this? Warnings to hold fast to the faith, scattered throughout the letter, reveal their growing doubts concerning God and his ability to care for them.[5] They felt abandoned by God and, in turn, were on the brink of abandoning him. The weight bogging down these Hebrew runners was the sin of unbelief.

When we're not sure about God—about his goodness, his love, or his control over our circumstances—when we begin to believe our lives are meaningless and beyond hope, when we lose the energy or the will to face another day, unbelief has set in. It confronts us every day in a hundred different ways. It was the hidden battle Mee-Yan faced daily as she went about her business and attended to family matters. It assaulted her openly as she wept beside two small graves in an English churchyard.

Unbelief never travels alone but brings bitterness and other sins of the heart. It exposes us to "all sorts of temptations, gives advantage unto all disheartening, weakening, discouraging considerations, and clogs and hinders us in our constant course of obedience."[6] Like the bowler's lead pin, it has the power to make a lot of other things in our lives topple over. Unbelief drains us of hope and undermines our courage at the very moment we need it most. When this happens, it is time to shed "everything that hinders and the sin that so easily entangles."

This is where we pick up our theology and begin to use it, for the best antidote for unbelief is truth. A malnourished faith is no match for the artillery that comes against us in the trenches of ordinary life. It will never do simply to have a stiff upper lip, close our eyes and try harder to believe, or force ourselves to dwell on happier thoughts. The writer to the Hebrews seemed to think combating unbelief by focusing on ourselves is getting things backward. Faith, according to his letter, must be fed, and truth is the only food it can digest. And so, instead of prefacing the command to throw off unbelief with the pep talk on self-improvement we were expecting, he spreads before his readers a lavish discourse on the greatness of God as reflected in his Son, Jesus. Fully three-fourths of his letter focuses on the person and work of Christ— some ideas that no doubt were new to his readers and certainly much that they knew already but needed to hear again. If you're looking for Christology (the doctrine of Christ), this letter is a must read. But, interestingly enough, though the content of this letter is deeply theological—perhaps the richest explanation of Christ that we have—it was not written as a seminary textbook. Its purpose was to fuel the faith of ordinary women and men who were afraid, hurting, and deeply disappointed with Jesus. The truth about God's character was as practical and soothing to these struggling believers as a mother's milk is to a malnourished baby.

The writer portrays Jesus with large brush strokes and bold colors to give his readers a clearer sense of the person they are called to trust. Jesus is the creator and sustainer of the universe, the Lord and King who reigns at his Father's side, the one to whom every knee in heaven and on earth will bow, and the heir who will inherit all things. Together, Father and Son are carrying out the plans they drew up before the beginning of time and which they will see through to the last detail. The God of these suffering Hebrew Christians is big, wise, and unstoppable. His power doesn't ebb and flow. His heart for his children is every bit as big as his power and never wavers. Unlike everything around us, he is "always the same" and will "never grow old" (Heb. 1:12 NLT).

But the writer doesn't stop here. After setting forth the proven changeless character of Jesus and the lengths he has gone in his love for them, he summons character witnesses for God. A vast cloud of witnesses gathers in response (Hebrews 11). Their stories have heartened believers for centuries. These are not fairy tales in which everything comes together magically in the end and everyone lives happily ever after. Even here our tendency to nail faith to a happy outcome is denied. These are accounts of real people whose hearts ached like Mee-Yan's and who struggled to trust God under the most appalling circumstances. Joining those who "conquered kingdoms . . . shut the mouths of lions, quenched the fury of the flames, and escaped the edge of the sword" is a less triumphant group of witnesses who "were tortured . . . faced jeers and flogging . . . were chained and put in prison . . . stoned . . . sawed in two . . . put to death by the sword . . . destitute, persecuted and mistreated" (Heb. 11:33–34, 35–38).

If I had been writing this letter, I would not have included this tragic group. But that's the point. It's easy to trust God when the story comes out right and all of the pieces line up. But throwing off unbelief is grueling when your world has collapsed and there's no resolution to the pain. The writer asserts in the strongest possible terms that even in darkness and in pain, Jesus has not lost control, has not compromised his goodness, and is worthy of our trust. Faith gathers fresh energy when it has this kind of God in its sights. These ancient runners knew their God and trusted him regardless of the outcome. He was working in all of their circumstances for his glory and for their good, and that was their hope. Some spectacular running resulted.

The tried and true method employed by New Testament Christians still works for us today. We throw off our unbelief the same way they did, by telling ourselves the truth about God. In the words of one wise doctor of the soul, "We must learn to take ourselves in hand, address ourselves, preach to ourselves, remind ourselves of who God is, what God has done, and what God has pledged Himself to do."[7] The payoff for everything we have learned about God comes when we embrace our theology and cling to him. It is a habit we must cultivate—one that gives our faith a solid footing and puts our unbelief to flight.

But there is something more we need to do to discard unbelief. We must affirm God's plan in the present moment—say yes to God and what he is doing in our lives today. "Trusting God in the midst of our pain and heartache means that we accept it from Him.... To truly accept our pain and heartache has the connotation of willingness. An attitude of acceptance says that we trust God, that He loves us, and knows what is best for us."[8] This is not to wave a white flag of surrender, resigning ourselves to the inevitable because we are helpless to do anything else. Trusting God means we embrace his goodness in this part of the race and determine, by his grace, to run.

It is important to emphasize again that affirming God's plan never gives us permission to take a casual view of sin. God calls us to join him in warring against sin in ourselves and in those around us—to "hate what is evil" and "cling to what is good" (Romans 12:9b) and never to confuse the two. Nor does this lead us to passivity or resignation; rather it mobilizes and emboldens us to confront problems and tackle opportunities because we know he has called us to this. Instead of shrinking from what lies ahead, faith emboldens us to face these challenges head on, for, as one runner remarked, "It is folly to think of escaping that cross which, being laid in our way, we ought to take up."[9]

I watched a woman throw off her unbelief after doctors told her she was in the advanced stages of cancer. As the terrible news spread through her circle of friends, her telephone began to ring. One call came from a close friend who was very upset over the terminal diagnosis. As they talked, the two women wept together. My friend understood the place (and also the need) for Christians to weep and grieve. But when this conversation ended, she was troubled by what had passed between herself and her friend. She knew, at least for herself, that these were tears of unbelief, self-pity, and bitterness against the Lord. It was a turning point for her when she reminded herself of God's character and privately resolved "never to cry like that again about my cancer." A runner threw off unbelief and purposed in her own heart to trust him as she ran the race he had planned for her. Would she never weep again? No doubt she wept many times, with friends, family, and also in private. Did she concede to her disease? To the contrary, she left no stone unturned in pursuing a cure. What lay ahead wasn't going to be easy, but she knew the one who was leading her through this dark valley.

What we believe about God—our theology—affects how we run our race. We can't run well if our feet are tangled with unbelief. Running by faith means believing God is good to me right now, regardless of how I feel or how things look.

Let Us Run with Perseverance

Susan was the first friend I made, shortly after our arrival in England. She was an English graduate student, a single mum, and my neighbor. We were a cultural contrast right from the start—she in dark winter stockings, well-worn walking shoes, loose fitting jumper and midcalf woolen skirt, with tousled copper curls reaching to her shoulders, and I in blue jeans, sweatshirt, Reebocks, and thick Lands' End jacket, with hair cropped short and neat. Our paths crossed one winter evening in the little convenience shop just around the corner from our flat. We had each stopped to pick up a small item to fill out the evening meal—supper for us and tea for her and her ten-year-old son. The resulting conversation—a mix of British and American expressions and accents—commenced a friendship that would add "colour" to my life and outlast the inevitable separation when an ocean came between us. Over the course of the next few years, we would spend hours in deep conversation over cups of dark English tea, sharing the world of Jane Austin and the Bronte sisters. Together we witnessed and pondered the fall of Margaret Thatcher, and Princess Diana's battle to survive a loveless marriage and the suffocating atmosphere of the British monarchy.

On Sunday afternoon rambles our two families took in and around Oxford, I learned even more about this remarkable woman. Despite getting off to a difficult start in her young life,

Susan had worked and struggled (sometimes fought) to make a life for herself and her child. It hadn't been easy. Money was scarce, and she knew the meaning of loneliness. But her commitment to her child was profound and selfless. She had battled hard to win a place for him at the prestigious Magdalen College boys' school at Oxford University, where he would receive the best education England had to offer. When I met her, she was searching for a church that would nourish him spiritually.

Susan had dreams for her son, but she also had dreams for herself. She dreamed of being an astrophysicist. She completed her undergraduate degree and then, against all odds and self-doubt, made application to Oxford University. The road to an Oxford doctorate wouldn't be easy. As she soon discovered, there is more than a little truth to the quip about Ginger Rogers and Fred Astaire that a woman can do anything a man does, only she does it backwards and in high heels. Not only did Susan keep up with the academic rigors of astrophysics, she did it without the support of a spouse and with the added responsibilities of a child. To complicate matters, she had chosen a male-dominated field, which made her task doubly difficult at times, especially when a male colleague or professor resistant to the idea of a female succeeding in the department decided to make life harder for her. Instead of going quietly about her research, she encountered roadblocks and conflict that drained her of emotional energy and took precious time from her studies. Here she was, finally at her dream's edge, and still she was struggling with life. More than once she was pushed to the limits of frustration and strength when a new complication disrupted the delicate balance she tried desperately to maintain between home and academics. Yet still she carried on. She had no choice.

Running is a vigorous demanding sport. The race God has marked out demands everything we've got and more. A lot of Christians are convinced God's sovereignty and human responsibility are mutually exclusive, that it is possible to hold only one or the other idea, but not both. For some strange reason this didn't seem to worry the writer to the Hebrews in the least. He put both ideas side by side without diluting either of them when he charged his readers to "run with perseverance the race marked out for us." God marks out our race, and we are commanded to run. If we follow the logic, sovereignty doesn't remove human responsibility. It actually increases it. Human responsibility depends on an ordered world in which God is sovereign. You can't be responsible in a world of chaos, chance, and blind fate. Sovereignty frees us to act because we know God has a plan. We are part of that plan, for we are the agents through whom he accomplishes his purposes. His plan is fulfilled and accomplished as we roll up our sleeves and get to work.

So what does it mean to run? According to the mechanics of running, it means taking the next step, doing what is right in the present circumstances. It is the opposite of passivity. God calls us to full-throttled, active, and creative living. Our decisions, attitudes, initiatives, effort, and actions matter. We make a difference because God has invested us and everything we do with significance. We don't need to diminish his powers to have significance ourselves.

But we are not only called to run; we are called to run *with perseverance*. Endurance is not a foreign concept to women. The instinct is born in us. Little girls listen in wide-eyed dismay to agonizing tales of childbirth with every intention of becoming mothers themselves. Feminine tenacity has a long and public history— from the relentless widow whose appeals finally wore down the unjust judge (Luke 18:1–5) to England's twentieth-century Iron Lady, Margaret Thatcher, whose determined bid for the office of Prime Minister awed her male detractors and led one columnist to remark that the Tories "needed more men like her."[10]

During the late 1980s and early '90s, while we were in Oxford, the United Kingdom was captivated by the tireless efforts of a young woman intent on securing the release of a British television journalist who was kidnapped by Islamic terrorists in Beirut in 1986. For five years, almost single handedly, Jill Morrell made sure that no matter how long his ordeal dragged on, John McCarthy would not be forgotten. One moment she was organizing a candlelight vigil and the next a publicity stunt. On day nine hundred of his captivity, she climbed Blackpool Tower in stiff winds to release hundreds of black helium-filled balloons while a friend gripped her ankles to keep her from being blown off. She even managed a meeting with Yasir Arafat. No one could guess what tactic she would try next to keep John's name in the public eye or to badger government officials into doing more to secure his release. Word of her efforts even trickled into the squalid cell where he and other hostages were held and lifted their sagging spirits. Despite numerous disappointments and frustrations, she never gave up until 1991, when John set foot on British soil again as a free man.

I saw a lot of endurance running in Oxford. Susan did it all the time. Sometimes it looked like her whole race was on a steep uphill slope. God calls women to run—to trust him and invest ourselves in the race he has marked out—to participate, contribute and fight for what is right. He calls us to do it with endurance. So, it shouldn't surprise us when we feel exhausted and pressed beyond our limits. It happens all the time: the young woman who fights for her marriage and single-parents her children, despite her husband's indifference and the raised eyebrows of Christian friends who are quick to pass judgment and slow to come alongside; the mom whose teenagers relentlessly test the boundaries and keep her on a constant state of alert for the sake of their souls; single and infertile women who press on year after year with unanswered longings and no promise of change on the horizon.

One of my favorite examples of running is the apostle Paul. How devastated he must have felt when a legal fluke abruptly ended his powerful ministry and restricted him to a Roman prison cell,[11] where he was unable to exercise the spiritual gifts God had given him. Missionary journeys were impossible now, and he could no longer attend to the overwhelming needs of the church. And as if this were not enough to discourage him, toss in the physical and mental suffering he endured.

But Paul told himself the truth about God and, by faith, affirmed the race marked out for him. He looked beyond secondary causes to the first cause. He did not see himself as the victim of his enemies but called himself the "prisoner of Christ Jesus" (Philem. 1:1). He never stopped hoping for release from prison and spared no effort to win his freedom. But in the meantime, he accepted his new assignment from the Lord. He seized the opportunities right before him in his prison cell. He gave the gospel to the Roman soldiers assigned to guard him and penned the New Testament epistles we hold in our hands. Far from being wasted, this was perhaps the most fruitful phase of Paul's ministry, even though he never knew how widely his writings would be circulated. It is hard to imagine where we would be without the letters he produced during his confinement.

Ultimately the race isn't a test of our stamina. None of us has what it takes to make it. The race is a test of our great God. We run well, not because of our own skill and determination but because we have a great God who is always at work for our good. It is only because he is on his throne that we can run with endurance.

Let Us Fix Our Eyes on Jesus

When Elizabeth and her husband first arrived from America, they had one adorable little toddler. Barely three years after their arrival (and following miserable pregnancies), there were two more mouths to feed. Their cozy little row home seemed to bulge as their family expanded. When the third baby arrived, Elizabeth placed a crib for her second child in the bathtub as a temporary solution for overcrowding. We laughed when she told us how nighttime visits to the bathroom had become delicate affairs that could easily turn chaotic. Without a car, errands to the grocery store were major productions, with babies and groceries packed into the stroller. Going into town was even worse, with the added complication of boarding and deboarding the bus.

Elizabeth's husband was on a tight schedule to complete his degree and resume pastoral duties in the States. While he focused on research, Elizabeth managed the domestic front and worked part-time as a cardiac care unit nurse to help cover expenses. She caught her sleep in snatches between night feedings, tending sick babies, and typing her husband's dissertation on the computer. I don't think I ever saw her fully rested. Although she savored the joys of her three bright-eyed children (my mental pictures are always of her laughing over something cute they had done) and the blessings of a strong marriage, her time in England seemed invariably to take the hard route. She would hit her limit when her back would go out from all the lifting in the hospital and at home.

Oxford can be cruel. Before leaving there, Elizabeth and her husband would face one last crisis when her husband took his viva—the final defense of a doctoral dissertation. At Oxford this is the moment of truth when the decision is made whether to award the degree. In a small examining room, three small desks are arranged according to Medieval tradition, with the student's desk placed a sword's length from the two desks where the examiners sit. In Medieval times, this was a necessary precaution to protect professors from the point of a desperate student's sword if things went badly.

Strict university rules require examiners to refrain from telling doctoral candidates how they have faired in the examination, to allow the decision to be relayed through proper (though often sluggish) administrative channels. You can just imagine the torture of awaiting those results. A few examiners, softened by memories of their own anxieties when they sat in the student's chair, send reassuring signals to the student throughout the process and drop hints regarding a successful outcome. One compassionate professor told a student, "If you happen to have a bottle of champagne at home, I wouldn't hesitate to open it."

But when Elizabeth's husband arrived for his viva, mercy vacated the room. The signals coming from his examiners were anything but reassuring, and the silence from university officials in the following week was unnerving. While they waited, Elizabeth and her husband lived with the very real possibility that all their efforts for the past three years had been in vain. After everything she had been through, this seemed like the last straw.

What keeps the runner on her feet and out of the ditch through the ups and downs of life? The writer of Hebrews exhorts us to fix our eyes on Jesus. There is so much ore to be mined in this brief exhortation that it deserves a chapter of its own, and we'll examine it more closely in the next chapter. So for the moment, a few words will suffice.

In a race, the runner who takes her eyes off the goal wastes precious time and courts disaster. What kept Elizabeth going through thick and thin was her determination to trust Christ to the very end. When her haggard husband emerged from his examination, her heart sank, but she struggled to keep her eyes fixed on Christ and waded into the struggle God had placed in her path. With her eyes focused on Jesus, she knew they were in safe hands and where they could find strength to make it through this ordeal. The cloud of witnesses can inspire and challenge. But only Jesus can help. He has gone before and done everything necessary to secure our happiness.

Jesus gives purpose and meaning to everything—even senseless moments like this endless wait for an outcome. Nothing we do falls outside the scope of the race. Everything matters. Even the cup of water that a weary Elizabeth takes to a little child in the dead of night is a significant act in God's eyes (Matt. 10:42). We look to Jesus, and we know all is well. With our eyes fixed on him, we remember why we can trust God, for Jesus is the proof of God's unfailing love for us. He is the reason God will never abandon us, and he will be the first to welcome us when we cross the finish line.

LIFE GOES ON

MY FRIENDS HAVE COVERED a lot of ground since I was living in Oxford, and all three of them are still running.

Shortly after we left for Florida, Susan sat a sword's distance away from two somber academics and successfully defended her contribution to astrophysics. She is pursuing her career as a lecturer in mathematics for Oxford's Open University. Her son has completed his studies in religion at the University of London and moved on to officer's training at Sandhurst, Britain's Royal Military Academy.

Some months after we left Oxford, Mee-Yan discovered she was pregnant again. It seemed too much to hope that God would bless them with another child. Yet nine months later, she was holding another baby. No one can imagine the anxiety of those early months when SIDS had invaded their life twice before, but they made it safely through. Even though the joys of two daughters are more than she had hoped for, there will always be an ache in her heart for the two little ones who died in their cribs.

In many respects, only Elizabeth's geography and the size of her children have changed. Her life is as busy as ever as she continues juggling her many roles. Dissertation days are past and the successful outcome of her husband's viva has dulled the memory of Oxford's cruel traditions. Now she works alongside her husband in a parish ministry that constantly sees new believers added to the flock they shepherd together.

Life goes on for all of us. Our theology helps us carry on through thick and thin. God is great, the race is good, and we can run. We can run well because we are in his hands. Hope is strong within us because we know the character of our God. He knows what he is doing with us, and we can trust him.

These three powerful instructions from the writer of Hebrews show us how to employ our theology in the everyday circumstances of our lives. But what made them stick for me was when I watched an Olympic athlete put them all into action in a run for gold. The adage "A picture says a thousand words" still holds true—at least for me. The image of a runner embodies what it means to live our theology. So does Jesus, the runner par excellence. If we are really serious about bringing our theology to life, we need to take a closer look at him.

7

FIXING OUR EYES ON JESUS

FOR A MOMENT I FORGOT I WAS AN AMERICAN. I WAS SITTING with my family on the gaudy sofa in our cramped student flat, watching the 1992 Barcelona Summer Olympics on the television we had borrowed. Heading into our fourth and final year in Oxford, we were indulging in a break from the grind of dissertation writing and software development projects. It was hard to tell which was more worn out, the sofa or its two adult occupants.

If anything, the frustration of watching the Olympics from English soil only heightened our American sensitivities, at least initially. British networks held us hostage and so, instead of seeing indepth coverage of our American team, we were compelled to follow the Queen's athletes and some rather obscure events we would have otherwise ignored. It was irksome at first. But during the men's 100-meter race, to my surprise (and despite a lineup of superb young American sprinters) I forgot about national loyalties and found myself cheering an over-the-hill Brit, thirty-two-year-old British team captain Linford Christie, who astonished everyone by seizing the gold medal victory from his younger Yankee competitors. It was a dramatic upset—one of those Olympic moments you never forget. *The Sunday Times* in London printed this description of the spectacle: "When Linford Christie came powering down the 100-metre track, ahead of the fancied Americans, some of us were privileged to be sitting close to the finish line. We saw our man, a Briton by way of the West Indies, catapult into history. We saw the eyes popping, the astonishing hypnotic concentration, the biceps rippling. The impression of speed, and the knowledge that this was a man reaching his peak for less than 10 seconds in a lifetime, was awesome."[1]

Christie's stunning performance caught everyone off guard, including the experts. But the most unforgettable aspect of his race (people would be talking about it for a long time afterward) was the half-crazed look of determination in his eyes. He was so focused on the finish line, one reporter observed, his "pop-eyed gaze made him look as if he was running away from mortal danger rather than towards his finest moment."[2] Christie would later describe a self-imposed tunnel vision that blocked out everything but the lane ahead. I suppose the exaggerated expression on his face made some spectators laugh, but who could argue with the result? Not that such a focused gaze ensures coming in first. But even an untrained observer could see that what he did with his eyes maximized everything else he did to run his race.

But for me this was more than a powerful exhibition of expert running techniques. Strange as it sounds (and now it's Christie's turn to laugh), when I saw that fierce, almost obsessive look in his eyes and the masterful way he ran, I thought of myself. The event was for me a vigorous reenactment of how seamlessly life and theology come together in a woman's life. Admittedly there is a world of difference between a less-than-ten-second sprint and the marathon I was running, not to mention the differences between Christie and myself. But I couldn't help seeing parallels between what was happening on the Olympic track in Barcelona and the race I was trying to run in Oxford. It was all there—the planned race; the power of unencumbered running; vigor, intensity, and perseverance; the riveted concentration on the goal; and one more thing I hadn't yet factored into my thinking: the unrestrained outburst of joy after he crossed the finish line.

Watching Christie run convinced me afresh of my need for theology. Here I was in my own race, facing challenges and stresses well beyond my limits, struggling just to put one foot in front of the other and keep going. How easy to lose my focus and center on myself or to gauge my progress by glancing sideways to see how well (or badly) I compared with other women instead of fixing my eyes on Jesus. As Christie's race flashed past and into the annals of Olympic history, he left behind a vivid reminder that what I did with my eyes would make a difference too.

EVERYDAY THEOLOGY FOR WOMEN

MOST OF US ARE better theologians in hindsight. We look at the struggles we have weathered and survived and testify warmly of God's goodness and faithfulness to us. But when a new crisis hits or we weary of the steady dripping of little problems and stresses, our theology collapses like a house of cards and we're faced with the task of reassembling it all over again. Yes, God *was* good, he *was* faithful, he *was* in control, he *did* show his love to me back then. But here and now? Somehow yesterday's theology doesn't look quite so glorious or reliable in the bleak light of today's cirumstances.

Fixing our eyes on Jesus is just the sort of down-to-earth advice we need to move our theology into the present. Rather than despairing of God's goodness until we see fresh evidence, fixing our eyes on Jesus helps us head into the current situation *banking* on his goodness. And the fact that this exhortation to "fix our eyes on Jesus" comes up in the middle of a race should tip us off that the benefits of a woman's theology are not restricted to the war zone. Knowing God has enormous peacetime value too. We need theology every day, whether we're carting our children to piano lessons and soccer practice, cooking a meal, listening to a friend, or shaping business strategy in the corporate boardroom.

The great women theologians I have come across cultivated the habit of using their theology in the here and now. What set these women apart—kept them from sinking when everything else was going down and strengthened them to lend a hand to others—was their unblinking focus on God. They were serious about knowing him and studied the Scriptures with that intention. They nurtured their faith on the truth of God's character so that, instead of starting over from scratch in each new situation, wondering if God's goodness had expired or if he had somehow lost control, these women fixed their eyes on him and actually put their weight down on the truth. No matter what the challenge or the adversity, their ironclad conviction was that he is always good, is always on his throne, is always working, always knows what he is doing, and that his love for them never stops. They were not passive with their knowledge but consciously took it up and confronted life with it. Their hearts were strong because they were sure of God. It made a difference in their running, and what is more, because their eyes were fixed on Jesus, they were better wives, mothers, daughters, and friends.

A cartoon appeared in the October 1998 issue of *Christianity Today,* next to a book review titled "Theology for the Rest of Us."[3] The reviewer was assessing Dr. Ellen Charry's book *By the Renewing of Your Minds,* in which she argues from Jesus and Paul through the writings of Augustine, John Calvin, and other church leaders that theology is (and always has been) good for every Christian in practical everyday ways.

The cartoon pictures a mother seated on a park bench with one hand resting on the handle of the stroller containing her wide-eyed, pacifier-plugged infant. Her other hand holds a book, balanced on her knees, which she is reading with the same undivided interest you would expect her to devote to the latest romance novel. The apprehensive look on the baby's face is explained by the title on the book jacket: "Theology for New Mothers." What the cartoonist intended as a joke (or at best a bit of satire on the notion that a mother would find any use for theology) is, in fact, an excellent suggestion. I have not yet attended a baby shower where the new mother unwrapped a systematic theology book, but upon reflection, that might not be such a bad idea. The value of reading Dr. Spock is negligible compared with the help a new mother would gain from focusing on her theology.

So how does a young mother, a grandmother, or a single fix her eyes on Jesus? What does it mean for the woman who hits the ground running in the morning and doesn't stop until she drops into bed late at night? How are we supposed to fix our eyes on Jesus? And what difference will it make anyway?

THE EYES HAVE IT

ON THE DAY of the Christmas pageant at Oxford's St. Ebbe's School, I was pressing toward a deadline on a software project. This would be a wild day for me, but a glorious one for my daughter, who was five and had been chosen from her class for a speaking part in the Christmas play. The headmistress announced there would be two performances, but as I explained to Allison, I would be able to make only the first program in the morning. At curtain time I was in my seat next to Frank, armed with video camera and beaming with a mother's pride. Less than an hour later, I was back at my computer pounding out the remaining lines of code, glancing periodically at the clock as the hour approached for the afternoon performance. I felt the heavy hand of guilt, and my resolve to stay away from the afternoon performance weakened. Suddenly I switched off the computer, grabbed my coat, and raced out the door.

Threading my way through Oxford's congested afternoon traffic, I took the shortcut across Christ Church Meadow and along the Isis River to the school. By the time I arrived, I was out of breath, and the program was already well underway. As I slipped quietly in the side door, several parents sitting nearby turned to look and nodded with disinterest, as if to say, "Oh, it's just the American mum." But I will never forget the look of recognition in the brown eyes of one small Bethlehem bell when she spotted me in the crowd or the zest that punctuated her lines when she realized mom was watching. The instant she saw me, everything changed. Her actions took on new meaning because one person in the crowd was there just for her, someone to whom she mattered and who would take delight in all she was doing.

Although it's obviously a whole lot easier to fix our eyes on someone who's physically visible, sometimes I think we make this matter of fixing our eyes on Jesus a lot more complicated than it needs to be. If we're not careful, it's easy for this to become some sort of mystical exercise in which we conjure up pleasant images of Jesus (whatever we happen to need at the moment, never mind if it is true or not) to soothe our frazzled nerves or jump-start our spiritual energies.

The letter to the Hebrews, which exhorts us to "fix our eyes on Jesus," takes an entirely different approach and actually reinforces the notion that fixing our eyes on Jesus means getting serious about our theology. Early on in the letter, the writer urges, "Fix your thoughts on Jesus" (3:1), indicating that we would do well to study Jesus. Following his advice, I have found it helpful to fix my eyes on Jesus by: first, focusing on knowing Jesus better; second, personalizing the truth I learn about him; and third, consciously viewing my fluctuating circumstances through the lens of his unchanging character. Once these become habits, they cease being separate actions and blend into a lifestyle.

LEARNING THEOLOGY FROM JESUS

FIXING OUR EYES on Jesus calls us to follow Mary's example and put ourselves under the tutelage of Jesus. Jesus is the best theology professor any of us will ever find, and he still warmly admits women into his school. He doesn't describe God in the abstract to us. He *shows* God to us through his own life. Jesus told his disciples plainly, "Anyone who has seen me has seen the Father" (John 14:9).

The prospect of taking up a thick theological volume or tackling some of those multisyllabic terms (something hopefully all of us eventually will do) may cause some women's knees to tremble, but theology in the person of Jesus sounds inviting right from the start. When we look at Jesus, heady abstract concepts about God suddenly become less formidable. We want to know Jesus better. And Jesus wants us to know his Father.

Fixing our eyes on Jesus means digging beneath the facts of Scripture to understand his character. What we see in Jesus is true of his Father too. Put yourself in the sandals of the thirsting Samaritan woman who expected insult and rejection but received grace and living water from Jesus. Sit at his feet with Mary of Bethany and hear him defend and affirm your desire to learn and to serve. Reach out covertly in your unworthiness, insecurity, and self-loathing, if only to touch the hem of his garment and hear him publicly call you "daughter" (Mark 5:25–34). Find yourself thrown at his feet with the woman caught in the act of adultery and discover a rich forgiveness that covers all and reinstates wholeness and purpose in your life. Jesus treated those who came to him exactly as his Father treats us now, for Jesus "can do only what he sees his Father doing, because whatever the Father does the Son also does" (John 5:19).

TAKING OUR THEOLOGY TO HEART

I NEVER WILL FORGET my first communion in Oxford. Prior to that service, I had always felt like one of many during the Lord's Supper as I served myself from the trays passed down the rows of fellow churchgoers. But the Anglicans, who serve each person separately, singled me out. When the person serving the bread looked me in the eye and said, "This is the body of Christ which was broken for you," the intimacy of those familiar words bowled me over. Two facts were inescapable—the enormity of *my* need and the immensity of his love for *me*. It was staggering and humbling to realize that Jesus suffered and died on the cross because there was no other way to deal with *my* sin; that what he suffered, *I* deserved. Suddenly the Lord's Supper was a personal matter.

The power of our theology comes alive when we take the truth personally. Holding God at arm's length—no matter how much theology we think we know—will never make us great theologians. We have to learn to write our own names into the plot. God will always be the subject of our theological sentences, but our sentences are incomplete until we make ourselves the direct objects of his attributes.

King David knew how to get personal with the truth about God. He loved nothing better than to put theology to music. He could have composed grandiose compositions to flaunt his mastery of deep truth. But theology was an intimate matter for David—the language of his own relationship with God. When he wanted to sing of God's omniscience, he wrote, "O LORD, you have searched *me* and you know *me*.... You are familiar with all *my* ways. Before a word is on *my* tongue you know it completely, O LORD" (Ps. 139:1, 3–4, emphasis added).[4] God's omnipresence comforted him, and so he sang, "If I go up to the heavens ... make my bed in the depths ... settle on the far side of the sea, even there your hand will guide *me*, your right hand will hold *me* fast" (Ps. 139:8–10, emphasis added).[5]

I do not simply fix my eyes on Jesus who died and rose again for sinners in general but on Jesus who died and rose again for *me*. God's goodness isn't some abstract principle; rather, God is good to *me*. Martin Luther was right to caution us that theology is never an end in itself, that we cannot truly understand it until we take it *pro me*. We need to take our theology to heart, and when we do, we often find that our hearts, like David's, spontaneously overflow in worship and adoration.

RUBY SLIPPER THEOLOGY

IN THE WIZARD OF OZ, homesick Dorothy trudges around the Land of Oz for days with her motley band of friends in search of a way to get back to Kansas and Auntie Em. Not until her wanderings come to a disappointing end in the Emerald City does she discover that the ruby slippers she has been wearing since her first moments in Oz possess the power to take her home. She only has to click her heels.

Perhaps one of the most tragic problems women have with theology is when we fail to connect it with what is happening (or has happened) in our lives. It is a problem that, oddly enough, surfaces often in women who describe themselves as avid lovers of theology. They find theology fascinating and jump at the chance to attend a theology class or join in a deep theological discussion. Some of them have been to seminary. Yet privately many of these women are just as defeated and despondent as women who only have a smattering of theology. They wander through life like homesick Dorothy in Oz, unaware that the theology they are wearing so prominently could make a difference in the problems that are getting them down.

An elementary school teacher once told me she couldn't get enough theology. She pored over theology books in her spare time and talked late into the night with friends who were studying too. At the same time, she was deeply depressed over changes in her life. Her roommate (who was also her dearest friend) had just announced her engagement and that she would, immediately after the wedding, move overseas with her new husband. She dreaded the departure of her friend, the breakup of their apartment, and the search for a new roommate. She couldn't help feeling left behind—watching God move someone else's life forward when hers seemed to be in reverse. I was listening to her saga (commiserating because of my own struggles) when it dawned on her that the things she had been studying about God had everything to do with her present struggle. It was an eye-opener for us both; it was the first time it had occurred to either of us that what we were learning ought to make a difference now.

Simply knowing a lot of theological ideas, no matter how orthodox and sound they are, will never turn us into great theologians. Theology isn't really theology for us until we live it. Not until we learn to make explicit connections between what we know about

God and the race we are running will we taste the transforming power of our theology. Fixing our eyes on Jesus means reminding ourselves of all that he is to us now. He brings meaning to our routines and energizes us to tackle the difficult tasks at hand. Fixing our eyes on Jesus gives us hope to offer disheartened husbands and hurting friends, and the wisdom we need to raise children who will fix their eyes on him too. The battle-weary mother who fixes her eyes on Jesus and reassures herself that nothing can stop God from accomplishing his good purposes finds the strength to go the distance with her wayward child whose heart seems hopelessly hardened. Knowing he has marked out all the days of our lives for our good and his glory fills the elderly widow's humdrum days with purpose, meaning, and value. Recalling the depth of his love, the lonely rejected wife and the despairing single know they are treasure in his sight. Dr. J. I. Packer writes, "He knows me. I am graven on the palms of His hands. I am never out of His mind. All my knowledge of Him depends on His sustained initiative in knowing me. I know Him, because He first knew me, and continues to know me. He knows me as a friend, one who loves me; and there is no moment when His eye is off me, or His attention distracted from me, and no moment therefore, when His care falters."[6]

The runner's theology goes straight to her feet. She makes sure it does by connecting what she is learning about God with the race he has called her to run. She fixes her eyes on Jesus and views the details of her life through what she knows to be true of him. This is when theology ceases to be merely intellectual and begins to transform our lives.

THEOLOGICAL SURPRISES

IN MY JOURNEY to become a better theologian, I have met two surprises. The first was the discovery that contrary to what we might expect, theology is not drudgery (like math homework or Saturday chores) but an enterprise overflowing with joy. The second was the realization that the state of my theology matters a lot, not just to me but to my friends, my family, and also my church.

Few things would sadden me more than for anyone to come away from reading this book thinking of theology as castor oil that women must swallow because "it is good for us." On the one hand, I'd be glad even for negative thinking if it moves any of us to get started. But having said that, how sad it would be if we *resign* ourselves to the pursuit of the one for whom we were made and in whom we will find our deepest delight and satisfaction. This is where I bump up against my limitations as a writer, for it would be easier for me to describe the delectable taste of chocolate, the splendor of a Florida sunset, or the exhilaration of skiing down the wintry slopes of Mount Hood than to put into words the unspeakable joys we discover when we apply ourselves to know our Creator. But where superlatives fail, I can at least leave hints to entice women to press forward in their pursuit of God, not merely to cope better with life but to flood our hearts with delight.

My first taste of the joy of knowing God caught me entirely by surprise because it was so contrary to what I had anticipated. I always expected to meet up with joy sooner or later—on the other side of a struggle, in the light that follows a dark phase, at the end of a long wait, and above all, after I crossed the finish line. I'd seen enough Olympic races to know that euphoria sweeps over even the most haggard, grim-faced champion when the race is over and the victory is in hand. Heaven is a precious hope cherished more fervently by the greatest sufferers among us, those who live with pain and brokenness, to whom heaven alone promises relief.

Joy on the far side of the struggle makes perfect sense and matches all the evidence. But the joy I encountered didn't have a leg to stand on, for it arrived ahead of schedule. The storm was still raging, none of my questions or prayers had been answered, my circumstances hadn't changed at all. Unlike finish-line joy, this midrace joy seemed more akin to a phenomenon often described by marathon runners. Running, they tell us, triggers the release of endorphins, chemicals from the brain that elevate the runner's mood, relieve tension, and give a deep sense of calm and pleasure during the race. The race isn't any less challenging, nor the effort any less taxing, but amazingly enough, that doesn't make the joy any less real.

Christian joy is more than a mood swing or a shift in hormone levels. Nor is it, as some have suggested, a choice or a duty to be happy, at least on the outside, even when we're miserable inside. True joy springs irrepressibly from the heart and is always rooted in our theology. Which explains why joy can appear in the middle of a crisis and coexist with pain, brokenness, grief, or loneliness. Joy isn't grounded in our circumstances; it is grounded in the unchanging character of God.

Fixing our eyes on Jesus keeps the big picture ever in front of us—that God is on his throne, that we are loved, that he is at work in the present moment accomplishing his purposes. Even *this* situation will work for his glory and my good. No matter how strong the enemy appears or how many wounds we receive, we already know how the story will end, and there is ample cause for joy in this.

But the most substantial reason for our joy is in the delight we find in God himself. Fixing our eyes on Jesus is, in itself, the single greatest cause for joy. The apostle Paul, an innocent on death row, wrote of midrace joy in a letter to the Philippians. Paul didn't explain his joy in terms of location or circumstances or prospects. Paul's joy was tied to a person, for he had fixed his eyes on Jesus. Compared to "the surpassing greatness of knowing Christ Jesus," Paul considered everything else (including all that he had lost and possibly his own life) to be "rubbish" (Phil. 3:8).

I may not have the soul of a poet to help me describe the joy that comes with knowing God. But King David was blessed with such a soul, and he used it freely to revel in the joys of the theologian. He longed for God like a parched soul staggering across a scorched desert in search of water. Tastes of God's unfailing love were, to David, more satisfying than life itself. He suffered from insomnia, but not because he feared the enemies who had driven him into the wilderness and were lurking somewhere in the darkness with murderous intent. David's sleepless nights were caused by joyous thoughts of God. "I lie awake thinking of you, meditating on you through the night. I think how much you have helped me; I sing for joy in the shadow of your protecting wings" (Ps. 63:6–7 NLT).

The joy that kept the king awake, that reverberated in Paul's prison cell, that draws women to study God more carefully, shone brightly at the deathbed of a middle-aged woman several years ago. Her family had summoned her young pastor to come to the hospital after doctors told them her time was short. When he arrived, her pain and labored breathing made it difficult for her to speak. Her words came slowly and were barely audible. As her pastor leaned nearer, he heard her whisper, "Why me?" At first he began thinking of Scriptures to comfort her; then he realized she wasn't complaining. This wasn't the "Why me?" of despair; it was the "Why me?" of incredulous joy—that God had set his love on her, that she was coming home. This side of the finish line, concurrent with the pain of dying and the grief of being separated from her husband and children, she knew real joy in Christ.

Even in the war zones of life, there is joy for us because our God is great and we are bathed in his love. The joy Jesus gives isn't grounded in our circumstances; it is grounded in him. We fix our eyes on Jesus and find in him every reason for joy, and he will never change. How can we suppress the joy this brings? This is the power of good theology in action.

THE RIPPLE EFFECT OF A WOMAN'S THEOLOGY

THE SECOND SURPRISE, that the quality of my theology matters to others, was evident right from the start when friends would drop by my apartment for a late-night chat or meet me for coffee. Sooner or later, one of us would start talking about her troubles, and together we would work through how our theology related to the issues that were bothering us.

Later, in marriage, my husband would need my theology for all sorts of situations that called for the best we both had to offer. When I held my infant daughter in my arms and faced the challenge of raising a little runner, my theology was (cartoonist's opinions aside) the greatest gift I had to offer as a mother. Now, hardly a day goes by when someone doesn't pass through my orbit in need of good theology.

A woman's theology is not a private matter. It is a public asset she is called to use for the good of her friends, her husband, her children, and her church. Whether I'm a good theologian or a poor one, my theology will always rub off on others, giving them new strength or dragging them down. "Curse God and die!" was the final blow Job received, from the lips of his despairing and agonized wife (Job 2:9). Naomi heard a very different message from Ruth, the daughter-in-law who shared her sufferings but, instead of shaking her fist at God, took refuge under his wing (Ruth 2:12). Instead of giving up on Naomi's God, Ruth's loyalty to him deepened when she vowed, "Your people will be my people and your God my God" (Ruth 1:16). These women weren't just venting their emotions. They were making theological statements to their loved ones that could dishearten or awaken hope in God. When someone's ship is sinking, it matters a lot to them whether we help them bail, dump more water in the boat, or stand by helplessly and watch them sink.

Recently two deaths have broken the hearts of the people at our church. One was a young mother who lost her valiant four-and-a-half-year battle to leukemia and a bone marrow transplant that never settled down. The second was less public but equally devastating: a miscarriage for another young mother—her third. Throughout these battles and in the aftermath of grief, women were on the scene. Oh yes, they arrived with their casseroles, but they also brought their theology. Some of them wouldn't say a word. But some would wade into the grief, listen to the wrestlings, get under the burden, and never relinquish their hope in God.

Women shoulder enormous responsibility to build up the body of Christ, whether we do it over coffee with a friend, in the privacy of our homes, or in the broader fellowship of God's people. Our theology equips us for this monumental ministry. It is sobering to realize that someone else is helped or hurt depending on the state of my theology.

STRAIGHT TALK FOR WOMEN

WHICH BRINGS US BACK to our earlier question: Is theology really important for women? The writer to the Hebrews answers with a resounding yes, perhaps more emphatically than we are prepared to hear. Abruptly and with a measure of exasperation, he halts his discussion and, like a well-informed surgeon general, stamps a glaring warning label on his letter—to warn us not of the dangers of theology but of the hazards of getting too little of it. I can't help feeling a bit shocked every time I get to this point in his letter. His words land like a punch, but it is straight talk women need to hear.

> There is so much more we would like to say about this. But you don't seem to listen, so it's hard to make you understand. You have been Christians a long time now, and you ought to be teaching others. Instead, you need someone to teach you again the basic things a beginner must learn about the Scriptures. You are like babies who drink only milk and cannot eat solid food. And a person who is living on milk isn't very far along in the Christian life and doesn't know much about doing what is right. Solid food is for those who are mature, who have trained themselves to recognize the difference between right and wrong and then do what is right.
>
> HEBREWS 5:11–14 (NLT)

This is where a lot of us act as though we are reading someone else's mail instead of a private letter addressed to us—a clever tactic to dodge the sting of this rebuke. But this letter isn't addressed to a gathering of church leaders or exclusively to men. The author is talking to Christians of all ages, including women. Instead of setting the letter aside as "too deep" or "not meant" for us, women need to close the door behind them and read as though the letter bears our name and was written by someone who knew exactly what we need to hear.

The writer is taking us to task for settling for a diet of theological pabulum—ideas about God that don't require chewing and go down easily. He urges us to tackle a meatier diet that will fortify us for the task at hand. And why is he so concerned? Our spiritual health is at stake, for starters. But the ramifications are greater. The facts are simple. A soft diet will stunt our spiritual development, stagnate our relationship with God, and weaken the body of Christ. When women neglect theology, the negative side effects ripple out from their private lives through their families and friendships, right on into the church.

Several years ago I visited a couple whose children were all grown, except for one. Their daughter, then in her midtwenties, had never physically or mentally matured beyond the age of a very young child. Anatomically undersized and grossly stunted developmentally, she could not walk, talk, or feed herself. Twenty-four hours a day, her parents lovingly and patiently took up the burden of her unending care—bathing, diapering, and dressing her, carrying her from bed to wheelchair and back again. Three times a day they spooned food into her mouth and wiped the excess dribbling down her chin. They poured never-ending care into her life and will for the rest of her life. They wouldn't dream of offering the same care to their healthy children. Had one of them resisted feeding themselves or refused to advance from pureed foods to eat meat and vegetables at the grown-up table, these parents would have been firm until the child ate solid food, not for their convenience but for the health of the child.

The letter to the Hebrews makes it abundantly clear that refusing solid food will stunt our growth. The assumption is that all of us are capable of a deeper understanding. But a light diet sentences us to a life of dependence. Fixing our eyes on Jesus means advancing from baby food—the basic concepts of Christianity—to an adult diet of deeper theological truth about Jesus. It means we have to learn to feed ourselves—reading and studying the Bible not in search of some tasty morsel to help us through the day but in search of God. Ultimately it means we should feed others as well.

Theology, to put it bluntly, is good for women, for the more we understand of Jesus, the more there will be for our faith to cling to when we are in crisis. Center on yourself, and discouragement is sure to set in. Look at circumstances or at someone else, and it's easy to feel overwhelmed and ready to give up. But make Jesus your focus—delve into his character, remind yourself that he is on his throne, that you are loved, that even now he is fulfilling his good purposes for you—and you will find a thousand reasons to keep going, even over the roughest terrain. We are stronger and have greater powers of endurance when we are properly nourished.

Theology also enriches our relationship with Christ himself, which ought to be reason enough for us to get down to business. Nothing depletes us more than trying to maintain a one-sided relationship with a husband or a friend who has lost interest in us. Yet we are the guilty party when our curiosity about Jesus cools and we think we've learned enough. Fixing our eyes on Jesus means that instead of always reaching into his pockets for something we want, we will reach for him. It means investing in Jesus the same ongoing levels of time, energy, interest, and listening powers that we ache for in our human relationships. It is the road to joy, drawing us closer to him and satisfying the deepest longings of our souls, no matter how empty the rest of our lives may be.

But the concern is more than personal, as the writer's warning intimates. Malnutrition impairs our ability to function as healthy members of Christ's body. The New Testament is emphatic. All women are called to be teachers, to live and speak the truth to those around us. When we are lackadaisical toward theology, too busy, too tired, or too fearful to wrestle with what the Bible says about God, we not only hurt ourselves and retard our relationship with Christ but we weaken other Christians who depend on us to be strong for them. The writer to the Hebrews makes about as pointed a statement of the importance of theology for women (and the serious consequences of neglecting it) as we will find anywhere in Scripture.

It may take a stern warning like this to shake us up and get us going. But higher motives will soon take over: the prospects of a deeper delight in Christ, along with improved strength and courage.

A WOMAN THEOLOGIAN FIXES HER EYES

NO ONE WAS MORE surprised than I when I stood and cheered Linford Christie in the 1992 Olympics. Since then another runner has captivated my interest—an American woman whose running leaves Christie in the dust.

Sara Pierrepont Edwards, wife of American theologian and preacher Jonathan Edwards, was a great theologian in her own right. They journeyed thirty-two years together in a marriage he described as "an uncommon union" and which was from the first distinguished by a depth of friendship only longed for in most marriages. "Her husband treated her as a fully mature being—as a person whose conversation entertained him, whose spirit nourished his own religious life, whose presence gave him repose."[7] One of their descendants mused that Sarah was "the resting-place of his soul."[8] The feeling was mutual.

Together they parented eleven children and weathered the ups and downs of life. On fair afternoons, they would slip away for a horseback ride in the hills and the luxury of a long uninterrupted conversation. She was his most intimate friend, his confidant and support. Her theology strengthened and supported him through many fierce battles in his pastoral ministries.

After years as an outcast, having been pushed out of his pastorate and rejected, Jonathan Edwards was vindicated somewhat when he was elected president of Princeton College. He had been away from home for several weeks to assume his presidency when on February 13, 1758, he was inoculated for smallpox. Unexpectedly the cure became the killer, and he died from the inoculation on March 22 at the age of fifty-four, leaving Sarah to raise their large family alone. It was the last and worst of a series of heavy calamities that had befallen Sarah. The kind doctor and friend who wrote to inform Sarah of her husband's death wisely urged her "to look to that God, whose love and goodness you have experienced a thousand times, for direction and help, under this most afflictive dispensation of providence."[9]

Sarah would never recover from her loss. But she took the doctor's advice. She fixed her eyes on God. Soon afterward she penned a poignant letter to her daughter Esther, who only a few months earlier had lost her husband to a fever.

> My very dear child!
> What shall I say? A holy and good God has covered us with a dark cloud. O that we may kiss the rod, and lay our hands on our mouths! The Lord has done it. He has made me adore his goodness, that we had him so long. But my God lives; and he has my heart. O what a legacy my husband, and your father, has left us! We are all given to God; and there I am, and love to be.
> Your affectionate mother,
Sarah Edwards[10]

With one hand Sarah grasped her theology, and with the other she reached out to support her daughter. Her theology bolstered her husband in the war zone, consoled her own bereaved heart, strengthened her grieving daughter, and lived on for generations in her children.

LOOKING AHEAD

AS I PUT THE FINAL touches on this chapter, the year 2000 is washing over the planet. Through television we witness the world welcoming in a new millennium with endless fireworks and festivities. The global celebration also brings somber moments of reflection, as people everywhere consider ways to improve themselves and the quality of their lives. People resolve to exercise more, eat less, stop smoking, take vitamins, get organized, and spend more time with family. Christians promise themselves to do a better job with quiet time, maybe even read the whole Bible this year. But it seems to me that the best thing a woman can resolve to do for herself is to get serious about theology, not just commit to read the Bible and pray more but to get to know the one who comes to us in the pages of Scripture. It's time to do some "pop-eyed" gazing of our own and work to know Jesus better in the days ahead.

As we turn one last time to Mary's story, we will see the difference her theology makes in her. This time we will not find her at Jesus' feet to listen or to weep. Instead her eyes will be fixed on Jesus, and she will use her theology for the benefit of others.

PART THREE

KNOWING GOD IN RELATIONSHIPS

8

A WARRIOR IN THE HEAT
OF BATTLE

Mary Anoints Jesus for His Burial

JOHN 12:1–8

SOME YEARS AGO I WAS IN THE SEMINARY LIBRARY, SURROUNDED by books and engrossed in my studies. I was in a state of mind my family calls "the zone," in which I tune out everything except the book or computer screen in front of me. As I pored over page after page in search of material related to my master's thesis, I failed to notice the approaching figure of a man until a large hand came down firmly on my Bible. I looked up with surprise and discovered the hand belonged to the same professor whose words had thrown me off balance earlier. Nodding at the place where his hand was resting, he whispered, "*This* is the book you need to study." It was another remark that managed to stick.

Now, as we add the third frame to our small collection of Mary's portraits,[1] a hand comes down on this final addition to our gallery. This time the hand belongs to Jesus. There is no library-correct whisper but a resounding declaration, "*This* is the portrait you need to study." Matthew recalled hearing Jesus say it this way, "I tell you the truth, wherever this gospel is preached throughout the world, what she has done will also be told, in memory of her" (Matt. 26:13). Studying Mary's third portrait is crucial for women, as well as for men like my professor who are dubious about a woman's theological acumen. According to Jesus, this is the defining portrait of Mary, the one we are supposed to carry around with us in our pockets and finger in reflective moments until its edges grow soft and worn and its image is permanently etched in our minds.

People with an untrained eye have been known to store priceless art treasures in the attic for years because the color didn't fit their decor, because they liked something else better, or because they simply had no clue it was worth so much. When I put Mary's three portraits side by side, I had to wonder why Jesus seemed to think this third portrait is the more valuable of the three. Most women prefer the portrait of Mary sitting at Jesus' feet to learn. I plead guilty to that myself. And now that we have examined more carefully the scene in which Mary weeps, we have drastically marked up the value of that painting too. The priceless value of the first two portraits and Jesus' assessment of the third should raise a flurry of expectation over what we will find when we reexamine this final familiar episode in Mary's life. Although we have always valued this painting of Mary, Jesus seems to see something in it that we have missed. Our inclination to store it in the attic, instead of hanging it prominently in the entry hall, is symptomatic of our need to investigate why Jesus would be so emphatic about its significance and why we have so grossly underrated it. In Jesus' eyes this is the defining moment for Mary as his disciple and as a woman. It is, as we soon shall see, the portrait of a great woman theologian.

THE LAST SUPPER IN BETHANY

OUR JOURNEY TAKES US again to Bethany, this time to the home of Simon the Leper, where a feast is given to honor Jesus.[2] On the surface, little has changed since our first visit to Bethany. Jesus and his disciples are back in town, Martha is bustling in the kitchen, and Mary is about to get herself into trouble again. But as our eyes adjust to the fire-lit room and the details come into focus, we get a chilling sense that everything has changed—Jesus' circumstances, his disciples, and Mary most of all.

This night in Bethany, a dreadful darkness closes in on Jesus. Only a few days remain until Passover. This ordinary marker in the Jewish calendar is full of foreboding here, for it signals that time is swiftly running out for Jesus. The approaching Passover meal will go down in history as the Last Supper. The uproar over Lazarus has ignited the fuse that will lead to Jesus' arrest, mistrial, and brutal execution. Only a few miles away at their headquarters in Jerusalem, Jewish leaders are readying for the final assault against the Galilean who has infuriated and eluded them for the past three years. This time they are determined he will not outwit them.

Anyone glancing around the dimly lit room this night could see that the eagerness and enthusiasm that characterized the Twelve during their early months with Jesus has been dampened by the things he has been saying lately and the mounting hostilities from Jerusalem. For the moment, the festive atmosphere and energetic rumble of masculine voices around the table may mask their uneasiness. But underneath, they cannot resolve the dissonance between their messianic expectations and Jesus' disturbing remarks about laying down his life. Only days earlier he had taken them aside and explained what awaits him. "'We are going up to Jerusalem,' he said, 'and the Son of Man will be betrayed to the chief priests and teachers of the law. They will condemn him to death and will hand him over to the Gentiles, who will mock him and spit on him, flog him and kill him. Three days later he will rise'" (Mark 10:33–34).[3]

This information had seemed to roll off the disciples, who responded by jockeying for positions of preeminence within his kingdom (Mark 10:35–45). Their political hopes had mushroomed along with the size of the crowds as Jesus' miracles continued and his fame spread throughout the countryside. Like drowning men, they would rather cling to their sinking ambitions than face the implications of his grim projections.

But a more sinister storm is brewing. Reclining only a few feet from the Rabbi, coolly sharing in the camaraderie of the hour, is one whose loyalties have shifted. Soon after the feasting is over and guests disperse into the night, Judas Iscariot, one of Jesus' closest companions and a leader among the Twelve, will steal behind enemy lines to cut a deal with Jesus' adversaries.[4] This is the break the Jews have been waiting for. What could be better than to have an insider working for them? For a price, Judas will hand Jesus over to Jerusalem authorities—an act that will close the net around Jesus and send his timorous band of disciples retreating in eleven directions.

"By instinct, we humans want someone by our side in the hospital the night before surgery, in the nursing home as death looms near, in any great moment of crisis. We need the reassuring touch of human presence—solitary confinement is the worst punishment our species has devised."[5] But as Jesus' ordeal escalates, those he should be able to count on for company and moral support are in denial or duplicity—unable to understand, much less enter the struggle with him. Probably no place on earth is as lonely this night as Jesus' place at the table.

OPERATION ALABASTER JAR

WHEN MARY ENTERS the room of men[6] this evening, nothing is plainer than the fact that she has changed too. She is no longer the eager novice working her way out of the kitchen to a place at Jesus' feet, nor is she the distraught young woman mourning the death of her brother and her disappointment with Jesus. You might say Mary has grown up. She has matured as a disciple and as a theologian. She has advanced from milk to meat, a diet that explains the change that has come over her.

It hadn't been a painless process. Twice before she had been at Jesus' feet—first to listen, ponder, and learn; then to mourn, wrestle, and believe. The potent combination of his teaching and her suffering had deepened her understanding of Jesus and her trust in him. It had also awakened her theological instincts. On this night, her theology will guide her actions as she encounters Jesus one last time. As evening settles over Bethany and Jesus contemplates the lonely road ahead, he will not be totally alone. If only for a moment, there will be a brave soldier at his side, a disciple he has trained for such a moment as this.

In her hands Mary clasps an alabaster jar that will shortly become the focal point of the evening's conversation. The jar contains the secret of her mission—a highly prized ointment extracted from pure nard and imported from India, a full twelve ounces.[7] In a strange twist, it will also distract everyone from the true significance of her deed.

Mary has several viable alternatives for ministry this night. She can sell her valuable perfume and give the money to Jesus for the poor (Judas Iscariot soon will suggest this, though his motives are thoroughly corrupt). Or she can join her sister, Martha, in serving the meal. Meaningful as either of these options are, once again Mary makes a better choice.

At first Mary's movements seem to escape notice as she silently approaches her Lord, breaks the jar, and pours its precious contents on Jesus.[8] In seconds a powerful fragrance fills the room, covering savory kitchen scents and exposing Mary's deed. As the rich aroma reaches the nostrils of the guests, conversation tapers into silence and all eyes turn to Mary. By now she has loosened her hair and is gently wiping Jesus' feet, which are covered in perfume.

Immediately her critics mobilize. Judas is first to fire off an accusation: "That perfume was worth a small fortune. It should have been sold and the money given to the poor" (John 12:5 NLT).[9] His reproach puts a pious face on his mercenary heart. As keeper (and pilferer) of the money bag, he is calculating how much money (a full year's wages by his estimate) has just slipped through his fingers.[10] With purer motives but blinded hearts, the other disciples follow his lead with a knee-jerk reaction of their own. "What a waste of money," they scold harshly, censuring her with a painful round of "friendly fire" (Matt. 26:8 NLT; Mark 14:5).

Jesus' displeasure is immediate and decisive—not with Mary but with his hardened disciples. "Leave her alone," he answers bluntly. "She did it in preparation for my burial. You will always have the poor among you, but I will not be here with you much longer" (John 12:7 NLT).

MARY, MARY, QUITE CONTRARY

NEVER HAD MARY BEEN more misunderstood. But the misunderstanding wasn't confined to that evening. Despite Jesus' resounding rebuke, we too somehow get stuck thinking about the cost of the perfume she poured out. Biblical scholars don't seem to grapple very well either with what prompted Mary to do such an outrageous deed. The typical evangelical scholarly interpretation of this event concludes that Mary's anointing was merely an act of piety. According to this interpretation, she acted out of devotion to Jesus but really didn't understand the significance of her own actions. One scholar writes, "Mary in her devotion *unconsciously* provides for the honour of the dead."[11] Scholars—both male and female—point to her love for Jesus and her gratitude for what he had done for her, or to her emotions, as sufficient explanations for her actions. Some are willing to credit her with having some "inkling"[12] of his death, but that's about as far as they are willing to go. No one seems to think she knew what she was doing. They include Mary in the theological ignorance and confusion of Jesus' other disciples and assume her understanding was no better than theirs. It's as though generous, kindhearted, grateful Mary inadvertently did something profound.

Something is not quite right about this. We hear ourselves (and preachers) praising Mary for her lavish generosity, as though a price tag would mean anything to Jesus. Sometime earlier, with his disciples in Jerusalem, Jesus denounced such thinking when he voiced admiration for the widow who dropped her last pennies into temple coffers (Mark 12:41–44). Her paltry coins wouldn't make a dent in the temple budget and were instantly lost among the money poured in by wealthy patrons, who donated a fraction of their assets. But the widow's contribution wasn't lost on Jesus. Her gift was monumental in his eyes. Nor would Jesus trivialize Mary's actions by placing a fair market value on them. He was mindful of her painful sacrifice, both of her property and of herself. Once again she had paid dearly for her boldness in making such an unconventional (and some would add undignified) gesture in a room full of men.[13] Although there was nothing indecorous about what she had done, she would have had to be made of stone not to be wounded by the rancor and hasty judgment of her fellow disciples. But for Jesus, there was more to this than sacrifice—costly as hers was.

And what about humility, love, and worship? One scholar writes, "Mary's actions express what she did not have the words to voice, but it 'filled the whole house' with the fragrance of her love and as such would continue to spread through the preaching of the gospel in the whole world."[14] To be sure, Mary acted from the fullness of her heart. Did anyone have greater reason for loving Jesus than Mary did? How could anyone mistake the loving worship that flowed from her as she knelt at Jesus' feet? He valued her love and worship. But there was more to this for him than adoration and love—lavish as hers was.

Sacrifice, worship, and love only partially explain Mary's actions. Nor do her actions provide a simple object lesson about maintaining right priorities, as the ensuing debate among the disciples over the place of ministry to the poor seems to suggest. If these explanations are the best we can do, then we haven't yet discovered why Jesus held such a high opinion of Mary's third portrait or why he crowned her actions with such an enduring legacy. Others made enormous sacrifices for Jesus, considerably more than a single year's wages. Jesus didn't argue when Peter claimed, "We have left everything to follow you!" (Mark 10:28), because it was the simple truth. Others offered heartfelt worship, from the magi who followed the star to Bethlehem, to his own disciples.[15] Yet none of them received this kind of commendation from Jesus. There would even be other women who, at great peril to their lives, would come to anoint his body (Luke 23:55–24:12). Why should Mary alone receive such a distinction?

A THINKING WOMAN IN ACTION

A VERY DIFFERENT PICTURE of Mary emerges when we put this last portrait alongside the two earlier episodes from her life and, following her example, stop to listen to what Jesus was saying. Contrary to what others have implied, her head is firmly on her shoulders and seems to be working in perfect concert with her heart and her hands. When we take Mary out of context—out of her *own* context—it isn't surprising that we would fail to recognize the mature theologian she had become.

Mary didn't arrive on this scene in a state of neutrality, with nothing more than good intentions and a jar of expensive perfume. We must not forget that Mary was Jesus' student. She had sat at the feet of Rabbi Jesus, and she had listened. She had heard him speak of his impending death and surely must have recoiled just like everyone else at such a suggestion. She, along with the other disciples,[16] had heard him speak of his resurrection and had marveled that anyone would claim such power over death. She had pondered and struggled with his words.

What is more, Mary had struggled with *him*. The deep theology she learned from him had been pounded into her heart in the darkest hour of her life, when her brother lay dying and there was still no sign of Jesus. She had seen Jesus in a new light through that excruciating disappointment. What she learned changed everything, including her. Jesus was no longer just a miracle worker to Mary. She now knew that he was Lord of life and of death, that he was, in fact, God in the flesh. He had shown her that he would not be governed by her expectations and opinions. She had wrestled with his character and learned that no matter what happened, how dark things looked, or how depressed she felt, the soundest and safest course of action was to trust him.

Jesus' words support the notion that Mary acted out of theological convictions. "She has done a beautiful thing to me ... to prepare me for burial" (Matt. 26:10, 12). If all she had had in mind was the inevitability of Jesus' death, how could her actions be called beautiful? Instead, wouldn't this anointing seem more like an act of weakness, unbelief, and despair, a caving in to the inevitable, conceding defeat before any of the others could think of giving up? Yet Jesus not only praised what she had done, he linked her actions with the gospel—the *good* news. "I tell you the truth, wherever this gospel is preached throughout the world, what she has done will also be told, in memory of her" (v. 13).

Others may not point to Mary's theology to explain her actions, but Jesus did. His response seems to indicate that this was something of a watershed moment in his ministry, for Mary evidently not only comprehended the gospel, her actions had just articulated the death, burial, *and* resurrection of Jesus. Everything Jesus had taught Mary, through his words and through the death and restoration of her brother, came together in this single act, which was her statement of faith. Mary's actions were born of deep theological insight and a heart for Christ. Of all his disciples, she was the only one who understood his mission. By anointing his body for burial, Mary was the first of his disciples to proclaim the gospel—that Jesus had indeed come "to give his life as a ransom for many" (Mark 10:45). Ever after when the gospel was proclaimed, it would be the same message Mary had been the first to announce at this feast.

AN ANGEL ON THE BATTLEFIELD

SEVERAL YEARS AGO I lay awake at night in a Philadelphia hospital. The bed was hard and strange, the night too still. No matter how long I lay there, I couldn't get to sleep. As I repositioned myself in the tightly sheeted hospital bed to try again, I could hear the sound of low voices in the corridor and the occasional footsteps of a nurse responding to a patient's call light. Desolation settled over me again as I contemplated the surgery scheduled for the next morning. The evening before, Frank and I had been with my cousin and her husband. Yet even though I felt bolstered by their love and support, I knew I would face the surgeon's knife alone. Finally, with the help of a sleeping pill, I drifted off to sleep.

When I opened my eyes the next morning, my husband was already there, along with a dear friend, Ruth Raisley, who was also the vice president of the hospital. It was like Ruth to show up at this early hour, just for moral support. She knew enough about surgery from her own medical history to understand exactly how I felt. In her typical fashion, she pressed the boundaries to go as far as she could to be there for me. This morning she would bend hospital rules to escort me right up to the doors of the operating suite. On my back, with an IV on one hand and Ruth on the other, I made the rolling journey down the hall, into the oversized elevator, and up to the OR. Even though I was already groggy from an injection, I didn't miss a drop of strength and comfort that flowed from her hand on my shoulder as she walked beside my gurney. It meant the world to me to know she understood and cared.

For Jesus there was such a moment—when his solitude was broken by the touch of a friend, someone who had some faint sense of the burden pressing down on him and, in her own gentle way, had come alongside to enter into his suffering. In the midst of a feast, when everyone else was looking the other way, trying not to think about the threat hanging over Jesus, Mary stepped into the middle of the room and raised the subject loud and clear. The fragrance that engulfed the room was the aroma of death—from a perfume the ancients normally poured on a corpse.[17] These were not the actions of an impetuous sentimental woman who accidentally did something meaningful and would be remembered ever after for having stumbled into it. She knew exactly what she was doing. Mary was a thinking woman, and her actions that night reflected her theology and were about as subtle as distributing funeral leaflets in a hospice.

The lessons Jesus taught had made their mark. Armed with a theology forged through pain and struggle, Mary confronted this new crisis as a theologian. This time the tables were turned. Jesus was the one who was alone, agonized, and grieving—for his followers and for himself. And Mary, instead of collapsing with grief, as those who knew her well might have expected, or sinking in denial along with the men, stared reality in the eye. With strong faith, extraordinary composure, and resolute courage, she moved beyond herself to think about someone else. Understanding Jesus prompted Mary to minister to him in a way no one else even considered.

Later in Gethsemane, while Jesus' disciples slept, an angel would minister strength to Jesus.[18] But on the front lines of the battle that night in Bethany, the angel ministering strength to Jesus was a woman. While everyone else retreated and denied, even tried to set up roadblocks to deter him from his mission, Mary came alongside and urged him forward. As darkness descended over Bethany and the shadow of the cross fell across his path, she alone encouraged him to obey his Father. She alone said yes to the cross. It is a stunning moment, for Jesus, for Mary, and for us.

LEARNING FROM MARY

THE NIGHT MARY WENT public with her theology, my search to find a great woman theologian ended. In Mary's ministry to Jesus, I found what I had been looking for and more. She was, as I have argued, not simply a great woman theologian. She was the *first* great New Testament theologian. On the dark side of the cross, she was the first to understand the gospel. She listened and believed, and so she was the only one who ministered to Jesus. But for me, this wasn't simply the answer to an old assertion from a professor. It was the birth of a whole new line of thought—not whether great women theologians existed but what I could do to become one.

When Jesus promised that Mary's extraordinary gesture would never be forgotten, it was as much for our instruction as it was to honor her. If we want to understand what theology is and why it is so vital for women, we need only to look at Mary with perfume dripping from her fingertips and the ends of her hair and with her face flushed once again from the disapproval of her critics and the endorsement of Jesus. *This* is the portrait of a great woman theologian.

Mary's interactions with Jesus demonstrate that nothing in a woman's life is more important than her theology. Knowing God is a woman's highest calling and her most pressing need. What we know of him, whether it is a little or a lot, is all we have to hang on to when the storm hits and we are being pulled into the downward spiral of worthlessness, despair, and defeat. It is also what energizes and guides us as we tackle the task before us—as mothers, daughters, wives, and friends.

The transformation we see in Mary, as our eyes scan these three portraits, is the same transformation we will see in ourselves when knowing God becomes our chief occupation. Some women are already seeing it. One of my friends, a breast cancer survivor, recently told me of the huge change she was beginning to see in herself. Several years ago, she heard the heart-stopping news that the lump in her breast was malignant. The physical ordeal of a mastectomy and its aftermath was nothing compared to the soul suffering she endured from mistakenly thinking God had turned his back on her or was evening the score for something she had done wrong. In the intervening years, she was not only cancer free but also hard at work on her theology. When a recent checkup uncovered a worrying abnormality and she faced another round with cancer, the same old fears and anxieties returned, as they would for any of us. But along with them was this difference—an unshakable confidence in God, that he is good, that she was the special object of his love and care, and that he was accomplishing his good purposes for her and for her husband through this devastating ordeal. Without a doubt, theology is good for women.

But a woman's theology is not only good for her; it is good for others. Despite what some might think, theology is never a private matter, no matter how shy and retiring a woman might be or what her convictions are about her role as a woman. What we learn from Mary at the feast honoring Jesus is that there were others who needed her theology almost as much as she needed it herself. In a social gathering of men, where women were supposed to remain in the background, the likelihood of Mary stepping forward to make such a bold theological statement was remote at best. Yet we have to ask, How different would that evening have been for Jesus if Mary had kept her theology to herself?

I would state it even more strongly. A woman's theology, regardless of the shape it is in, affects others. Whether she holds it passively or exercises it actively like Mary, others feel the effects of her theology. It can't be helped. Mary's theology delighted the heart of God, refreshed and strengthened Jesus, and conveyed a crucial message to everyone else in the room. All of us have stories to tell of places where the good theology of a woman helped us over a hump or comforted us in a crisis, as well as times when a woman's weak theology drained our spirits or left us without the helping hand we needed. The bold theological action of a young woman in Bethany two millennia ago is a sobering reminder of the importance of a woman's theology and of the powerful opportunities it creates for us to minister to others.

MARY AND THE MEN

STUDYING MARY'S FEATURES on their own in this famous portrait would give women plenty of food for thought. We can see how her theology steadied her in the crisis and how it directed her to minister encouragement and strength to Jesus when he needed it most. But Mary is not portrayed alone against the marbled background of a studio portrait. She is drawn in sharp relief against the backdrop of the glaring failure of twelve confused men. If the source of Mary's story had been a woman, such a contrast would no doubt be suspect. But the sources in the three Gospel accounts of this anointing are disciples: Matthew, Peter through the pen of Mark, and John, men for whom this story brought back painful memories but who portrayed themselves in this honest but unflattering light. They set up the contrast and intended for their readers to study and compare Mary's behavior with their own, and her solid theology with theirs, which was by their own admission clouded and twisted by nationalism, ambition, and an unwillingness to set aside their inferior plans for God's. We would be remiss to move on without calling attention to the contrast.

In comparison with the disciples who saw the death of their leader as the end of their hopes for Israel and themselves, Mary had begun to grasp the meaning of the atonement[19] and the true hope it brought her, which she expressed in a way Jesus approved. She embraced the gospel. They politicized it. Even after the resurrection, they would still be talking politics. "The questions [they asked Jesus before his ascension] appear to have been the last flicker of their former burning expectation of an imminent political theocracy with themselves as its chief executives."[20] Mary's eyes were fixed on Jesus. Theirs were fixed on Rome and on themselves. The convictions and conduct of Mary and of the disciples were shaped by the focus of their eyes. The disciples rejected out of hand any mention of death and distanced themselves from Jesus. She knew it had to be and stood with him on the front lines of the battle.

If you want to feel the full impact of Mary's actions, compare her response with Peter's. Given the same information, Peter temporarily defected to the enemy, responding with an adamant, "Never, Lord! This shall never happen to you!" Would Peter ever forget the sting of Jesus' rebuke? "Get behind me, Satan! You are a stumbling block to me; you do not have in mind the things of God, but the things of men" (Matt. 16:22–23).

One male writer, Philip Yancey, openly disgusted with the blundering of Jesus' disciples and the contrast of the men's behavior with that of the women who remained near his cross and who were up at the crack of dawn to return to his tomb, reflected on Gethsemane: "Perhaps if women had been included in the Last Supper, Jesus would not have spent those hours alone. . . . But only male friends accompanied Jesus. Drowsy with dinner and wine, they slept while Jesus endured the crucible, alone."[21]

Tempting as it is to attribute Mary's actions to her gender, the explanation for her insightful sensitivity to Jesus does not lie in her being a woman. Recall, first of all, that she had learned compassion and sympathy from a man—Jesus himself. The theology anyone would learn from Jesus is characterized by compassion and sympathy for the downtrodden and afflicted. He not only taught it; he lived it before them every day as he related to them and to others. But even speaking from experience, I would be hard pressed to say the ability to empathize and enter into someone else's struggle are female attributes, or that it would seem odd or out of place in a man. For most of my life, I have been surrounded by men—five to be exact; my father, three brothers, and now my husband—and have on many occasions noted these same sensitivities in all five of them. At different times in my life, I have seen each of their faces drawn with concern and felt their arms go around me as they entered into my struggle. When I was in trouble, not one of them held back. My burden suddenly felt lighter because one of them was under it with me.

Sympathy and tenderness are not gender traits. They are *Christian* qualities the Holy Spirit generates in both sexes, qualities he intensifies through our theology and calls us to express in our ministry to one another. The fruit of the Spirit, even kindness and gentleness, are never divided up by gender. These are attributes of Christ, which all of his followers are called to emulate. Perhaps one of the reasons the Holy Spirit enlightened Mary and left the disciples in the dark was to cultivate these very traits in them. These undershepherds of God's flock would be kinder, gentler, and more patient with the weaknesses of others having felt their own dullness and hardheadedness in such a painful way.

But having said that, we would do well to ponder some important issues raised by Mary's actions that night. Her actions poke all sorts of holes in the notion that it is ungodly, unfeminine, insubordinate, and pushy for a woman to take the initiative. Here we see Mary taking the initiative in public, on a theological matter, and in a gathering of male leaders. What is more, she did it right in front of Jesus. And to everyone's astonishment, Jesus praised her for her actions. Jesus taught a brand of theology that was living and active. It did not lead Mary to withdraw into passivity or wait for a man to do the job; it led her to accept responsibility, step out, and take action where she saw a need.

Under the umbrella of Jesus' approval, it is clear that Mary's decisive actions did not in any way violate headship. What may come as a surprise is the fact that her actions actually modeled godly submission, the kind of submission Jesus also displayed. She is not mindlessly resigned to what Jesus has purposed to do. That would degrade the meaning of biblical submission and is certainly not the kind of submission Jesus desires of his followers. Christ (the standard of true submission for all Christians) never modeled a passive unthinking submission to his Father, and Mary did not offer that kind of submission to him. She had applied her mind and heart to understand what God required of Jesus and wholeheartedly threw herself, as well as her resources, into embracing and promoting Jesus' obedience to the Father. Submission did not reduce her to passivity but actually drew her out to participate in God's will. Her submission to God united her to Jesus, and as a result, she flourished and took the kind of bold action such a moment calls forth. Biblical headship does not ask less of us. It asks more. Headship is not so fragile that women must walk on eggshells for fear of threatening or destroying it. Jesus did not look askance at Mary's behavior nor rebuke her for making the Twelve look bad. To the contrary, he applauded her.

And did she make the men look bad? One would be hard pressed to resist arguing that they looked bad enough on their own. They saw it that way themselves later and wrote with great integrity of their failure that evening. Ironically, the disciples were the ones who violated Christ's headship with their unsubmissive rebellion against the will of God. But the fact is, Mary's actions that evening certainly did expose their failings. Although clearly Mary's intent was not to embarrass or shame the disciples, neither did she show any interest in covering for them. Mary's primary allegiance was to Jesus, not to the disciples. But the outcome was beneficial for them as well. Imagine what she would have denied Jesus and what great harm she would have brought on his disciples had she restrained herself to protect their sense of masculine leadership. Their masculinity didn't need to be shielded by her holding back but needed rather to be jolted by her obedience.

This is not to suggest, however, that Mary's actions leave room for women to be offensive, insensitive, or cavalier toward others. Mary didn't elbow her way into the room or behave disrespectfully toward the disciples, although they were in fact offended by her actions. Her conduct was above reproach, filled with grace and graciousness. The fruit of the Spirit must always govern how Christians interact with one another. This underscores the importance of fixing our eyes on Jesus to know him and his ways, so we will reflect him when we step out. Mary was not putting herself forward, fighting for herself, her rights, or her sex. She was fighting for her Lord. The issues involved were much bigger than Mary or the disciples. Her eyes were fixed on Jesus alone. Knowing Jesus prompted her to initiate and act on the truth in a way and with a spirit that would honor him. Her actions were costly and difficult for her, but it was the right thing for her to do, if Jesus' words mean anything at all.

MUTUAL DEPENDENCY

THE POINT OF MARY'S story is not, as Yancey suggested, that women will do a better job of things than men but that in the body of Christ, men and women need each other. That was one of the important messages Jesus highlighted that night in Bethany when he affirmed Mary's actions. The mysterious blending of God and man in the one person Christ is something we will never fully understand. But we do know this: Jesus' humanity was real. And along with his humanity he drank deeply of our weaknesses and our needs. As a baby he depended on his mother to care for everything. And as a man he thirsted, hungered, and grew weary. At the feast in Bethany, Jesus suffered isolation and dread. Strange as it sounds, Jesus needed Mary that night. The encouragement and ministry Mary offered him must have felt like balm to an aching heart. Mary literally ministered to the body of Christ that evening, and Jesus gladly accepted her ministry.

But Jesus wasn't the only one who needed Mary that night. The disciples needed her too. How much better it would have been for them if they had been willing and interested enough to sit down, listen, and weigh what this woman was thinking about Jesus instead of restricting her behind rigid lines of social demarcation. They had much to learn from Mary, as their later writings seem to admit. The point is not that women are better theologians than men but that men and women need each other to understand the truth and fulfill their calling as God's people. Nothing was more important that evening than Jesus. His friends needed to understand and stand with him in his hour of suffering. Mary did that when the men didn't. Instead of ridiculing and criticizing her, they would have benefited by including her in their conversation.

Once again the meeting of Mary and Jesus marks a crucial turning point for women. When Mary sat at Jesus' feet for the first time, the door to learning theology opened wide to women. But when she knelt at his feet this last time, the door to ministry swung open for women too. The need Mary sensed in Jesus wouldn't have been answered by the sumptuous plate of food on the table before him. Nor would it have been good enough for her to wait passively on the fringes, praying for one of the male disciples to notice what was needed and do something. The Holy Spirit had opened her eyes to the need. Jesus had trained her to be active and to contribute, and so she stepped out to anoint Jesus, not to shame anyone else or because there wasn't a man who was willing to do it but because this job belonged to her. Mary offered pastoral ministry to Jesus, which he warmly and publicly accepted. Jesus' response to Mary's critics gives women permission to think in wider categories for how we can minister to others. On this momentous night, Mary set a precedent for us to follow. A woman's theology opens new spheres of spiritual ministry in which she can readily engage—spiritual ministry to other women, to children, and also to men.

WOMEN IN COMBAT

HISTORICALLY WHEN A NATION was at war, the women stayed at home to run the family, the farms, and the factories and to write letters laden with love and moral support to their brothers, sons, and lovers on the battlefield. While the men were under siege, the women waited at a safe distance for lists of casualties and news of which way the battle was going. During the Vietnam War, my family breathed a sigh of relief when a damaged knee, medical service, and a high draft lottery number spared my three brothers from the horrors of war. My name never once came up in discussions over who might or should enlist. Until recent years the thought of a woman going to war alongside the men occurred only to rare figures like Israel's Deborah and France's Joan of Arc.

But no gender lines spare women from active duty in God's army. As little girls we marched and sang "Onward Christian soldiers" and "I'm in the Lord's army" right along with our brothers. No one ever batted an eye. The call to arms—sounded by the apostle Paul—doesn't segregate the men from the women but commands both sexes to "put on the full armor of God" (Eph. 6:11). I suppose it shouldn't have surprised me when, as part of his marriage proposal to me, my husband quoted the old warrior's words to Timothy, "Endure hardship with [me] like a good soldier of Christ Jesus" (2 Tim. 2:3).

Some military organizations ban women from their ranks. But Jesus wants them in his. Furthermore, female recruits, such as Mary, are not in the way or a liability to the troops, as some might fear. Neither are they a disgrace to their sex. In the trenches of the war zone, God's army is stronger for its female theologians. It is the crown of our womanhood, the essence of true femininity, the highest praise ever accorded a female that it should be said of any of us, she was "a brave and godly soldier in the army of the Lord."[22]

The war zone is no respecter of gender. The inclusion of women in the ranks of God's army is not to meet some affirmative action requirement or to ensure women receive the same treatment as the men. The simple yet revolutionary reason for including women is because the army needs them. God never intended for women to sit on the sidelines and await the outcome of the battle the men are fighting. He meant for us to be theologically active and engaged right alongside the men on the front lines of the battle.

We can't afford to take this lightly. We must arm ourselves with good theology, for our own sakes, as well as for the soldiers who are next to us in the trenches. Our fellow soldiers bear a double burden if women march unarmed into battle. And they are doubly protected if we prepare ourselves for combat. In a battle fierce as this, brave warriors are indispensable whether they are male or female. And it is on this battlefield that a woman will discover the power and usefulness of her theology. Mary's third portrait should have a profound impact on how we see ourselves as women, in the home and in the church. When we take this definition of ourselves seriously, the home, the church, and the men will only benefit. Conversely, to walk away from this hurts us all.

Climb the stairs to the attic with me and help me brush the dust off the portrait of Mary anointing Jesus. It's time we mounted it in the entry hall where it belongs. The battle rages all around us. *This* is the portrait we need to study as we soldier on in our homes and in the church.

9

GOD CREATED AN INTIMATE ALLY

WHEN LUCY MADE HER WAY THROUGH THE OLD WARDROBE AND into the snowy white world of Narnia, a Fawn by the name of Mr. Tumnas (upon learning she was human) promptly identified her as a Daughter of Eve. Although in our world this label gets hung like an albatross around our necks, in Narnia it was a badge of honor, conveying dignity to its wearer and inspiring trepidation or hope in the hearts of all who met her, depending on which side of the battle they were on.

When we are designated Daughters of Eve, the stigma we feel can be traced to the fact that it is usually the fallen Eve who comes to mind. The original Eve—the crowning touch of God's creative masterpiece and the inspiration of man's first poetry[1]—is long forgotten. Sadly, all anyone seems to recall is the "ambitious" hand that grasped the fruit, dragging Eve herself, her husband, and all the rest of us into a sea of depravity.

No matter how uneasy we are with the legacy of Eve, or how much the barbs and jokes hurt and offend us, we are well advised to acquaint ourselves with both Eves—the sinless Eve in Eden and the banished fallen Eve. Though Mary showed us that women are called to employ their theology for the good of those around them, including men, we cannot make an airtight case for this without considering Eve. Is there a link between Mary's actions and God's original design for women? Was Mary acting out of form, or was she actually fulfilling her calling as a Daughter of Eve? Eve's story brings our discussion of theology home, where we find the most intimate of human relationships—that of husband and wife. If a woman's theology benefits others, the first to feel these benefits should be her husband.

A WOMAN FOR ALL SEASONS

SINGLE WOMEN (at least some, I fear) might be tempted to skip this chapter. Either they suspect what comes next will be of little relevance or interest to them or else they just prefer to pass on the sense of alienation that comes from getting left out of the conversation one more time. I have been forewarned of this from my own memories of being on the outside looking in when I was single. I have since learned that every Christian needs to understand marriage, regardless of their marital status. Just as the sinless Eve provides the pattern for our calling as women, so marriage provides the paradigm for every other human relationship. More important, marriage is a picture of the church and teaches us how we are to relate to one another within the body of Christ.

But another reason we should resist the urge to skip ahead is that Eve's story takes us deep into theological territory. Questions over our identity and calling as women fall under the theological subheading of anthropology, or what God has revealed in his Word about humanity as male and female.[2] Our goal as theologians is always to see things from God's point of view, to understand him and his ways. That is no less true when it comes to something as personal as who we are as women. We owe it to him to wade into the discussion and see for ourselves what he wants of us. Our immediate objective is to figure out what God had in mind not merely for the first woman but for every woman after her. No woman is excluded from this discussion. The Bible doesn't teach a theology of women that applies only to a subset of the female population or fits only certain seasons of a woman's life. God's calling for women applies to all of us from the cradle to the grave, whether we are single or married, divorced or widowed, childless or moms, infirm or able bodied. Our conclusions (if they are true) should fit any woman's life, under any circumstance, at any point in history, and at any location on the planet. That is the nature of truth and the reason we need to stick together as we study.

ABOUT THAT RIB ...

LATE IN LIFE, C. S. Lewis, a confirmed old bachelor, met and married a Daughter of Eve. Four brief but intensely happy years later, she was gone. Cancer had severed Lewis from his beloved Joy. With pen in hand, he cataloged his grief and the emptiness of his heart, paying eloquent tribute to the love of his life. "For a good wife contains so many persons in herself. What was [she] not to me? She was my daughter and my mother, my pupil and my teacher, my subject and my sovereign; and always, holding all these in solution, my trusty comrade, friend, shipmate, fellow-soldier. My mistress, but at the same time all that any man friend (and I have good ones) has ever been to me. Perhaps more.... Did you ever know, dear, how much you took away with you when you left?"[3]

Swallowed by grief, Lewis amened the verdict spoken first by the Creator on the threshold of time, God's prelude to the creation of the woman: "It is not good for the man to be alone" (Gen. 2:18). It is as true today for men like Lewis who feel the ache of their aloneness as it is for diehards, such as Professor Henry Higgins in *Pygmalion,* who tell themselves that the last thing on earth a man needs is "to ever let a woman in [his] life."

The drama of the creation of the woman is lost on those of us who have grown overfamiliar with the Genesis story. But if you were reading it for the first time, you would be in for a surprise. The story sets the reader up for a shock with a refrain that is repeated (seven times in all) each time God completes a phase of his handiwork: "And God saw that it was good." After two or three times, even the youngest reader catches on and anticipates the phrase. By the seventh time, we're in rhythm and primed to hear it again. Then God created the man and placed him in the garden. And just as we're about to chime in one last time, God disrupts the rhythm with the startling words, "It is *not* good for the man to be alone" (2:18, emphasis added).

It was a showstopper. And this was not just overblown theatrics, for there truly was a problem in Eden. God hadn't caught himself in an oversight, for he never makes mistakes. He purposefully injected a poignant interlude between the creation of the man and the creation of the woman at least in part to impress upon the man the depth of his need for her. But it was also for our benefit, for it causes us to stop and ponder the relationship between the man and the woman.[4]

One thing is clear, the man *needed* the one God was about to create. God wasn't indulging his favorite creature with a luxury or a perk. God had diagnosed an inadequacy, something the man lacked and could not overcome. The remedy would come from God as well, not a smorgasbord of options but a single perfect answer to man's need: "a *helper* suitable for him" (2:18, emphasis added).

Rather than explaining this to Adam, God used a simple object lesson to cause him to feel his aloneness. As God passed all the creatures before Adam to see what he would name them, a consistent pattern emerged. Every creature had its partner, another creature who corresponded—all of them except Adam. Aloneness settled over him. It was a beautiful first enactment of the words Jesus would speak millennia later: "Your Father knows what you need before you ask him" (Matt. 6:8). Already God had planned what he would do. And so while Adam slept, God took a rib from his body, fashioned it into a woman, and brought her back to his side. Then for the eighth time, the refrain sounded with greater resonance than ever, "God saw all that he had made, and it was *very* good" (1:31, emphasis added).

THE WOMAN AS *EZER*

THE LINK BETWEEN the New Testament single Mary of Bethany and the sinless Old Testament married Eve of Eden turns on the meaning of the word *helper*. Despite what we are often told, the operative word in the Bible for women is not submission but the word *ezer*, which God uses here. Helper comes from the Hebrew word *ezer*, an interesting word choice loaded with significance.

Ezer appears twenty-one times in the Old Testament. Twice, in Genesis, it describes the woman (Gen. 2:18, 20). But the majority of references (sixteen to be exact) refer to God, or Yahweh, as the helper of his people.[5] The remaining three references appear in the books of the prophets, who use it to refer to military aid.[6] If language means anything, the *ezer*, in every case, is not a flunky or a junior assistant but a very *strong* helper.[7]

Usually at this point the discussion of women degenerates into a debate over just how strong a helper she might be—a controversy over power and rights in which the woman's strength is gauged with reference to the man. One side argues that the association of *ezer* with God means the woman is superior. The other side argues that her rank is unaffected, for she is clearly the man's subordinate. Like kids caught in a custody battle, we feel tugged at by both sides and sometimes pulled apart in the middle. We end up wrangling and taking sides among ourselves over marriage, motherhood, homemaking, and careers—spheres of life we all hold dear and are fiercely committed to uphold. Despite the fact that the *ezer* has become a battleground, we must brave the subject anyway.

I can almost hear a groan as we roll our eyes and brace ourselves to hear the ground rules explained one more time. We've gone over this so many times before, it hardly seems worth mentioning again. Besides, what does this have to do with theology and women? Just when we were beginning to make some progress, discovering new ways for women to live out their theology, this old topic has to come up again.

I would groan myself (and probably wouldn't have brought it up in the first place) if I hadn't started paying attention to what Hebrew scholars were saying about the word helper. They piqued my interest. What I learned from them surprised me, I'll admit. But even more amazing was the discovery that the call for women to be strong theologians in our relationships with men was part of God's original blueprint. The first great New Testament theologian wasn't an aberration; she shouldn't have caught anyone by surprise. Even as a single woman, Mary was following the paradigm set forth in the creation of the woman. Mary was an *ezer*.

A JOB DESCRIPTION FOR THE WOMAN

HISTORICALLY THERE HAS BEEN a strong inclination to nail the definition of helper down to a specific job description for women. Some people (most of us, I suspect) feel more comfortable when the division of labor between the sexes is clearly spelled out and we know which tasks belong to women and which ones don't. Usually the details center on three main aspects of the relationship between the husband and wife—sex and procreation, domesticity and motherhood, friendship and companionship.

Besides the overarching rule of thumb that our primary purpose is to understand what God requires of us, four principles must govern any further discussion. The first is that whatever we conclude about the strong helper, we must not make light of God's assessment of the situation. In God's eyes the man's aloneness was a major problem, critical enough to warrant waving a red flag over it. This was not much ado about nothing but a seriously important matter to God.

Second, our conclusions must not trivialize or demean the man or the woman. Genesis sets forth an astonishingly high view of both sexes, which we must not in any way diminish. We cannot reduce the man to his biology or his aloneness to the need for someone to pick up after him. The woman was not an afterthought or an embellishment to creation. God didn't describe her as a mate, a junior assistant, a follower, or a dependent. Definitions of the woman which cast her as a passive responder who does only what she is told (someone the man would have to think for, supervise, and guide) create *more* work for Adam instead of providing him with help. Eve was introduced as a significant, active, and welcomed contributor to the man and to the work they were both called to share.

Third, as we have already noted, our conclusions must have universal application. The strong helper isn't a role a woman puts on like a white veil as she heads down the aisle to the altar. It is a *lifetime* calling for us all.

Fourth, we need to be honest with the text. Our goal is truth, to understand what God has revealed, not to score points for one side or the other in the perpetual debate over women or to preserve some long-cherished view on the subject. If I have learned anything from my seminary professors, it is this: no matter how many times we study a passage or how thoroughly we know it, we always need to be prepared to learn something new, to discover we were wrong or perhaps not as clear in our grasp of things as we had thought. None of us has everything figured out. Everyone has more to learn.

The first time I spotted a flaw in my understanding of helper (and I have found a good many more since), I was single and had just heard that my cousin, whose child was less than a year old, had taken a job. Her young husband simply couldn't earn enough to support them. In my heart I felt critical of her decision to work outside her home. But her courage in this tough decision commanded my respect and helped me realize my narrow views actually would have tied her hands behind her back and prevented her from being the strong helper she was called to be. She wasn't abandoning her home, as I first thought. She was fighting for it. It was good preparation for my own marriage, for I have learned over the last twenty years that a wife's job description encompasses a whole range of responsibilities and adventures I never would have thought of listing under the heading of helper.

Usually, the responsibilities that top the list center on the home. The man's helper is his companion and sexual partner, a childbearer, mother, and homemaker who under certain conditions supplements the family income. Certainly no one would question that the helper role encompasses all of these important responsibilities and more. But they do not, either separately or altogether, satisfy the meaning of the *ezer*.

If we go further, as many have done, and *equate* these functions with the *ezer*, we will, in effect, exclude a large number of women from God's calling to them as a woman. Women who are single, childless, or disabled are either morally or physically prevented from carrying out such responsibilities. And women whose children are leaving the nest see their usefulness diminish steadily with each child that passes through the door. The effect on working women is considerably more overt, for they are condemned for having skewed priorities, for having turned their backs on the home for selfishness and greed. Some have even blamed them for the moral decline of the country. Recently, an advertisement for a book on Christian parenting listed indicators that our culture has "rejected biblical standards of morality." It named "working mothers" first on that list, which also included child abuse and pornography. Such statements devastate godly working mothers who, like my cousin, are pouring themselves out for the sake of their families. We forget that historically women have always worked alongside the men and that selfishness, greed, and poor parenting are pitfalls for either sex, no matter where we spend our time.

Strangely enough, Adam didn't need someone to do most of the tasks we usually associate with the role of the helper. His physical needs were abundantly met in the shelter and bounty of Eden. A wide variety of food was readily accessible in Eden, his well-stocked pantry. There were no menus to plan, groceries to buy, or meals to prepare. There was no house to decorate or clean, no table to set or children to nurture. There were no socks to pick up, not a stitch of laundry. What is more, the first sewing project was a joint effort. Adam didn't wait behind a bush for Eve to sew fig leaves together for him. He did his own sewing. Hard to imagine that God would announce with fanfare a helper who would do things the man could just as easily do for himself. Defining helper in terms of domestic activities also implies (and this is surely not good news) that women who hire domestic help are abdicating their calling as strong helpers. And if motherhood comprises the heart of the helper role, then Eve wouldn't begin to function at full capacity until months later when her first child was born.

Companionship and friendship come closer to the meaning of helper but still don't go far enough. Considering the likes and habits of modern males, even this possibility will seem implausible to a lot of women. Most men (even married ones) find their need for companionship amply satisfied by *Monday Night Football* or an afternoon with the guys on the golf course. But in God's eyes, a fraternity of male companions would never remedy the man's aloneness. Only the *ezer* would do, and although she would certainly keep him company, she was far more than a warm body or a partner for tennis. Her companionship would reach the man at a much deeper level than his best male friendships would approach, just as C. S. Lewis discovered. The woman's task requires much more than anything we have suggested so far.

THE WOMAN AS WARRIOR

TWO THINGS STAND OUT to me as I keep coming back to the text and in particular to this word *ezer*. The first is that the word itself is so *generic*. Perhaps this explains its resistance to our efforts to come up with an official to-do list that works for every woman. The very nature of the word would indicate that any attempts to narrow this down to specific tasks violate the intent of the word. We aren't told what Eve's job description included, and my guess is it was as fluid as the day is long. As helper she would rise to the challenge of each new circumstance and challenge of life. And in a sense, isn't that the very essence of a helper—to see and do what is needed, rather than confining herself to certain prescribed tasks?

The beauty and the complexity of *ezer* is the fact that it is so non-specific. It is purposely so, for it opens the way for the strong helper to enter into every arena of life with the man—at home, at work, and on the frontiers of knowledge and exploration. The commands to multiply, fill, subdue, and rule the earth mean the sky's the limit for what a woman can do as strong helper. Jesus' command for us to love one another even down to the washing of dirty feet means no task is too menial for anyone, male or female, who desires to reflect his image. The parameters for a woman seem to be *expansive*, rather than constrictive, flexible and dynamic in each new situation, rather than woodenly prescribed. Together, male and female would prove daily in a hundred different ways the wisdom of the ancient proverb that "two are better than one" (Eccl. 4:9).

But the second thing that impresses me about this word and opens a whole new vista for women to explore in every relationship is the way this noun functions in the Bible. Usually, in commentaries and also in books on both sides of the debate over the role of women, the discussion of the word *ezer* ends with a breakdown of the twenty-one times this word appears—similar to what I have done. Two for women, sixteen for God, and three for military powers. But when I reexamined each of the sixteen references to God, I discovered to my surprise that powerful military language permeates every passage. God is the helper, deliverer, shield, and sword of his people. In battle he is more trustworthy than chariots and horses. He personally stands on sentry duty, guarding his own from their enemies. His strong arm overthrows all their foes.

Next I looked at the verb form of the word and found that *azer* ("to rescue or save"), which appears in the Old Testament approximately eighty times, "generally indicates military assistance."[8] Checking the math, in nineteen of the twenty-one times that *ezer* appears in the Bible, and in nearly 100 percent of the uses of the verb form, there is an overwhelming military connotation. But for some strange reason, when the same word refers to a woman, we end up talking about making babies, submission, and cleaning house.

Considering the evidence, it makes sense that this military imagery would carry over to the woman too.[9] That possibility grows stronger when we see the same imagery used for women elsewhere in the Bible. Although some may be uneasy using military language to describe a woman, biblical writers clearly didn't share this phobia. One of the best known passages concerning women—the ideal wife of Proverbs 31—uses military language extensively, the same language used elsewhere in the Bible to describe the military exploits of Israel's heroes.[10] English translations of the Bible downplay the military flavor, but Hebrew scholars have demonstrated that heroic military imagery sets the tone for our understanding of this woman. According to Old Testament scholar Bruce K. Waltke, the poet portrays her "going out to battle" (v. 29), "her arms are strong for her tasks" (v. 17). "She arises [like a lioness] while it is still night, and provides 'prey' for her household" (v. 15). She "girds her loins with strength" (v. 17), "an act that prepares one for heroic or difficult action, often for warfare."[11] She "laughs [in victory]" (v. 25). She is bold, courageous, valiant, battling fiercely for God's glory in her marriage, her family, her household, and her community. Everyone around her, and above all her husband, benefits from her wisdom, determination, and strength. "The valorous wife is a heroic figure used by God to do good for his people, just as the ancient judges and kings did good for God's people by their martial exploits."[12]

The military language associated with the word *ezer* ties the same bold imagery to the strong helper. She is a valiant warrior conscripted by God, not to fight against the man but to fight at his side as his greatest ally in the war to end all wars. Even before creation, the battle lines were drawn between God and the powers of darkness. In the Garden, God wasn't weaving a great romance. He was building an army, and the enemy was waiting to launch his first assault. Adam and Eve were not simply our first parents. They were

God's first recruits, and both of them would soon be in the line of fire. Their mission was overwhelming—more than the two of them could handle together, much less face alone. They would need each other, not just for the sake of company but for strength to fight the battle that lay ahead. The aloneness of the man and the creation of the woman converge in the first great lesson in God's school of human relations: that men and women need each other.

AN INTIMATE ALLY

AT A FAMILY GATHERING, my daughter (who had just learned to crawl) headed across the living room carpet for her preschool cousin, who was engrossed with his toys. The howl that erupted from him seconds later alerted everyone in the room that an unwelcome little intruder was spoiling his game. But when Adam's eyes blinked awake to the discovery that there was a woman in his garden, there was no complaining howl, only an outburst of poetry.

> "This is now bone of my bones
> and flesh of my flesh;
> she shall be called 'woman,'
> for she was taken out of man."
>
> Genesis 2:23

She was no intruder, but, at every level, the perfect answer to his aloneness. She was his intimate ally.[13]

In Genesis 1 the woman stood beside the man in union and equality. They shared a common identity and a common calling.[14] *Both* were created in the image of God—an identity that, apart from Christ, no human has ever yet lived up to. This designation invested them and their actions with dignity, honor, and meaning because God conferred his own significance on them. *Both* were commissioned to multiply and fill the earth. As coregents, *both* were called to subdue and rule the creation. The scope of their joint mission encompassed the whole earth and every sphere of life—home, work, and the vast unknown regions beyond. The man would not be alone in any dimension of life. But the daunting task before them was never simply, or even primarily, a physical enterprise, for from the outset all of life was centered in God.

The command to be fruitful, multiply, and fill the earth was never simply about populating the earth with human beings but with filling it with *worshipers* of the living God. Every child we encounter, every adult we meet, is an opportunity for us to be fruitful, multiply, and fill the earth. Most of us (women and men) can name several godly women, besides our mothers, who have had a major formative influence on our walk with God. Singles and childless women must assume an active role in nurturing children and young people to know and trust God if we hope to fulfill this divine mandate.

Likewise, the mandate to subdue and rule was never purely about government, science, technology, and exploration. It too was theological—a call to apply God's truth to every sphere of human life and to uphold the Creator's honor throughout all the earth. Adam and Eve's calling, as male and female, was to reflect and fight for God's glory (not their own) throughout the world. They would face stiff opposition on every front—not just from the enemy without but also from the enemy within. It would demand much from both of them.

The battle would be fought and won not on the global stage of human achievements but within the solitary chambers of the human heart. And this place, more than any other, was where the man's need was greatest and where he was utterly alone. How beautiful God's design, for no other creature was so uniquely suited to end the man's solitude than the *ezer*—the wife of his heart.

Within the sacred intimacy of marriage, the man's wife would know his struggles, fears, and failures. He might (and would) conceal his weaknesses from others. Never from her. Such vulnerability would not pose a threat to him, for she was not his competitor, his critic, or his adversary. She was his help, his ally in the battle. The bond between them was "as strong as death" and as "unyielding as the grave" (Song 8:6), stronger even than the bond between parent and child.[15] Their "bone of my bones" union meant no one shared a greater interest in his welfare or a deeper concern for his struggles. She was his rib, formed to protect and defend his vital organs. God did not create her to let her husband do the thinking while she flattered, cajoled, complied, and shored up his male ego. Her mission was to build him up in God, to stand with him in truth and to oppose him whenever he veered onto wrong paths.

Recently a young seminarian who was preparing for the pastorate asked me whether I thought it mattered that the young woman he was dating had no interest in theology. (I seem to hear that question less and less these days.) His pastor thought it *might* pose a problem because often in the church the pastor's wife is called upon to counsel *other women* in the church. I watched the color drain from my young friend's face as I explained that the person she would counsel most would be her husband. A lot of men assume that when they need advice, they'll turn to their pastor or one of their male colleagues. But the truth of the matter is that a man's lowest moments and biggest struggles come when he's at home and the only one around to help him is his wife.

The greatest asset a woman brings to her marriage is not her beauty, her charm, her feminine wiles, or even her ability to bear a child. It is her theology. Every wife is her husband's partner, pastor, spiritual counselor, motivational speaker, and his fellow soldier in the war zone. With her eyes fixed on Jesus, she is less inclined to make her husband, herself, or her children the center of the universe. With head and heart filled with the knowledge of God, she will find strength to enter the fray and wrestle with all of life's problems alongside her husband. As she lives in the light of God's sovereign goodness, she will radiate hope and courage to him in the darkest hours. With her feet firmly planted on God's holy character, she will find boldness to stand up to her man when his disobedience is tarnishing God's glory. And her husband will only be the better for it.

And here's something to contemplate. Contrary to the message we get from our culture (and from ourselves whenever we look in the mirror), the *ezer,* like a fine wine, only improves with age. One of the most beautiful *ezers* I have ever known was a widow in her eighties. Mrs. Willies (I spoke of her in chapter 4) used to hobble around supported by her cane and breathe courage and strength into the hearts of men and women who were much younger. It wasn't theory with her. The words she spoke came from long years of soldiering through difficult battles and proving the goodness and faithfulness of her God. As her physical strength declined, her confidence in God burned brighter. "I know him too well to think he would ever let me down," she told a friend who was visiting her in the hospital. There is hidden treasure to be mined in God's church, in the wisdom and theology that reside in the hearts of older women—not just for the benefit of younger women but for the good of the whole church.

WHERE EVERYTHING WENT WRONG

BUT WE DID SAY there were two Eves. Which brings us to the second half of her saga, the part where instead of sailing off into the sunset to a blissful happily ever after, both hero and heroine are cut down in the first assault of the great war. It is one of those tragic epochs in the Bible that lovers of happy endings dread to read—like Israel's worship of the golden calf so soon after crossing the Red Sea (Exodus 32), the catastrophic failures in the book of Judges, or the capture of the ark of God by the Philistines (1 Samuel 4). The bottom falls out, God's glory departs, and we're confronted once again with the sinfulness of our own hearts.

Certain tragic moments in history have extraordinary power over the human memory. People who were old enough at the time can tell you exactly what they were doing when they heard the news of the bombing of Pearl Harbor, the assassination of President John F. Kennedy, or the death of Princess Diana. No doubt if we were to ask them, the angels of heaven could give a similarly precise account of the moment they learned that Adam and Eve had eaten the forbidden fruit. It was a catastrophe of unimaginable proportions. The battle had been joined, and the casualties were heavy. Forever after, the name of Eve would be blackened by the shame of her treachery: "For that first marriage was our funeral; / One woman at one blow, then kill'd us all."[16]

The first conversation on human record is a theological discussion between the woman and the serpent—a painful reminder of the importance of a woman's theology. The topic centered on the motives and truthfulness of God, and doubts were already beginning to take root in the woman's mind. Does God have a right to tell us what to do? Is he good, or is he depriving us of something advantageous? Does he really care about what is best for us? We all know what happened next.

Two explanations are typically offered to explain the fall of the human race. The first is straightforward: Adam and Eve violated God's law. They rejected his authority and his goodness. Eve, we are told in 1 Timothy 2:14, was deceived and disobeyed. The second view, while affirming this first explanation, sees a "deeper" problem—the origin of the battle between the sexes. "Eve usurped Adam's headship and led the way into sin. . . . And Adam, who (it seems) had stood by passively, allowing the deception to progress without decisive intervention—Adam, for his part, abandoned his post as head."[17] Eve made a power grab, and Adam's sin was in "being led by his wife rather than leading her."[18] Commenting on God's rebuke of the man, "Because you listened to your wife and ate from the tree about which I commanded you, 'You must not eat of it'" (3:17), one advocate of this view writes, "Adam sinned at two levels. At one level, he defied the plain and simple command of 2:17. That is obvious. But God goes *deeper*. At another level, Adam sinned by 'listening to his wife.' He abandoned his headship. According to God's assessment, this moral failure in Adam led to his ruination."[19]

This line of thinking creates a serious dilemma for men as well as for women. It has led some to conclude that a man is abdicating his headship when he listens to his wife. In making important decisions, the man should assume full responsibility, take the lead, and make the call.[20] "Listening to his wife" somehow weakens his headship. But this arrangement walls the woman off from functioning as his strong helper and returns the man to his original state. Once more, he is alone. The question becomes all the more serious for us because the nature of Eve's contribution was theological; she was drawing and acting upon conclusions (false ones to be sure) about the nature and character of God.

So where does this leave us? Is a woman never to speak? Never to speak on important matters? Never to speak on biblical or theological matters? The implication is that God will never lead through the woman, that her input is theologically suspect and she should never be given the opportunity to create such havoc again. But this notion doesn't seem to square with the rest of Scripture, which instructs men to listen to their wives and commends women who speak words of truth and wisdom. Consider some examples.

During Abraham's heart-wrenching crisis over his sons, Isaac and Ishmael, God told Abraham, "Listen to whatever Sarah tells you" (Gen. 21:12) with regard to banishing Ishmael and his mother, Hagar. When Abigail intercepted an enraged David with wise counsel and prevented the bloodbath nearly provoked by her wicked husband, the future king praised her godly initiative, even though she was acting in subversion to her husband. "Praise be to the LORD, the God of Israel, who has sent you today to meet me. May you be blessed for your good judgment and for keeping me from bloodshed this day and from avenging myself with my own hands. . . . Go home in peace. I have heard your words and granted your request" (1 Sam. 25:32–35).

King Josiah consulted Huldah the prophetess, even though Jeremiah was available (2 Chron. 34:22; 2 Kings 22:14). Ruth and Naomi instigated and initiated, and godly Boaz responded willingly and energetically to their wise proposals (Ruth 2–3). In the New Testament, Apollos listened to Priscilla and Aquila as they "explained to him the way of God more adequately" (Acts 18:26). Even infamous Pilate would have been well-advised to listen to his wife when she counseled him concerning Jesus, "Don't have anything to do with that innocent man, for I have suffered a great deal today in a dream because of him" (Matt. 27:19).

On the flip side, Sapphira was held accountable for listening to her husband. Instead of being granted leniency for submitting to her husband and for her failure to disobey his headship, the judgment of God fell with equal force on her for complying with his schemes to lie to the Holy Spirit and defraud the church (Acts 5:1–11). In disbelief the apostle Peter asked, "How could you agree to test the Spirit of the Lord?" (5:9).

It seems to me that in every case the issue is not so much *who* is talking but *what* they are saying. Would anyone condemn Eve to silence if Adam had been first to reach for the fruit and she had forcefully opposed him? Was God condemning Adam for allowing his wife to speak and thereby sentencing the woman to a life of silence? Or was his displeasure due to the fact that Adam heeded her counsel when her words went against God's command?

The suggestion that Eve was trying to overthrow her husband fails to take into account the fact that before the Fall, harmony and union characterized their relationship, not tension and frustration. She wasn't oppressed by his dominion, for his dominion (as well as hers) was directed outward at the creation, not inward toward each other. Furthermore, had she been bent on gaining the upper hand, she never would have shared the fruit with him but would have hoarded the benefits for herself. She would have made herself like God and left Adam as he was.

THE *EZER* IN FAILURE

I WOULD LIKE TO SUGGEST an alternative explanation for the dynamics between the man and the woman in the Fall. Rather than seeking to overthrow the man, it seems that from her words to the serpent and also her actions toward Adam, Eve was actually functioning as Adam's helper. She was hearing a sales pitch about something that promised to benefit both of them. According to the serpent, eating the fruit would advance them higher than they had ever dreamed, putting them on a par with God.

On the surface, her actions are perfectly in keeping with her calling as a strong helper. Surely there was nothing wrong with bringing her husband something to eat. Nor would anyone suggest that she was wrong to pursue something that would advance and benefit her husband and herself. Her sin began when she shifted her first loyalty from God to herself and to Adam. Here was an opportunity for the strong helper not to place her sword in its sheathe or retreat in silence, leaving the battle to her husband, but to stand with him, to wield her theology like a gleaming Excalibur, slicing through the barrage of lies with the truth and drawing strength from God to do the right thing.

What we would prefer to read is that the woman fixed her eyes on God; that she was still humming the eightfold creational refrain that all God does is good; that she steeled herself with the knowledge that God is good, that allegiance to him is always the right course of action, no matter what the cost; that she and her husband picked up sticks and together drove the serpent out of Eden.

Instead of making God the center of her thinking, she removed him from the equation, making his voice only one of many. She fixed her eyes on the fruit and its alleged benefits for herself and her husband. *She* became the reference point. Despite what God had said, she judged that "the fruit of the tree was good" for them (3:6). Instead of being a help, she began to destroy.

There is an added twist to the story, for the text reads, "She also gave some to her husband, *who was with her,* and he ate it" (3:6, emphasis added). This seems to indicate that the man was present and heard the whole conversation with the serpent. "Adam was not only silent with the serpent; he was also silent with Eve. He never reminded her of God's word. He never called her to a larger vision. He did not join his wife in battling wits with the serpent. He passively listened to her speak, rather than speaking with her in mutual respect."[21] Clearly, listening *was* part of Adam's sin—not because the speaker was a woman but because the message urged rebellion against God. This fact points up the responsibility for both of them to think through what the other was saying and to act according to the truth.

This is further supported when God came to interrogate the pair for what had transpired. He was not gathering information (he knew full well what had transpired). He came to call them to account and compel them to see their actions within the framework of their relationship to him. Recognizing headship—an important biblical concept—God addressed the man first. But he also held the woman fully responsible for her actions. When we put this scene together with the tragic outcome of Sapphira's compliance with a sinful husband, clearly neither headship nor submission absolve a woman from full responsibility before God.

It isn't wrong for women to think, speak, or act. And men are not supposed to plug their ears at the sound of a female voice. This tragic disaster simply reinforces the need for good theology. It underscores rather than discredits lesson one in God's school of human relationships: men and women need each other to know, trust, and obey God. Even in a sinless world, being a good theologian wouldn't be easy or instinctive for either of them. The challenge is even harder in a fallen world. Unless they resisted, selfishness, weakness, passivity, and disobedience would always rise to the surface. It would take their combined energies—both mental and physical—to live by faith.

THE *EZER* AS A FRIEND

AS I WRITE THIS chapter, I am haunted by the faces of women I know who are caught in difficult marriages and who could easily feel overwhelmed by all we have been saying. I have described the ideal situation. But life since the Fall has never matched that standard. In a dysfunctional world, being her husband's strong helper is asking the impossible of some women. He's perfectly happy to accept her help in the traditional sense of the word. But when it comes to deeper matters, or to his relationship with God, he is as resistant as granite. Women—some of them are my own friends—tell me their husbands are dismissive of anything they say and wouldn't think of looking to them for counsel on any subject. Sometimes what a woman faces is worse than resistance. One woman, whose husband was emotionally and physically abusive, needed an *ezer* for herself, to protect and guard her and her children from the unpredictable rage of her husband. Sometimes, even in marriage, the one who is alone is the woman.

These women draw enormous comfort and strength from knowing God is their helper. But if there is one message in the story of creation, it is that all of us need human help. When God raised the problem of Adam's aloneness, he never said, "I am all you need." Instead of giving Adam a lecture on contentment or a sermon on God's sufficiency, God formed a woman—a tangible, flesh and blood human being—to come alongside and, in her own imperfect way, enter into his struggles. He commissioned a person to stand in the gap and be there for the man. But women aren't somehow better suited to cope with aloneness than the man was. Everyone needs an *ezer*—especially women who are living in crisis. The *ezer's* ministry is not simply about the role of women in marriage. It is something all Christians are called to do for one another.

There are plenty of times in my life that I look back on and hate to think what would have happened if someone hadn't been there for me. Often the friend who reached out didn't have any experience with my particular struggle. But that didn't seem to stop them from trying or hinder them from getting through. Elderly women were strong for me when I was a teenager and a young adult. When I was single, my greatest support came from three women who had married in their teens. Sometimes, the one who is an *ezer* for me is my daughter. There's no minimum age for this. God works in mysterious ways, especially when he uses us to do his work. The Holy Spirit is alive and well, and people are his preferred method of giving strength, encouragement, and hope to those who are alone.

IMPLICATIONS FOR WOMEN

SO WHAT ARE the implications for us? For starters, the Bible sets forth the highest view of woman you will ever find anywhere. She is the image bearer of God. It doesn't get any higher than that. She is equal to the man and entrusted, along with him, with enormous responsibility to fill and rule the earth. Debates over superiority and inferiority die on the doorstep of Genesis 1. The issue is not how we compare with one another but how we measure up to God's standard. When God made male and female in his image and put the whole world under their rule, he raised the bar so high for both sexes that we should all have crooks in our necks from trying to see where it went. Instead of searching for boundaries to curb a woman's activities, we ought to spend a good deal more time talking about the possibilities for women, for our mission in this battle requires the best we have to offer.

Second, God has called women to a monumental task—not just in marriage but in all of our relationships. It is a heavy responsibility to know our theology benefits or weakens others depending on what shape it is in. This knowledge reinforces the urgency of pursuing a deeper knowledge of God, wrestling with the truth and keeping our eyes fixed on him. A woman's theology can make the difference between "stumbling and blundering" (dragging others down with her) and being a well-armed soldier girded with strength and dignity for the difficult task at hand. Knowing God keeps us focused on what really matters, helps us steer a steady course through troubled waters, and equips us to minister to others.

Third, God's calling for women should put to rest any fears we might have of taking things too far or getting ahead of the men. No Christian—male or female—will ever be accused of being overqualified for the job God has given them to do. I can still recall the sinking feeling I felt when the speaker at a singles meeting in my church stated unequivocally that women who spend a lot of time in the business world will find it hard to be good wives. I was spending my days as a systems writer in a large bank in Oregon and would be doing more of the same in the foreseeable future. According to his theory, every day I worked reduced my chances of being a good wife. The same fear crossed my mind when I headed off to seminary. But God doesn't plant the seeds of paranoia in a woman's heart, leading her to walk on eggshells, fearful of learning, thinking, or doing too much. God requires more of us, not less. A soldier who takes the conservative approach in preparing for war isn't helping anyone. She's creating weakness in the ranks.

Ironically, many husbands openly acknowledge that much good has come from their wife's education, theological maturity, career skills, and life experiences. The husband of the valiant woman of Proverbs 31 certainly did. His wife didn't hold back in any sphere, and her value as a wife skyrocketed as a result. Instead of hurting her marriage, her full-fledged efforts strengthened the bond between them and brought honor to her husband in the community.

The *Ezer* Brings Her Theology Home

THE LEGACY OF THE FIRST Eve lived on when Mary knelt to anoint Jesus for his death. And it lives on in us today, bringing courage and hope to husbands and friends and striking fear in the enemy, who knows his time is short. The message of Eve's legacy is not that women outrank men but that neither sex is adequate for the task God has given us without the help of the other.

When my mother was recuperating from the surgery that had left her coping with pain, she faced an uphill battle to regain the use of her leg. For a long time, her simplest movements required the aid of a walker or someone's strong arm to keep her from falling. After spending several weeks in Portland caring for her, I reluctantly boarded the plane for Orlando, leaving my dad on duty in the kitchen and first in line to care for my mom, on top of his responsibilities as a pastor. And my mother, in addition to her physical difficulties, faced the added frustration of being physically unable to be of any help. Their situation brought the *ezer* question closer to home: What does it mean to be the strong helper of a husband who must cook, clean, run errands, and care for her?

She answered that question one evening when they were both feeling haggard and battle worn from the relentless pain and the endless household chores. She asked him to read aloud to her (and also to himself) from Jerry Bridges' book *Trusting God*. These are the words she wanted him to read, words she knew would bring them both the encouragement and strength they needed: "God never wastes pain. He always uses it to accomplish His purpose. And His purpose is for His glory and our good. Therefore, we can trust Him when our hearts are aching or our bodies are racked with pain. Trusting God in the midst of our pain and heartache means that we accept it from Him.... An attitude of acceptance says that we trust God, that He loves us, and knows what is best for us."[22]

The legacy of the *ezer* lives on whenever women use their theology to strengthen a comrade in battle. What was true before the Fall is truer still today. "It is not good for the man to be alone," in the home, in the trenches, and also in the church.

10

BODY BUILDING IN THE CHURCH

NOT LONG AGO THE PASTOR OF A LARGE AMERICAN EVANGELICAL church rose from his plush high-backed chair and mounted the steps to the historic pulpit he occupies every Sunday. Gazing out over his congregation and taking mental note of the large number of men in the pews, he remarked with satisfaction, "If you walk into a church and it is filled with women, then you know it's a weak church. But a church filled with men—now that is a strong church indeed."

What was intended to encourage the men came at the expense of the women. His words, which sent a shudder through many of the females sitting in the pews that Sunday morning, would cause any *ezer* to wonder if her usefulness expires on the doorstep of the church. Imbedded in his comment is the common perception that the strength and health of the church rest on male shoulders, and that consequently a woman's theology is not all that important in the church. Even more troubling is the unfortunate impression that there is an inherent link between women and weakness. But perhaps the greatest indignity is the implication that weakness in women is of no real consequence to the church, so long as there are men around. Some have even argued that it is *better* for the church when women keep a low profile and allow the men to take care of things. A woman may minister to other women, to children, or to people with physical or material needs, and perhaps her theology may come in handy in those areas. But men will handle the spiritual ministries of the wider church. Women are not expected or needed to help shoulder the burden at this level. A woman's theology may prove useful on a private level or behind closed doors in women's ministries, but when she enters the corporate life of the church, she might just as well check her theology at the door, for it won't be needed in here.

We have seen how indispensable a woman's theology is for her own sake, and we have also explored the value of a woman's theology to others. Now we have finally arrived on the doorstep of the church where we must stop to ask ourselves, What happens when the *ezer* enters the church? How does a woman in the pews utilize her theology for the good of the body of Christ?

CORPORATE WOMEN

A FRIEND AND I sipped cinnamon iced tea from tall glasses as we sat in wicker chairs on her porch and talked away the hours between the women's Bible study at our church and the time when we would hurry off to pick up our children from school. Our conversation wasn't filled with the idle talk or whispered gossip that some might expect to pass between two women on a warm Florida afternoon. As a matter of fact, we were wrestling with the down-to-earth implications of our theology in a crisis we were witnessing in our church.

During the previous year in our congregation, five marriages (four which had celebrated double-decade anniversaries) had come unraveled and wound up in divorce court. Our pastor and elders spent countless hours in disappointing counseling sessions. Their tireless efforts to understand the problems and reconcile the couples were to no avail. Everyone was heartsick over these breakups, and my friend and I knew from our interaction with other women in the church that these five divorces were just the tip of the iceberg. It was just a matter of time before other troubled relationships would consume the elders' time.

Fresh from a study of the woman as a strong helper and from examining the lives of women in the Bible, like Mary of Bethany, who took their corporate responsibilities seriously, the question on our minds that afternoon was, What could we do to help? Both of us were up to our necks in ministry to women. But these problems crossed the boundary lines of women's ministry, spilling over into areas traditionally considered out of bounds for women. We were committed to continue our ministry to women, but our efforts seemed disjointed and hampered if we remained confined to the feminine side of these problems. Was there some way we could come alongside the elders and help lighten their load? Better still, was there anything we could do to address such problems *before* they reached crisis proportions?

In the end we would answer our questions at two levels—as individual members of the body and as a group of women who care deeply about the church. The church needs the theological contributions of each individual woman in the lives of other members of the body, and the church needs the collective participation of women in the spiritual life of the church if it is to remain strong. At both levels a woman's ministry is vital, not just among other women but also *with* and *to* men. Our corporate identity and responsibilities would lead my friend and me to explore ways we could do more to help others in our church, for "we are all one body in Christ, we belong to each other, and each of us needs all the others" (Rom. 12:5 NLT). If we take Paul's language seriously, the simple truth that emerges is that even in the church, men and women need each other.

Similar conversations are taking place all over the country as women rethink their responsibilities to Jesus Christ and his church.

These discussions are not prompted by worries over rights, a determination to "have a say" in things, some private agenda, or even an interest in gaining power—motives detrimental to the church regardless of which gender has them. Rather, the discussions are prompted by an increasing awareness of our biblical calling as women, an honest desire to find ways women can contribute in substantial ways to the spiritual life of the church, and a growing uneasiness that the passive role we have accepted in the life of the church may not be so godly after all. The issue here is not women's ordination to the ministry but the responsibilities of women in the pews. While ordination is an important issue for Christians to work through, I am raising a different issue, one of profound importance to every woman (indeed to every Christian) in the church regardless of denomination. The truth is that the vast majority of Christians will never serve as pastors or hold offices within the church. Yet New Testament writers believed *every* Christian shared significant responsibility for the spiritual welfare of the church.

"WOMEN'S WORK"

THE TOPIC OF A WOMAN'S spiritual responsibility to the wider church seems to be missing from our ecclesiastical thinking—a major blind spot recently felt by a single parent who joined her local church. Whenever a woman raises the question of how she can serve the church—a question this woman began asking church leaders—she is inevitably directed to restricted zones where it is permissible for a woman to exercise her gifts. This particular woman was precluded from the women's ministry because of her working hours, and the Sunday school wasn't an option because the teaching posts were filled. She was left with the uneasy feeling that she had no way to contribute. But even if women can find slots in these official ministries, this limited ministry in no way satisfies our obligation to address the spiritual needs of the wider church. The church is not, in reality, simply a volunteer organization in which everyone finds a job description with an appropriate title. It is an organism—a body—that is only as strong and healthy as each of its respective members. This means a woman either strengthens or weakens the church, depending on whether she invests herself in or withdraws from spiritual ministry to her fellow believers.

Ultimately, women's work in the church is not a gender issue but a theological matter. To help us understand who we are as the church and how we are to relate to one another as members, the apostle Paul employed the language of human anatomy. He called us the body of Christ, describing individual believers as the various parts of his body. This metaphor places a uniform burden on every believer—male or female—for the overall spiritual condition of the church.

Fitness-conscious Americans should have little trouble grasping the implications of this biblical imagery for the church. Health is a *whole* body concern that is jeopardized if any organ or limb is weak or not functioning properly. The person who has one strong leg and one that is weak is not viewed as strong because they have a strong leg. To the contrary, they are lame and in need of physical therapy to restore the weak leg to full strength. Having one spare kidney or one spare eye is little consolation when the other kidney shuts down or the other eye is blind.

A short time ago, a business colleague of mine suffered a severe stroke that rendered him unable to speak and left half of his body paralyzed. Although his speech has returned, his consternation is indescribable over what has happened to his body and the prospect of the long and uncertain convalescence. When women are encouraged to take a passive role, the church becomes more like a stroke victim shuffling down the road, dragging a limp and lifeless leg along behind. All of us, including the pastor who spoke of women as inevitably weak, would react with great alarm if half our body shut down. Weakness and atrophy are never okay for those who care about their health. These conditions do not enhance the other limbs and organs of the body but place an inordinate burden on them, causing strain, injury, and further breakdown. If women are supposed to be seen and not heard in the church, then we are promoting weakness and atrophy in Christ's body. But if this biblical imagery of the body means anything, then the church cannot reach maturity so long as women are marginalized.

When it came to building up the body of Christ, New Testament writers didn't let anyone off the hook. They took a dim view of weakness in the body of Christ and called every Christian, both female and male, to vigorous spiritual ministry to the entire body. Weakness was always a condition to be remedied, whether it resulted from newness in the faith or to the immaturity, disobedience, and passivity of older Christians.[1] Strength or maturity, on the other hand, was not simply a matter of getting along with other Christians or even of adding numbers to the congregation. The strength of the church was always couched in theological terms—tied to our *unity*—a theological condition that centers in our knowledge of Christ and how men and women live out that knowledge together. Unity cannot be achieved when some individuals understand and the rest just fall in line. True unity comes from a deep shared knowledge of Christ and an active commitment to build each other up. It entails striving to attain Christ's likeness, not simply as individuals but as a body. Paul spelled out this lofty goal when he urged all Christians to "let the words of Christ, in all their richness, live in your hearts and make you wise. Use his words to *teach* and *counsel* each other" (Col. 3:16 NLT, emphasis added). These responsibilities fall on all of us. If Paul is to be taken at his word, then every woman has a responsibility to "teach and counsel" others in the body of Christ so that all will mature in their faith. This is not simply the task of pastors, elders, deacons, and Sunday school teachers. Teaching and counseling are the ongoing *normal* interactions between believers, regardless of age or gender. The task of church leadership is to equip God's people—male and female, young and old—for this all-consuming task of building up the body of Christ until we are perfectly unified in our faith and knowledge of Christ, a knowledge reflected as much in who we are and how we treat one another as it is in the beliefs we affirm.[2] One New Testament scholar puts it this way: "Christians must break the monopoly the clergy has on the tasks of ministry. The body of Christ does not have two classes of members—clergy and laity—or two sets of expectations. Everyone has the same task of building up the body, even though responsibilities vary. Certainly some tasks are more appropriate to pastors and require professional expertise, but even with those tasks pastors should include and train church members. Ministry is the only profession that retains nothing to itself, gives away all its knowledge free, and invites those served to do the same work."[3]

The simple fact is that the job of building up the body of Christ cannot be accomplished by the efforts and theology of a few. It is a responsibility every Christian shares, for "from [Christ] the *whole* body, joined and held together by *every* supporting ligament, grows and builds itself up in love, as *each* part does its work" (Eph. 4:16, emphasis added).

Ultimately the ratio of males to females in the church is simply not the issue. What is profoundly significant is how well men and women work together in the church. According to New Testament teaching the church as a whole *cannot* reach spiritual maturity without the theological and spiritual contributions and ministries of women. Those around us need our words of wisdom and encouragement if the body of Christ is to reach maturity and persevere. This extraordinary task demands, as we have said before, *more* of women, not less.

Women never know when an opportunity to minister will present itself. Not long ago, my phone rang, and when I picked it up, I heard a masculine voice on the other end of the line—a young man calling to ask us to pray for his wife, who was undergoing a battery of medical tests and surgical procedures to enable them to conceive a child. The infertility problems were severe; their odds were about fifty-fifty; the biological clock was ticking away; and the longings of two hearts were on the line. What was I to do? "Yes, of course, we will pray," I heard myself say. But was there something more I could and *should* do when part of the body of

Christ is hurting and faith needs nurturing? Should I simply pray that the pastor will arrive on the scene to say the right words, or tell my friend that my husband will phone him once he returns home? Or should I also pull out my theology and draw from my own history of God's faithfulness to build up the faith of my brother in Christ? Should any Christian do less?

What was true at the dawn of creation is no less true in the church today—"it is not good for the man to be alone." New Testament teaching concerning the body of Christ calls women to step up to the plate because edification is "women's work." Edification comports perfectly with who we are as members of Christ's body and also with our calling as *ezers*. Everything we said in the previous chapter about the woman as warrior, called to come alongside the man and join him in fulfilling God's great mandate to subdue and rule the earth, to multiply and fill this planet with worshipers of the living God, remains in full force within the church. Indeed, the marriage paradigm plays out most fully within the bride of Christ. Yes, even in the church, it is "not good for the man to be alone." In fact, the ideal established in Eden ought to find its closest fulfillment on earth within the body of Christ. How tragic, then, that instead of going into the battle along with the men, women grow fearful of doing too much and overstepping their bounds, or they are branded as pushy, troublemakers, or feminists when they seek to become more involved and contribute in more substantive ways. With the monumental task before us in the church—"to measure up to the full stature of Christ"—can we afford for anyone to hold back?

New Testament Role Models

The clear teaching of the New Testament, which exhorts all Christians to teach and pastor their fellow believers, is backed by numerous examples of New Testament women who took seriously their responsibility to build up the body of Christ. Beginning with role models like Mary of Bethany, the New Testament is peppered with the names of women who were strong theologians and who freely lived out their theology within the church in ways that some may find surprising. Paul gives us an impressive roster of *ezers* who were "brave and godly soldiers in the army of the Lord."

The conclusion of Paul's letter to the Romans, a section many readers are prone to skip over, reads like a hall of fame of women and men who were active valued participants in the mission of building up the church. Phoebe heads the list, and Paul deems her "worthy of high honor" because she was a great help to many people, including the apostle himself (Rom. 16:1–2 NLT). She performed the work of a deacon and, according to many scholars, held the office of deaconess. Four women, Mary, Tryphena, Tryphosa, and Persis are commended for being hard workers in the Lord (vv. 6, 12). Priscilla, always named in tandem with her husband, Aquila, because evidently they ministered as a team, was called a fellow worker in Christ Jesus and had risked her life for Paul (v. 3). This husband-wife duo were activists for the gospel, teaching Apollos, "a learned man, with a thorough knowledge of the Scriptures" (Acts 18:24–28), and hosting a church in their home.[4] Paul notes that all of the Gentile churches were indebted to them both for their ministry.

Another prominent woman, Junia, would no doubt be dumbfounded at all the modern ruckus surrounding Paul's commendation of her.[5] According to Paul, she, along with Andronicus, who may have been her husband, was "respected [or outstanding, NIV] among the apostles" (v. 7 NLT). Battle lines have been drawn over her name and her designation as an apostle, with the central issue being precisely how significant a role this woman actually played in the early church. While there is greater consensus among scholars that Junia is a female name, the jury is still out on what Paul meant by identifying her as an apostle. For our purposes, the importance of Junia does not turn on whether she held the office of apostle. Even if Paul employed the word apostle here in the looser sense (as opposed to the official office held exclusively by the Twelve and Paul), it cannot be denied that Junia was an outstanding and significant representative of the Lord and that her contributions in ministry to the New Testament church merited Paul's hearty commendation. The honor Paul pays her in calling her an apostle puts her in the company of others who were also loosely designated as apostles—such familiar names as Barnabas, Epaphroditus, Apollos, Silvanus, and Timothy,[6] individuals who were evangelists and itinerant missionaries and who risked their lives along with Paul for the work of the gospel. Junia, who had been a believer longer than Paul, also put her life on the line and suffered imprisonment for her public activities in spreading the gospel. Like England's Princess Diana, whose loss of royal title did not diminish or discredit her efforts on behalf of the crown, Junia needs no title to authenticate her significant contributions to fortify and nourish the body of Christ. Truly a remarkable woman whose stature within the church, according to Paul, was unquestionably well deserved.

The Philippian church, one of the leading New Testament churches, had female roots. Paul and Silas founded this major church with the help of a group of committed women who met for prayer along the banks of the river near Philippi. Perhaps the apostles expected to find more than women when the Holy Spirit employed a powerful vision to bar their way to Asia and redirected their steps toward northern Greece and the Roman colony of Philippi in Macedonia. But there is no mention of disappointment when their steps led them to a small gathering of praying women instead of men. Although one pastor described these women as "the perfect anti-climax" for the travel-weary apostles, obviously neither the Holy Spirit nor the apostles were hesitant to build a church with female help.

Lydia, a Philippian business woman and a member of the small band of women, took bold initiative by urging Paul and Silas to stay at her home to minister to this fledgling body of believers. According to Luke's report, she wouldn't take no for an answer and didn't retract her invitation when violence erupted and lives were in danger. It turns out she was only one of several women who hosted churches in their homes.[7] Nor was she the only woman honored for her work in Philippi with Paul. He also singled out two other women, Euodia and Syntyche, as Philippians who "contended at my side in the cause of the gospel" (Phil. 4:2–3). Later Paul wrote to the flourishing Philippian church, which Lydia and her female associates helped to start, "I thank my God every time I remember you . . . because of your partnership in the gospel from the first day until now" (Phil. 1:3–5). What a revealing light this sheds on the pastor's comment that a church filled with women is weak.

Paul's intent in naming women in his letters was neither to minimize or inflate their contributions to the spread of the gospel and the building up of the church. Nor was he trying to cast aspersions on men by including women in the list. Rather, he was paying tribute to these women for their worthy and significant contributions, expressing his own conviction that their partnership with him in the gospel was indispensable. More important for us, he was holding them up as role models. These women weren't breaking the rules, nor were they odd exceptions. They were setting a biblical pattern that women today should not hesitate to follow.

It is also worth noting that these women weren't inhibited by the fear that their actions might upset some precarious balance of leadership or that they might offend Paul's sense of masculinity. If Paul is to be believed, their bold actions actually strengthened his leadership, advanced the gospel, and fortified the church beyond anything he could have accomplished on his own. Surprising as it may seem, the fruitfulness of Paul's apostolic ministry multiplied and spread through the efforts of women. Women who worked with Paul were willing to stick their necks out and risk rebuke, rejection, and even their lives because something greater was at stake than their personal comfort and honor. Their activities demonstrated what members of Christ's body are called to do. In effect Paul was looking over his congregation in the first century and saying that a church filled with theologically active women is a strong church.

As my friend and I sat and talked on that long warm afternoon, our conviction deepened that as stewards of Christ, we were obligated to fan the flames of our passion for him and for his church. The problems we were seeing weren't just the problems of the pastors and elders. They were our problems too, and we had a responsibility to do what we could, individually and also with the other women in our church, to address them. To bury our concerns, gifts, and ideas in the ground when there was so much to be done would be to dishonor Christ, overburden and abandon the elders, and deliberately allow part of Christ's body to atrophy. We could see the need to rehabilitate our definition of "women's work" to meet the New Testament standard. Edification ought to be the first task on a woman's to-do list in the church—pastoring, teaching, encouraging, stepping out to take the initiative and build up the faith of the person next to her. The answer we were seeking to the question, What happens when the ezer enters the church? was just this simple. But as is often the case, one answer leads to new questions, and for us, the next question was, How do we make the transition from long-term passivity into a more substantive role in the life of the church?

A DEEPER VISION FOR WOMEN'S MINISTRY

ONE OF THE MESSAGES that came through loud and clear (and at times even hotly) in responses to my informal internet survey of why women are inclined to avoid theology was concern over what is happening in women's ministries in the church. Words like light, fluffy, and superficial came up with disturbing regularity. Women often tell me the same thing in person. At a conference just a few weeks ago, some women expressed indignation over a women's retreat they attended during which a major session included a discussion of the use of feather dusters.

These women all voiced longings for more substance and an eagerness to probe into the character of God along with other women. They were frustrated that in so many women's groups women are unable to find the depth they need for the hard questions and difficult problems that confront them in life. Many women openly admitted that they deliberately avoided women's gatherings because they felt offended and let down by the shallow content of the meetings. Their comments underscore the need for us to bring our theology into the church by using it to build up women.

The last thing I want to do is dishearten anyone or to question the sincerity of those who pour themselves into women's ministries. Nor do I want to disparage in any way the many indispensable and often behind-the-scenes ministries that women do in the church. But I believe we all need to take a long, hard, reflective look at what we are doing (if anything) in women's ministries to help women become better theologians. Our spiritual ministry to the church will only be as deep as our own relationship to God. To walk in the footsteps of women like Mary of Bethany and the other women Paul named, we must begin by following them in the relentless pursuit of a greater knowledge of God. The truth they were learning about him not only transformed their lives; it informed and enriched their ministry to others. It will do no less for us today.

But along with a deeper knowledge of God comes a responsibility to employ that knowledge in ways that enrich the whole church. Ministry to women is never an end in itself. Yet often in women's ministries there is an insular tendency where we are inclined to partition ourselves off from the rest of the church, particularly when it comes to spiritual ministry. There is an expectation that a woman's deepest ministries will take place within the confines of a woman-to-woman ministry, and there is little or no discussion of how women are called to spiritual ministry in the wider church.

At least part of the reason for this tendency was pointed out by one internet respondent who remarked that "in the church we have been conditioned that the men should pursue the 'thinking' ministries while the women pursue the 'caring' ones." The underlying assumption is that one sex is better than the other in performing certain ministries and that therefore each should focus on what they do best. The fallacy of dividing ministries by gender is nowhere more apparent than within women's ministries. There *both* aspects of ministry—the thinking and the caring—are consistently and effectively carried out by women. But the fatal flaw is the failure to acknowledge that Christ calls every Christian *both* to think and to care and that there is a necessary relationship between thinking and caring. Some of our most hurtful problems in the church stem from presuming it is biblical to do either one without the other. Christ-likeness necessarily means doing both.

Jesus taught Peter, a man who at first was not particularly good at thinking or caring, to wash the feet of his fellow disciples, to feed his lambs and take care of his sheep (John 13:1–17; 21:15–23). These activities—both to teach and to nurture—reflect the shepherding practices of Jesus and are the natural outworking of a love for Christ. Later the apostle Peter would blend heart and mind when he wrote to the church, "All of you should be of one *mind,* full of sympathy toward each other, loving one another with tender *hearts* and humble *minds*" (1 Peter 3:8 NLT, emphasis added). Peter urged both men and women to develop as mercy givers and as thinkers, to "grow in *grace* and in the *knowledge* of our Lord and Savior Jesus Christ" (2 Peter 3:18, emphasis added).

A second impediment to the ministry of women in the wider church results when the segregation of women's ministries from the rest of the church takes on physical dimensions. Women's ministry becomes a world unto itself, a self-sustaining pocket in the church. Instead of joining our efforts to the rest of the body, women run parallel church ministries on the side. It is not uncommon for a women's group to have their own programs for pastoral care, evangelism, missions, mercy, and community service. Within the parameters of our own gatherings, we have complete freedom to contribute ideas, develop ministries, exercise gifts, and act where we see a need. We may assume a passive role in mixed company, but when we are off to ourselves, we pull out all the stops and invest ourselves in each others lives without wondering if we're doing too much. If you have ever been on the receiving end of such an outpouring, you will know how incredible it is and the good it can do.

As I have been hammering out the chapters of this book, I cannot count the times different women have phoned, e-mailed, or caught me by the arm at church to ask how I am doing and give me a word of much needed encouragement. More often than not, their words were just what I needed to keep pressing. Plenty of women live from week to week on the encouragement, spiritual nourishment, and support they receive from other women in a women's Bible study. Inside women's ministries you will find skilled burden bearers who seem to read the signs of discouragement in someone else's eyes. These women theologians have learned how to listen and have a rich storehouse of comfort and truth to offer a hurting heart. Outside of the women's ministry environment, however, it's a different story. There these same women are reticent to carry out their powerful ministries to others in the congregation, particularly if those others happen to be men.

The picture we are seeing in the church today seems strangely out of step with the portrayal of the church in New Testament times. Instead of joining forces and doubling our efforts in the church, men and women run on separate tracks. The apostles didn't envision a church in which the women would work separately from the men. The picture they portrayed, and this comes through especially in Paul's writings, is of men and women who are colaborers in all aspects of the ministry.

Rest assured, this in no way diminishes the vital ministry of women to women—a biblical ministry that, if anything, needs to be promoted and deepened even more. I wouldn't be writing this book if ministry to women weren't high on my list of priorities. But our ministry to women should inevitably move beyond women. We do not build up women simply so they will be better off themselves, although we certainly hope that will be the case. A major part of our ministry to women is to build them up so they will have wisdom and strength to offer the rest of the church. The task of women's ministry is to equip women for ministry in the body, a calling that goes well beyond any official ministries a woman may volunteer to do. The church cannot reach full matu-

216 Part Three: Knowing God in Relationships

rity if women minister only to segments of the body as if they were knotted off by a tourniquet.

A woman's ministry in the church (and the principle holds true for a man too) is defined in concentric circles, beginning with those nearest to her and moving out until the entire church is encompassed. This principle isn't taken from some book on ministry methods and guidelines but from the Scriptures that establish marriage and family as the primary ministries both for men and for women. During certain phases in a woman's life, her family may be her only ministry. But who can overstate the importance of investing ourselves in our marriages and in the lives of our children? Ministry to the family is kingdom work that edifies the body of Christ. A mother rocks the next generation of the church in her arms, and one way or another, the church to come will feel the effects of her spiritual influence. Her husband and her children will either draw strength from or be weakened by her efforts as a pastor, teacher, and counselor at home.

Beyond the immediate family, a woman's options for ministry are limitless and, more than likely, staring her in the face. Every Christian needs a friend—someone who will listen, understand, and encourage. Sunday after Sunday, lonely struggling people wander into our fellowship only to walk out again carrying the same old heavy burden that no one seemed to notice. One woman told me, "I feel like a little lost bottle bobbing up and down on the ocean's waves whenever I walk into the church." Sometimes a genuine "Are you okay?" is all it takes to open a door of ministry.

Christianity always flows both ways—giving and receiving. We all are needy, and we all have much to offer others. None of us should be content to remain on the receiving end and never reach out to others. No member of the body of Christ is outside the scope of a woman's responsibility to minister. Having grown up in a pastor's home and now that my husband is an elder, I know how weary and discouraged church leaders can get. A single phone call can break their hearts and turn their world upside down. It means a lot, even to those who seem strongest, when someone comes alongside to help them remember that God is good and knows what he is doing, even in a church riddled with problems. Even the pastor needs to be built up in the Lord. The plain and simple fact is that the church needs women—a fact the apostles outspokenly affirmed.

On a plane trip once, I sat beside a scientist who was legally blind. During the first leg of the flight, only a couple of sentences passed between us. But in the second half of the journey, we entered into some pretty intense conversation about God. I discovered that I was the latest link in a chain of other Christians who had engaged this intelligent man as he searched for meaning in his life and investigated the claims of Christianity. No one in the church would question me for joining the efforts of other Christians I didn't even know in fighting for this man's soul. Yet if this same man walked into church on any given Sunday, would I feel the same sense of responsibility (and would anyone encourage me) to promote his spiritual well-being? Or would I shrug off such thoughts with impunity because I am a woman or because I didn't think my particular gifts were suited for such a need?

Godly women in Scripture had acutely sensitive theological antennae, activated by their deep relationship with God and their love for his church. Their relationship with Christ and their own struggles to trust him alerted them to the needs of others around them. They devoted themselves to making his body strong and to lending a hand wherever they sensed a need. One need only recall what Mary would have denied Jesus if she had not responded to the opportunity God put in her path to anoint him, or what the New Testament church would have lost without the contributions of women who sacrificed, evangelized, taught, and ministered alongside their brothers in the church. Sadly, in the church today, important ministries are overlooked or done poorly because the feminine perspective is missing. Again the point is not that women have superior gifts to offer the church but that men and women need each other in the church and that we harm the church when we minister selectively rather than freely to anyone who needs our help. Can we do any less for our generation than

New Testament women did for theirs and arm ourselves to engage actively in "the work of the Lord" with our brothers in the faith?

THE NEWS FROM LAKE WOBEGON

IN HIS WEEKLY BROADCAST from St. Paul, Minnesota, Garrison Keillor regularly reminds his listeners that Lake Wobegon is a place "where all the women are strong, all the men are good looking, and all the children are above average." A pastor from Europe recently told me that when he looks out over his congregation, at least part of this midwestern slogan comes to mind, for among the sea of faces are at least a dozen women he is thankful to say are strong. They are hungry to know God better, eager to drink in the deep theology their pastor preaches to them week after week, and determined to live out that theology in their hearts, their homes, and in the church.

When the *ezer* enters the church, her calling and identity are unchanged. She is the strong helper. Her eyes are fixed on Jesus, and she knows she has a job to do. Her calling in the church, as in the home and in friendship, is a spiritual calling. She is called to arm herself for the battle and to fight valiantly alongside her brothers in the faith for the souls and edification of others. Paul charges women as well as men to "be strong in the Lord and in his mighty power" (Eph. 6:10). Christ grants no exemptions from his army based on gender, age, or any other reason. The battle is for Christ's kingdom and for his glory. The *ezer* will not turn her back on God's call. Even in the church, she is the answer to the man's aloneness. In the church there is a void only she can fill. Without her help, the church is weak. If she is passive, the church is lame. Apart from her wisdom and contributions, the church has blind spots in its thinking, in its understanding of the truth, and in its ministries. Where she utilizes her theology and participates in body building, the church gains strength and makes strides toward maturity. This is what it means to be a woman in the church. More important, this is what it means to be a Christian. When women are good theologians, the church only stands to benefit.

We could say more. Hopefully, what we have said will challenge women to think and to explore ways they can take a more active role in the church, both individually and as a group. But before we conclude our discussion of women and theology, there is one person we need to revisit. We left her long ago when we set out on our journey with her sister, Mary. And so we make our way back to the kitchen to take one last look at Martha.

EPILOGUE

"Martha, Martha"

THE LAST TIME WE PAID MUCH ATTENTION TO MARTHA, DINNER was steaming, and so was she. Her sister's sudden disappearance from the kitchen crew at a crucial moment had been the last straw. Since then the elder sister essentially dropped from our discussion as we traced Mary's roller-coaster journey, which, in the end, established her as the first great New Testament theologian. In the meantime, whatever became of Martha? Did she just get left behind, stranded in the kitchen, while her sister made the journey to theological greatness?

To help us answer those questions, the gospels give us three portraits of Martha too, which although not drawn with the same precision as those of Mary, are nonetheless sufficient for us to piece together Martha's story. Ironically, Martha's portraits will also provide us with a fitting conclusion to our exploration of the importance of theology for women.

A TALE OF TWO SISTERS

WE ALL HAVE points in our personal history that we would just as soon forget. Even years afterward, some ridiculous comment, clumsy moment, or social gaffe stays fresh in our memories and has the power to make us blush. The good thing for those of us who live our lives in relative obscurity is that probably no one else remembers what we did. But Martha's faux pas, even though it occurred within the privacy of her home, didn't slip from anyone's memory quite so easily. Hers was memorialized in the Bible and has been the frequent topic of public sermons and private discussions ever since. Martha must have groaned with chagrin in heaven when she learned about Johannes Gutenberg's invention of the printing press. Now the episode she would most like to forget would be publicized more widely than ever.

Not only was Martha's behavior a problem for her, she poses a serious problem for us as well. Normally, her actions are used to justify the existence of two types of women—the thinkers and the doers—a thesis which this book set out to refute. If Jesus' words are a call for Marthas to step out of character, suspend their activities at least occasionally for a moment's quiet reflection in the Word, the theory that there really are two kinds of women remains firmly intact. But are there really two kinds of women? Was Jesus actually classifying us into two irreconcilable camps? Perhaps the best person to address that question for us is the elder sister herself.

In fairness to Martha, return with me one last time to Jesus' first visit in Bethany, when Martha challenged Mary's choice to sit and listen to Jesus. This time let's look at things from Martha's point of view. Usually that means commiserating with her for getting in a huff because major dinner preparations were underway that she could not possibly manage without some help from her distracted sister. But that's not where I want us to focus. I want to revisit the uncomfortable moment immediately *after* Jesus' gentle rebuke, "Martha, Martha . . . you are worried and upset about many things, but only one thing is needed. Mary has chosen what is better, and it will not be taken away from her" (Luke 10:41–42).

In the minds of many readers, Jesus' words signaled the end of the story. Mary wins. Martha loses. The curtain drops, and we move on with Luke to the next scene in the life of Jesus. In real life, however, it wouldn't have happened that way. Others might easily move on to other episodes, but neither of the sisters would casually walk away from such a moment as this. We have already explored what this meant to Mary. What did it mean to her sister?

Usually this is where we draw a solid line between the two sisters and choose which one we identify with most. Are we thinkers like Mary or doers like her elder sister? This is, as we have said before, a serious misreading of the text. Jesus wasn't drawing lines or categorizing women by personality type and interests. He was defining priorities for all of us and, more important, drawing *Martha* into a deeper relationship with himself. His unexpected response would have been enough to get Martha's attention. A defense of Mary's actions was the last thing she or anyone else expected to hear from him. In that culture, it would have been obvious to everyone that Mary was out of place. Jesus didn't see things that way.

But more than what he said, the very nature of his response would have made it even more improbable that Martha would dismiss his words. Jesus didn't act like a supreme court justice handing down an objective opinion filled with legalese. His was the kindhearted personal appeal of a friend for Martha to rethink her priorities. "Martha, Martha . . ." the directness of his words must have deflated her anger and penetrated her agitated heart. Instead of shrugging her shoulders and turning back to the kitchen with a sigh of defeat, my guess is that she stopped cold in her tracks because she realized she was missing out. Which was exactly his point. In a way, Martha had been set up. Jesus used that aggravating moment when she discovered she was working alone, to throw his net over her and draw her into the theological conversation he was having with her sister. The issue, after all, wasn't dinner or the urgency of household chores. The issue was Jesus and whether Martha would take the time to know him better for herself.

The same reasons that prompted Jesus to defend Mary motivated his appeal to Martha. The road ahead would be rough for Martha. The life of faith is never easy. To trust him in the days ahead and to serve him well (clearly her heart's desire), Martha needed to know him better. If she heard him right, she would have realized Jesus was sending her a message—not that her service to him was unimportant but that building a strong relationship with him was far more pressing than anything she could do for him.

Luke doesn't tell us what happened next, but I have a hunch that Jesus got through to her. He wasn't putting Martha down or siding with Mary in a family dispute. Jesus was guiding Martha to join her sister. For the moment, dinner could wait. Martha would see that too. No woman in her right mind would turn away from such an invitation. In the end, two women would be sitting at Jesus' feet. Neither sister could or would resist the opportunity to come and learn from him.

HOPE FOR THE HERE AND NOW

EVIDENCE THAT MARTHA may have joined her sister as a student of Jesus appears in Martha's second encounter with him. Here we find a conversation between Jesus and the elder sister from Bethany that hints of earlier deep discussions. Jesus doesn't treat Martha as though she is a newcomer to theology, and she in turn doesn't act like one. No novice would come up with the profound theological statements about Jesus that spill from her lips as she talks with him about her brother's death. She isn't reading a script, and we can be fairly certain she didn't learn such things slaving over pots and pans in the kitchen. Contrary to our stereotyped expectations of Martha, she actually offers verbal proof of her theological understanding, something her sister Mary never does. Mary displays her theology through her actions. But Martha's theology shows up first in her words. In contrast with Mary's verbal silence, Martha is articulate, reflective, and advanced in her theological understanding of Jesus. This icon for feminine domesticity is unquestionably a thinking woman.

Furthermore, the significance of the interaction between Jesus and Martha is intensified by the timing of their meeting. Martha is raw with grief, having just lost her beloved brother, a pain exacerbated by the inexplicably slow response of Jesus to her frantic appeal for help. Now that Lazarus lies decaying in the cold darkness of a hillside tomb, word finally reaches Martha that Jesus has arrived. Instinctively, she runs to meet him, leaving her despondent sister behind. Her first words to Jesus reveal how torn and bewildered she is by what has happened. She is caught in a theological dilemma of the worst possible sort. On the one hand, she cannot deny the finality of her brother's death or Jesus' role in the tragedy. Yet at the same time, she is unwilling to relinquish what she knows to be true of Jesus.

It is a familiar conflict that catches us all off guard, when our prayers go unanswered and God seems strangely indifferent to our pleas. A baby drowns, a LearJet falls from the skies, throbbing pain persists, the wounds of old emotional injuries fester, marriages disintegrate, children rebel, loneliness swallows us up, and hope vanishes in a puff of smoke. The question that bothers us most is not whether God's power is on the decline but why he seems unwilling to use it to spare us from such agonies.

Martha, with characteristic forthrightness, blurts out what is on her mind. "Lord, . . . if you had been here, my brother would not have died." Her next sentence finds her backpedaling in an attempt to recover what she has lost in admitting Jesus' failure to avert her brother's death. "But I know that even now God will give you whatever you ask" (John 11:21–22). Despite the tragic ending of Lazarus' story, Martha is staunchly unprepared to relinquish what she understands about Jesus. She possesses conflicting information—the preventable death of her brother and the undeniable power of Jesus. Although she has buried her brother and, in her heart of hearts, knows Jesus could have saved him from death, she would rather live with this miserable tension than bury all her hope in Jesus along with Lazarus. Unable to bring these two contradictory realities together, Martha hangs on to Jesus and pushes her hopes for her brother and for herself into the far distant future.

You would think that, under the circumstances, Jesus would somehow redirect their conversation to more comfortable subjects or begin with gentle reassurances and loving words of comfort, such as he had been known to say before. "Blessed are those who mourn, for they will be comforted" (Matt. 5:4) would have sounded better here. But Jesus is no more predictable in dealing with Martha than he was with her distraught sister. Instead of offering polite condolences, a heartfelt apology for his delay, or even expressing his profound sense of sorrow as he would do with Mary, Jesus counters Martha's statement with a theological assertion: "Your brother will rise again" (John 11:23). His comment, which on the surface sounds like what we often say to those who grieve, is the bait he would use to coax Martha into deeper theological waters.

Her response discloses the far off but no less real location of her hopes: "I know he will rise again in the resurrection at the last day" (v. 24). She looks, as we all do, to a future resolution of her pain— the final resurrection of her brother. Like any believer who has known grief, Martha's future hopes have grown dearer through the loss of a loved one. But in the present there is only the pain of bereavement and unanswered questions about Jesus. Often, it seems, we try to salvage our theology by propelling it into the future.

But Jesus isn't content for Martha to close her eyes to his hand in the present. With his words, he challenges her to open both eyes and confront the dilemma he has created by his unexpected behavior. He helps her see that he never postpones his goodness nor allows his glory to be tarnished, even in a dark episode like this. Gently, for he knows the pain she is in, he guides her to confront the unpleasant issue at hand.

We must not gloss over what is happening here. Not only is Jesus talking to a woman about theology again, the woman he is talking to is *Martha*—the women who has come to represent those who prefer to pass on such a heavy subject. Yet Jesus doesn't make an exception for her because she, and women like her, neither need nor have the personality for grasping deep theology. What is even more remarkable, Jesus doesn't seem to think theology is off limits as a topic for conversation with someone in the throes of grief. Clearly Jesus believes Martha needs theology now more than ever. His conversation with her is not unlike the one he had with the Samaritan woman at the well. His remarks, which take her to the heart of deep theology, this time focusing on his identity and his power, seem strange at first, almost insensitive and a bit too abstract. But upon further examination, it becomes clear that Jesus, in his wisdom and compassion, is speaking the very words this struggling woman needs most to hear.

Instead of sidestepping the turmoil in Martha's mind with appropriate civilities or by changing the subject, Jesus spotlights the very question his delayed arrival has provoked. Without hesitation, he boldly reminds her that he is everything she hoped when she first called for his help—and more. "I am the resurrection and the life. He who believes in me will live, even though he dies; and whoever lives and believes in me will never die. Do you believe this?" (v. 25).

I cannot imagine how painful it must have been for her to hear those words. Resurrection power and life? Precisely the attributes so tragically absent when her brother's condition deteriorated. Yet despite her discomfort, Jesus compels Martha to look him in the face and affirm, even in her pain, his power to do what he has withheld from her brother. He is not merely the great healer. He is the Lord of life itself—the giver of life to the dead and the enemy of death for the living. Martha might try to sweep the conflict between his power and this terrible outcome under the rug. Jesus, to our amazement, pulls it back out and sets it starkly in front of her. He wants her to make connection between who he is and her present grief. And so he speaks the very words that seem least believable under the circumstances: "I am the resurrection and the life."

When Jesus trains great theologians, their hope is not just in the far flung future or in the distant but settled past. Hope for the theologian is also in the very real and often painful present where the pieces do not fit neatly together and agonizing questions about Jesus will not go away. Jesus calls Martha to hope in him in the present, to take what she believes about him and cling to it in her distress. It is a call not simply to affirm the truth about Jesus' power but to affirm his right to exercise his power according to his own purposes. She will never have the answers to all her why's, but in his character she will find enough of an answer to sustain her faith.

No matter what might happen next (and it is certain Martha has no inkling that Jesus will restore her brother to life), Jesus calls Martha to trust him now—trust that he is good even here, when her losses are insurmountable and when Jesus, who had the power to prevent it all, had chosen not to act. In this brief but profound conversation, Jesus will bring Martha's hope back into the present crisis. Will she affirm that Jesus is the resurrection and the life now, while her entombed brother lies decaying? The words she speaks to him in scene one may have been hasty and misguided. But here, in scene two, her words will mark her as a great theologian.

Instead of backing away, Martha moves toward Jesus with powerful words of faith. Mary may have the privilege of anointing Jesus for his burial. But Martha claims the honor of being the only woman in the Gospels to proclaim his true identity. Martha's confession ranks her as one of the few individuals who, before the resurrection, affirmed Jesus as the Son of God.[1] "Yes, Lord," she tells him, "I believe that you are the Christ, the Son of God, who was to come into the world." Astonishing words from a woman usually thought of as an anti-intellectual domestic. In a sentence, Martha violates her own stereotype and joins the growing circle of great women theologians. But even she will not grasp the full meaning of her own words until she puts her convictions about Jesus alongside the baffling loss of her brother.

It will take time before the rest of Martha catches up with her words. But the encounter with Jesus sets that process in motion. The discrepancy between what she affirms in her head and what she believes in her heart is nowhere more apparent than when Jesus orders the removal of the stone that covers the mouth of Lazarus' tomb. Once again, she will try to stop him. But this will be the last time Martha reaches out to stay his hand. She is learning by degrees that she can trust him, no matter what.

OF POTS AND PANS AND FEATHER DUSTERS

WHEN THE CURTAIN rises for Martha's final appearance, Jesus is back in Bethany for the feast in his honor. Martha is back in hostess mode. True to form, the elder sibling of Mary and Lazarus is bustling in the kitchen, putting in little more than a cameo performance. The scene that would star her sister, Mary, seemed to leave only a bit part for the familiar figure preparing dinner. Two words sum up her part in the evening's drama: "Martha served" (John 12:2).

Some might wonder if we aren't a bit disappointed, after seeing all the progress she had made, to find Martha in the kitchen once again. But if, as we have consistently asserted, true theology moves from head to heart to life, it is probably more fitting for us to find her here than anywhere else.

Just as the portrait of Mary anointing Jesus takes on new and deeper meaning when you place it side by side with her earlier two portraits, so these two words, which have come to define Martha and women who think of themselves as carrying on her legacy, are redefined by Martha's two earlier portraits. In a way, that is the point. Theology doesn't disconnect women from life or diminish our willingness to tackle our next assignment. To the contrary, knowing God mobilizes us. Those who know God find deeper meaning in the ordinary and extraordinary moments of their lives. They know that he is in control and that he is good here and now, no matter what is happening. Strange as it sounds, theology belongs in the kitchen every bit as much as it belongs in the pulpit or the seminary classroom, perhaps even more. Wherever

God's people live, knowing him deeply is a boon to what they are doing and the truth about him energizes everything they do.

Martha of Bethany is about as powerful an argument as you could want to prove that women need theology. Not only that, but her life argues forcefully that theology is good for us. Take a careful look at Martha in this final scene, if you are skeptical. Here is a woman who devoted herself to cultivate the relationship with Jesus that we are calling theology. Knowing Jesus had become Martha's highest priority, even when she had hungry guests, a dinner to prepare, and a hundred unfinished items on her to-do list. She took time out of her hectic schedule to listen to him, to wrestle with the meaning of his words, and to study his character. Nothing was more urgent, the death of her brother proved that point. Trusting Jesus would be the hardest thing she ever did. Jesus didn't want her to do that based on secondhand information from Mary or with her eyes blindfolded. He drew her in to confront the questions she was trying to forget and to connect his hand with the unhappy personal circumstances of her life. As the truth began to sink in, her faith in him took on a different quality. To be sure, like the rest of us, Martha would always have an opinion about what she hoped he would do and how each situation would turn out. But she was learning to trust his good purposes, even when he withheld his powers and didn't respond within her time frame.

Look closely at Martha in this last scene and see the good it had done her to know Jesus better. The two words used to describe her activities here would mean less to us if we hadn't traced her journey from the start. But in light of her outspoken objections in the two previous episodes, here, as the worst crisis of all began to escalate, Martha seems to be a woman at peace. No one who understood her even slightly would wonder for a moment if she had simply lost track of her sister's whereabouts. In all likelihood, Martha knew exactly what was happening—that Mary had ditched her again and, as before, she was working solo in the kitchen. Remarkably, there was no explosion from Martha. This time she doesn't charge up to Jesus with instructions to intervene

and rectify this injustice. Even with the shadow of the cross loom-
ing over him, Martha knows enough to trust him. Knowing him
preserves her from thrashing about and frees her to focus on the
task at hand.

But Martha is not only a woman at peace. She is also a woman
of purpose. Although Mary commanded the spotlight for the
evening, Martha's actions did not go unnoticed. This wasn't a
remake of the primeval story of two siblings, Abel and Cain, who
presented their early offerings to God and one was accepted while
the other was not. Both sisters' gifts to Jesus were warmly received
and highly prized. We must not forget that according to God's system of weights and measures, there are no bit parts. Meaningless
acts of obedience or service are unheard of in his kingdom. God's
Oscars don't go to the high-paid actor who thrives in the attention of the press and the flashing lights of cameras and basks in
the applause and acclaim of the crowd. In God's kingdom the
honors go to an unnamed child who shared his lunch, to an
obscure widow who dropped in her last pennies, to the one who
offers something so mundane as a cup of cold water, to the
unknown intercessor lying helplessly on a bed of pain, to a woman
who poured out a flask of perfume, and to her sister who served
dinner. Theology manifests itself in everything we do, and God
invests our slightest actions with enormous significance, because
we do it all for him. Martha was back in the kitchen because good
theology finds expression in service and ministry to others, no
matter what form that ministry takes. Her eyes were fixed on
Jesus, and she knew what she was doing mattered to him.

Some of my closest friends think of themselves as Marthas—
masters of culinary arts, gracious hospitality, and people skills. An
invitation to dine in one of their homes has a way of lighting up
the eyes of the pickiest eaters. Their tables live up to everything
implied when fine dining experts say that "the first bite is always
with the eyes." The flower arrangements and candles, tantalizing
platters of food, garnishes and embellishments, a fire on the hearth
(yes, even in Florida), plus all the little touches that create the

atmosphere—the most critical observer would have to concede there is nothing lacking here.

But even Marthas need theology. The blows of life fall indiscriminately on Marys and Marthas alike. Marthas I know, like their patron saint from Bethany, face their fair share of bereavements, trials, and challenges. When the crisis hits or life becomes unbearable for whatever reason, they bump up against the same imposing questions that baffle all of us. Can God be trusted? Does he know what he is doing here? Is he good?

But as we've said before, a woman's theology always affects others. And for Marthas, the repercussions of having good or bad theology are staggering. Whenever there's a crisis, it is the Marthas who are often the first to arrive on the scene, and, long after the funeral is over, the uproar has died down, and everyone else has resumed their routines, it is the Marthas who remain behind to pick up the pieces and render a plethora of ministries to bruised and aching hearts.

If you were to post watch in the shrubs across from the home of one family in our church that was hit several weeks ago with a tragic loss, you would still report sightings of Marthas going in and out of the house, carrying pies, chicken casseroles, and even feather dusters for an hour or two of cleaning. What many Marthas are discovering is that the most important dish they serve is their theology. Their ministries are golden opportunities to come alongside those in distress with encouragement and hope. They are, in their own gentle way, pastors of the wounded and the broken, and their knowledge of God gives them strength and equips them for this difficult role.

TAKING A LONG HARD LOOK AT OURSELVES

YEARS HAVE PASSED since I first felt stung by the claim that "there have never been any *great* women theologians." Since that time, and especially during the writing of this book, my conviction has grown stronger that whether we think of ourselves as Marys or as

Marthas, every woman's first and highest calling is to become a great theologian. For all of us, nothing approaches the importance or the urgency of pursuing a deeper knowledge of God—a knowledge that makes thinkers and doers out of all of us. As *ezers*—Daughters of Eve—we were created to know God, to probe his character and ponder his ways. We hurt ourselves and make life far more difficult when we try to subsist on inadequate ideas of God. No wonder we are discouraged and suffer from the notion that he doesn't care or has abandoned us. We all suffer from this. We have sentenced ourselves "to stumble and blunder through life, blindfold, as it were, with no sense of direction and no understanding of what surrounds [us]."

We need to be better theologians for our own sakes. In writing this book, I have told stories about women theologians I know—real stories of real women living everyday lives full of real heartaches, real tears, and overwhelming challenges. No doubt every woman reading this could add her own story. Life is hard. Not one of us will make it through unscathed. We ask too much of ourselves and go against our own instincts when we try to trust a God who is essentially a stranger to us. Even when his plan for us makes the least sense from our point of view, our faith will find a foothold when we know his character, when we are confident that he never drops his scepter but rules all things for our good and his glory. Hope in that kind of God is impossible to extinguish.

We need to be better theologians for those we love—for our husbands, our friends, and our children. Whether our theology is good or flawed, those we love most will be first to feel the effects. As *ezers* we are called to join them in the trenches, to help them fix their eyes on Jesus and run with endurance the race he has marked out for them. We can't do the job if our own faith is anemic and wavering.

And without a doubt, we need to be better theologians for the church. The church is weakened and vulnerable when women take lightly their responsibility to think, study, and gain a deeper knowledge of God. But a church filled with women who are growing as theologians is a church that is gaining strength.

But the greatest and most compelling reason for us to get serious about theology—the argument that no one can ever refute—is the one who longs for our fellowship, who delights in us and promises to be our delight. He alone can quench the thirsting of our hearts. He is the joy that nothing can destroy. He is the satisfaction of our deepest longings. Jesus longed for Mary and Martha to come aside and know him better. Likewise, our heavenly Father longs for us to make knowing him our chief desire. We are not orphans. We have a Father who loves us and who over every inch of the race is drawing us into closer fellowship with him. We were made for this. As C. S. Lewis wrote, to live in pursuit of anything less is to be "like an ignorant child who wants to go on making mud pies in a slum because he cannot imagine what is meant by the offer of a holiday at the sea. We are far too easily pleased."[2]

A Professor Gets the Last Word

I SEEM TO HAVE a knack for inspiring zingers from professors. Little did I know two years ago, when I learned that Professor J. I. Packer of Regent College was coming to Orlando for a series of meetings, that I was about to hear another one.

As a step toward encouraging the women in our church to get serious about their theology, our women's ministry periodically invites leading theologians and biblical scholars to speak to us, a practice which has not surprisingly piqued male interest in attending our women's meetings. Already we have had unforgettable evenings with author and conference speaker Jerry Bridges, Old Testament scholar Dr. Bruce K. Waltke, and Scottish pastor, theologian, and author, Dr. Sinclair Ferguson. We were due for another such gathering when I received the news that Dr. Packer would soon be in town. Although I knew his time was at a premium, this was too good of an opportunity to pass up. Getting him to see things that way, however, would prove more difficult than I expected.

With high and no doubt slightly unrealistic hopes, I jotted off a letter to Dr. Packer, inviting him to speak to the women of our church on the importance of theology for women. Never thinking how that topic might sound to a busy man with a full schedule, I was naturally very disappointed when his secretary phoned from British Columbia to inform me Dr. Packer had declined.

Back to the drawing board I went, this time to write a more impassioned letter to Dr. Packer, explaining why this was so important to us and trying to persuade him to change his mind. I threw in the strongest arguments I could think of and begged him to reconsider. A lengthy silence followed. I had nearly given up hope when a letter postmarked from Canada arrived. Inside, on Regent College letterhead, was the following cryptic letter, typed on what I suspect was the same typewriter Dr. Packer had used when he was a student at Oxford University.

> Dear Mrs. James,
> All right. I will speak to the ladies on Wednesday evening
> May 6, on the non-sexist topic "Everyone Needs Theology."
> Sincerely,
> J. I. Packer
> Professor

Professor Packer's letter brings us full circle. The journey that commenced with one professor's remark, "You know, there have never been any great women theologians," concludes with the unqualified assertion of another that "everyone needs theology."

The quest for great women theologians is pointless until it compels us to take a long hard look at ourselves and ask, What kind of theologian am I? It's time we rolled up our sleeves and took our responsibilities seriously. The price for turning our backs is higher than any of us can afford. Dr. Packer is right, and his words are meant for all of us: everyone needs theology.

Recommended Reading

In many ways, my book is only a beginning. What happens next—what you do to pursue a deeper relationship with God—will tell the real story. I would encourage you to explore resources and relationships that will help you go deeper in your walk with God. For those interested in resources to know God better, I have assembled a list of suggestions and books that have helped me.

Suggestions for Reading and Studying the Bible in Search of God

Reading the Bible with Theological Eyes

The Bible heads the list of books we need to read. My professor couldn't have offered better advice when he said, "*This* is the book you need to study." The purpose of the Bible is to help us know God. It is God's revelation of himself to us—through history, biography, poetry, prophecy, and the teachings of the apostles. God is the true hero of the Bible, and we understand it best when we look first for him.

Three simple questions transform our reading of the Bible from a hunt for some comforting morsel to get us through the day into an active enriching search for God:

What does this tell me about God?
What does this tell me about myself?
What difference does it make for me to know this?

238 Recommended Reading

What Does This Tell Me about God?

What does this tell me about God? is the burning question that ought to drive all of our reading and study of the Bible. It focuses our thoughts on God first, rather than on ourselves. Many times I've been surprised at how much richer a passage becomes when I spend my time trying to understand what God is revealing about himself.

What does God say directly about himself? What do God's prophets want the people to know about God? How does God look through the eyes of Abraham, Ruth, David, or Peter?

The Bible is God's revelation of himself to us, and by seeking its primary message, we can better understand what it is saying about us and the life God calls us to live.

What Does This Tell Me about Myself?

The words of reformer John Calvin underscore the fact that by turning our attention toward God, we will begin to see everything else—ourselves, our struggles and frustrations, other people—in a truer light: "It is certain that no man [or woman] ever achieves a clear knowledge of himself unless he has first looked upon God's face, and then descends from contemplating him to scrutinize himself."[1]

The Bible teaches that God knows us better than we know ourselves. His intimate knowledge of us is our security as we study. He knows the full truth about us—warts and all—yet he will never turn away or reject us. His knowledge and understanding of us invites our honesty before him. There is no safer place for me to admit who I really am than in my relationship with God. Here I can be honest about my sin, my weaknesses and failings, my hopes and fears. And it is in the light of his character that I will begin to see myself more clearly and learn in deeper ways how much I need him and his redemptive work in my life.

What Difference Does It Make for Me to Know This?

Our digging in the Scriptures is incomplete, no matter how much deep truth we unearth, until we take what we learn to heart.

God never reveals himself simply to satisfy our curiosity or even simply to give us greater insight into ourselves. His purpose is always to transform us. And so we must always probe and ask why he would want us to know what he has revealed about himself. What difference does this make? Theological ideas are never fully comprehended until we live them out in our circumstances and relationships.

In the blazing light of God's holiness, I see the true depths of my own sin and am drawn to him in repentance. This teaches me not only to cling to Christ's work on the cross with renewed tenacity but to forgive those who have wronged me. His sovereignty, wisdom, and love shed the twin lights of hope and purpose on the struggles dragging me down today. And the cumulative effect of all that I learn about him is that I have greater reasons to trust, obey, and worship him.

It is worth noting that not everything we learn about God in the Bible is going to go down easily. The Bible isn't a reflection of our thoughts and ideas. Often what it teaches is contrary to our point of view. God himself warned us that this would happen. His Word compels us to rethink our beliefs and to "be transformed by the renewing of [our minds]" (Rom. 12:2).

> "For my thoughts are not your thoughts,
>   neither are your ways my ways," declares the LORD.
> "As the heavens are higher than the earth,
>   so are my ways higher than your ways
>   and my thoughts than your thoughts."
>   Isaiah 55:8–9

Sometimes, from the vantage point of his people, God doesn't look so good, and they wrestle and even resist his ways. Consider Abraham when God called him to offer his son as a sacrifice. Or Job and Naomi when only rubble remained of what had once been a full life. Habakkuk and Jonah agonized and argued over God's purposes for the cruel enemies of God's people. He seemed unjust to them. And what about Mary when Jesus failed to arrive in time to heal her brother? Our tendency when we come upon difficult passages like these is to sugarcoat them or reduce God's people to cardboard characters who are very different from ourselves. But they were real people with real emotions and a sense of justice that was sometimes violated by what God was doing.

The Bible is a powerful and sometimes unsettling book. However, God gave us his Word not to make us comfortable but to transform our minds, hearts, and lives. Real growth and understanding will occur only when we engage the Scriptures—give ourselves permission to ask honest probing questions and wrestle with what it all means.

God is a revealing God. He does not hide in the Scriptures. His purpose is to disclose himself to us there. His Holy Spirit is alive and well, and the Scriptures are his domain. He specializes in helping us understand and know God better through his Word. So we can read and study with the expectation that he will open our eyes to a greater vision of our God.

Reading to Your Children

Busy moms rarely enjoy the luxury of a quiet moment in the day for prayer and Bible study. A mother once told me she couldn't even take a hot bath without one of her little ones bursting into the room because she needed mom for something.

One way to overcome this chronic lack of solitude (and at the same time help your children become better theologians) is by reading the Bible to your children. *The New Living Bible* (Wheaton: Tyndale House Publishers, 1996) is an excellent modern translation that captures the attention of the youngest reader and gives weary adults a fresh read of the Scriptures.

Read Marian M. Schoolland's *Leading Little Ones to God: A Child's Book of Bible Teaching* (Grand Rapids: William B. Eerdmans Publishing Company, 1962) and learn theology with your child.

Getting the Big Picture of the Bible

To a lot of us, the Bible is a confusing book to read. Old Testament, New Testament—so many smaller books? It helps to see how the Bible hangs together, how the Old Testament prepares the way for the New, and how the New explains the Old. If you want to understand the big picture of the Bible and how the sixty-six different books form a cohesive unit, try Dr. Tremper Longman III's *Reading the Bible with Heart and Mind* (Colorado Springs: NavPress, 1997).

Finding Experts to Help

When reading a particular book of the Bible, commentaries written by Old and New Testament scholars often unlock the meaning and help you dig deeper. Commentaries walk you through a book of the Bible one verse at a time, explaining things from the original languages and the biblical culture that the untrained reader would not know. The *NIV Application Commentary Series* (Grand Rapids: Zondervan Publishing House) was designed to help Christians understand the text and bring the truth of Scripture into the present by applying the message of the ancient text to life today. These commentaries are an invaluable tool.

Putting the Pieces Together

Because the Bible wasn't written as a theological textbook, it can be difficult to distill theological ideas from the historical narratives, poetry, prophecy, and letters without some help. How do we find out what the Bible teaches about God's holiness? Where does the Bible explain the trinity? What is the Bible's view of human nature?

Dr. Wayne Grudem has written a superb theology book, *Systematic Theology: An Introduction to Biblical Doctrine* (Grand Rapids: Zondervan Publishing House, 1994) in which he summarizes biblical teaching on major theological topics. This book is user friendly—intended for the nonacademic reader—and maintains an important balance by addressing both the mind and the heart. The author explains theology in easy to understand language, includes questions for personal application, and guides the reader into worship and praise. On page 16, Dr. Grudem outlines his personal theological convictions so the reader can be aware of the particular point of view he affirms in each section.

Knowing God Is Not a Private Matter

Theology has never been a private matter. Historically, Christians have always explored and interacted with the Scriptures within the context of the church. This means that, rather than hatching new ideas or moving in maverick directions, the church today is building upon the foundations that were laid by the apostles and the church in previous generations. Granted, there are points where correction is warranted and reformation occurs and also where godly Christians agree to disagree. But on points of crucial beliefs, the church has affirmed the same truth for millennia. My point is that we need each other if we hope to understand the Scriptures properly. Together, we stimulate and challenge each other's thinking, hold ourselves accountable to the Scriptures, and guard each other from falling into theological ditches.

In the present, certainly this highlights the importance of choosing and becoming involved in a church where the teaching of God's Word and the fellowship of Christian friends will promote our efforts to know God better. And looking back, this ought to increase our interest in the writings of godly leaders from previous generations. Here are a few titles you might want to consider:

Augustine. *Confessions: Books I-XIII.* Translated by F. J. Sheed. Indianapolis: Hackett Publishing Company, Inc., 1993. Augustine (354–430 A.D.) is generally thought to be one of the greatest thinkers of the Christian church. In his *Confessions,* Augustine gives us the passionate saga of his spiritual autobiography, confessing the restlessness, futility, and despair of his early life without Christ and his praise to Christ who redeemed him and led him to a lasting peace in God. It is the story of every Christian; a story one person described to be "as living as molten lava."

Calvin, John. *The Institutes of the Christian Religion.* Edited by Tony Lane and Hilary Osborne. Grand Rapids: Baker Book House, 1987. The name "John Calvin" (1509–1564) sends a shiver down the spines of a lot of Christians. Maybe you are one of them. This much-maligned reformer is surprisingly unlike what many of his detractors would have us believe. Instead of being harsh, intolerant, and oppressive, his writings are warmly pastoral and full of love for Christ, which will appeal to the heart of any reader. Our pursuit of a deeper understanding of God's character will be impoverished if we shun the wisdom this man has left behind.

Calvin's major work, *The Institutes of the Christian Religion,* while an undisputed Christian classic, recognized for its value in nurturing Christians who are "hungering and thirsting for Christ," is still a bit daunting to the average reader. Most of us don't have the stamina or the time to tackle this large two-volume work. Calvin scholar Tony Lane, editor of the edition of the *Institutes* cited above, devised a way to expose us to Calvin's writings in modern English and in a more manageable serving. Who knows? Maybe this sampling of Calvin will whet your appetite for the full version.

Packer, James I. *A Quest for Godliness.* Wheaton: Crossway Books, 1990. Another group of writers who will help us along are the Puritans (1550–1700). Dr. James I. Packer writes, "They were great souls serving a great God. In them clear-headed passion and warm-hearted compassion combined. Visionary and practical, idealistic and realistic too, goal-oriented and methodical, they were great believers, great hopers, great doers, and great sufferers." They understood that what they believed had to be lived, and they lived out their beliefs in God in every sphere of life. Read Dr. Packer's *A Quest for Godliness* to make friends with the Puritans.

BOOKS TO HELP US KNOW GOD BETTER

Allender, Dan and Tremper Longman III. *The Cry of the Soul: How Our Emotions Reveal Our Deepest Questions about God.* Colorado Springs: NavPress, 1994. A Christian psychologist and an Old Testament scholar combine forces in a rich study of the Psalms that explores how our struggles and the emotions they arouse ultimately deepen our relationship with God.

Bridges, Jerry. *Trusting God: Even When Life Hurts.* Colorado Springs: NavPress, 1988. The author is a kindred spirit to those who struggle to trust God because of personal adversity. Writing as a fellow struggler because of his wife's battle with cancer, Jerry Bridges points our faith to the solid ground of God's unchanging character. There is rich encouragement to be found here.

Packer, James I. *Knowing God.* Downers Grove, Ill.: InterVarsity Press, 1973. A classic book about the importance of theology in the Christian's life. Dr. Packer walks us through a discussion of the importance of studying God, the wonders of God's character, and what God has done for us through Christ.

Piper, John. *The Pleasures of God.* Portland, Ore.: Multnomah Press, 1991. John Piper shows us the attributes of God through the lens of what delights God's heart. Anyone who reads this book will derive fresh comfort and hope when they explore why God is the "blessed" or happy God.

Sproul, R.C. *The Holiness of God.* Wheaton: Tyndale House Publishers, 1985. A glimpse of God's holiness has a way of transforming our perspective on a lot of things. Dr. Sproul pulls back the curtain to show us a God who is worthy of our worship and who calls and enables us to follow him in pursuing holiness in every corner of our lives.

Tada, Joni Eareckson and Steve Estes. *A Step Further.* Grand Rapids: Zondervan Publishing House, 1978. For those of us who are visual learners, Joni's story provides a powerful picture of the importance of theology in a woman's life. After a swimming accident that left her paralyzed, Joni wrestled with God. Through the process, her deepening understanding of his sovereign love lifted her out of despair to run boldly the race he had marked out for her. Hers is an unforgettable testimony to the power of knowing God.

For those who are wrestling to trust God in times of adversity, the following two books offer an honest discussion of the troubling issues and lead the reader to a deeper rest in God, even in the midst of the storm. These are deep and powerful books that minister to the battle-weary soul.

Carson, D. A. *How Long, O Lord? Reflections on Suffering and Evil.* Grand Rapids: Baker Book House, 1990.

Tada, Joni Eareckson and Steve Estes. *When God Weeps: Why Our Sufferings Matter to the Almighty.* Grand Rapids: Zondervan Publishing House, 1997.

BOOKS TO HELP US KNOW GOD IN OUR RELATIONSHIPS

Allender, Dan and Tremper Longman III. *Intimate Allies.* Wheaton: Tyndale House Publishers, 1995. This book breaks from the pack of books on Christian marriage by grounding Christian marriage on our identity as God's image bearers. Instead of settling for ways to help couples get along better, these authors paint an expansive vision of marriage as an endless process of discovering the wonders of one's spouse, of growing intimacy, passion, and union, and of increasing glory as "each spouse invites the other to become more like Jesus Christ."

Tripp, Paul David. *Age of Opportunity: A Biblical Guide to Parenting Teens.* Phillipsburg, N.J.: Presbyterian and Reformed Publishing, 1997. With a high view of parenting and an equally high view of teenagers, Paul Tripp describes the teen years as "years of unprecedented opportunity ... the golden age of parenting." The author (a parent of four) combines solid theology and down to earth practical experience to highlight the heart issues that emerge during the teen years. He shows parents how to lead their daughters and sons into a deeper relationship with God.

————. *War of Words: Getting to the Heart of Your Communication Struggles*. Phillipsburg, N.J.: Presbyterian and Reformed Publishing, 2000. Our theology is nowhere more exposed than in the words we speak to one another. Dr. Tripp shows how theology transforms our interaction with one another. Knowing God lifts our relationships to a higher level as we learn to serve God's agenda instead of our own.

Tripp, Ted. *Shepherding a Child's Heart*. Wapwallopen, Pa.: Shepherd Press, 1995. The author takes parents beyond behavioral issues to understand and minister to the needs of their child. I wish I had known about this book when my daughter was little.

BECOMING A THOUGHTFUL READER

In New Testament times, the apostle Paul's listeners put his teaching to the test of the Scriptures. It wasn't good enough that "the apostle Paul said it." They wanted to be sure that what he was telling them was corroborated by the Scriptures. And so "they received the message with great eagerness and examined the Scriptures every day to see if what Paul said was true" (Acts 17:11). This did not offend the apostle. Their caution was admirable and responsible; they were not sponges who mindlessly absorbed everything they heard.

The point is well taken, for if it was important to check up on what the apostle Paul was teaching, then we are well advised to examine every word we hear or read. No one has perfect theology or is above such careful scrutiny. All of us have blind spots. We are all learning, growing, refining, and correcting our understanding of God and his Word as we continue to read, study, and mature. Passive listening is always risky—to the learner as well as to the teacher. All of us must take what we hear and read from other people to the Scripture to see if it holds up there.

Some of the books which I have recommended contain views with which I personally take issue. But overall, the strengths far outweigh the weaknesses, enough so that I feel strongly about recommending them. These writers provide us with excellent opportunities to develop critical thinking and test their teachings in light of Scripture.

NOTES

Introduction

1. Michele Guinness, *Is God Good for Women?* (London: Hodder and Stoughton, 1997), 2.

2. James I. Packer, *Knowing God* (Downers Grove, Ill.: InterVarsity Press, 1973), 14–15.

Chapter 1: In the School of Rabbi Jesus

1. Gordon H. Clark, *Defense of Theology* (Milford, Mich.: Mott Media, Inc., Publishers, 1984), 7. "This English word comes from two Greek words: *theos-logos*. As bio-logy is the study of the bios, life; and as anthropology is the science of *anthropos*, man; and as sociology is the knowledge of society—so *theo-logy* is the study of knowledge of *Theos*, God."

2. Peter Kreeft, *Three Philosophies of Life* (San Francisco: Ignatius Press, 1989), 99.

3. Luke 10:38–42; John 4:7–29.

4. James B. Hurley, *Man and Woman in Biblical Perspective* (Grand Rapids: Zondervan Publishing House, 1981), 83, emphasis added.

5. James I. Packer, *Knowing God* (Downers Grove, Ill.: InterVarsity Press, 1973), 14–15.

6. John Piper, *The Pleasures of God* (Portland, Ore.: Multnomah Press, 1991), 101.

Chapter 2: The Dreaded T-Word and Why Women Avoid It

1. James B. Hurley, *Man and Woman in Biblical Perspective* (Grand Rapids: Zondervan Publishing House, 1981), 72.

2. Ibid.

3. Mary Pipher, *Reviving Ophelia: Saving the Selves of Adolescent Girls* (New York: Ballantine Books, 1994), 22.

4. Deborah accompanied Barak into battle against Sisera and his forces when Barak's faith faltered at the prospects of so fierce a battle.

5. David and his men had protected Nabal's flocks from thieves and marauders. Their request for food in exchange was both reasonable and customary. It was an opportunity for Nabal to express his gratitude and hospitality. Instead, he refused and insulted them. When Nabal's wife, Abigail, heard

what her husband had done, she knew David and his men would avenge themselves on her wicked husband. They were all in grave danger. Abigail quickly prepared a feast and traveled to David to appease his anger. David received her and acknowledged that God had sent her to prevent him from taking revenge on his enemy.

6. The letter of the law permitted the poor to gather what was left and harvest the edges of the field after the landowner harvested the crop. The spirit of the law intended for the poor to be fed. Ruth's request to glean after the harvesters, rather than wait until the women had gathered up the grain, prompted Boaz to grant permission, instruct his harvesters to put plenty of grain in her path and leave her alone, and provide her with lunch and water. She returned home in the evening with twenty-nine pounds of grain (far more than any of his workers took home for their day's work) and a pocketful of ready-to-eat cooked grain for Naomi.

7. Deborah is called "a mother of Israel" (Judg. 5:7). David's response to Abigail affirms her theology: "Praise be to the LORD, the God of Israel, who has sent you today to meet me. May you be blessed for your good judgment and for keeping me from bloodshed this day and from avenging myself with my own hands" (1 Sam. 25:32–33). Boaz esteems Ruth: "Everyone in town knows you are an honorable woman" (Ruth 3:11 NLT).

8. Sapphira joined her husband Ananias in selling a piece of property and giving a fraction of the proceeds to the church while taking credit for giving all. The apostle Peter called both husband and wife to account for their actions, and judgment fell on each of them separately. Sapphira was not given special consideration because she was following her husband's lead.

9. Bruce Milne, *Know the Truth: A Handbook of Christian Belief* (Downers Grove, Ill., InterVarsity Press, 1982), 5.

10. Ibid.

11. John 4:4–42.

Chapter 3: Colliding with God

1. Joni Eareckson Tada and Steven Estes, *When God Weeps: Why Our Sufferings Matter to the Almighty* (Grand Rapids: Zondervan Publishing House, 1997), 12.

2. Harold S. Kushner, *When Bad Things Happen to Good People* (New York: Avon Books, 1981). Rabbi Kushner chronicled his struggle with God over the issues raised by the suffering of his young son Aaron, who died at the age of thirteen of progeria or "rapid aging."

3. Dan Allender and Tremper Longman III, *The Cry of the Soul: How Our Emotions Reveal Our Deepest Questions about God* (Colorado Springs: NavPress, 1994), 63.

4. If you are not familiar with this compelling story, see Recommended Reading, which lists books in which Joni Eareckson Tada records the saga of her accident and her subsequent wrestlings over God's hand in her paralysis.

5. David F. Wells, *Losing Our Virtue* (Grand Rapids: William B. Eerdmans, 1998), 205.

6. John R. W. Stott, *The Cross of Christ* (Downers Grove, Ill.: InterVarsity Press, 1986), 204.

7. John 19:25.

8. The Hebrew word for glory *(kâbôd)* means "to be heavy, weighty." It represented both the reputation and the character of the individual. In the Hebrew mind, a person's glory was inexorably tied to their worth and character. A weighty person in society was "someone who is honorable, impressive, *worthy* of respect" (emphasis added). Any discrepancy between glory and character would strip a person of glory and place them in the category of hypocrites. R. Laird Harris, Gleason L. Archer Jr., Bruce K. Waltke, eds., *Theological Word Book of the Old Testament,* vol. 1 (Chicago: Moody Bible Institute of Chicago, 1980), 426–27.

9. See Ex. 33:18–19; 34:6–7.

Chapter 4: Surviving the War Zones of Life

1. Diane Mandt Langberg, preconference keynote address and "How to Make the Church a Safe Place for Women" seminar, 1999 Presbyterian Church of America Women in the Church Conference, Atlanta, Georgia. Dr. Langberg is the author of *On the Threshold of Hope: Opening the Door to Healing for Survivors of Sexual Abuse* (Wheaton: Tyndale House, 1999).

2. Wayne Grudem, *Systematic Theology: An Introduction to Biblical Doctrine* (Grand Rapids: Zondervan Publishing House, 1994), 332.

3. Dualism is the belief that in the universe there are "two equally ultimate powers, one good and the other evil." It leaves God and evil, or God and Satan, locked in a battle with victory within grasp of either combatant. Dualism forgets Satan's rank as a creature and God's sovereignty over all his creatures—in heaven and on earth—and leaves us hanging in the balance, sometimes with the power to cast the deciding vote. Grudem, *Systematic Theology,* 492. See also pp. 269–70.

4. Jerry Bridges, *Trusting God: Even When Life Hurts* (Colorado Springs: NavPress, 1988), 102.

5. Glenda Revell, *Glenda's Story* (Lincoln, Neb.: Gateway to Joy, 1994), 31.

6. For Rahab's story, see Joshua 2; 6:17, 22–23.

Chapter 5: Disappointed with Jesus

1. James I. Packer, *A Grief Sanctified: Passing through Grief to Peace and Joy* (Ann Arbor, Mich.: Servant Publications, 1997), 159.

2. A. Moody Stuart, *The Three Marys* (Edinburgh: The Banner of Truth Trust, 1984), 192.

3. The song of Mary, Jesus' mother, is rich with theology taken from Old Testament allusions (Luke 1:46–55), and Anna, the prophetess, acknowledges that the infant Jesus is the fulfillment of God's ancient promises to Israel (Luke 2:36–38).

4. C. S. Lewis, *A Grief Observed* (New York: Bantam Books, 1961), 4–5.

5. Packer, *Grief Sanctified,* 160.

6. Lewis, *Grief Observed,* 1.

7. John Piper, *The Pleasures of God* (Portland, Ore.: Multnomah Press, 1991), 104.

8. Ibid., 109.

9. Thomas Watson, *A Body of Divinity* (Edinburgh: The Banner of Truth Trust, 1970), 55.

10. Joni Eareckson Tada and Steven Estes, *When God Weeps: Why Our Sufferings Matter to the Almighty* (Grand Rapids: Zondervan Publishing House, 1997), 131.

11. John Angell James, *Female Piety: A Young Woman's Friend and Guide* (Morgan, Pa.: Soli Deo Gloria Publications, 1999), 257.

12. Herman Ridderbos, *The Gospel of John: A Theological Commentary*, tr. John Vriend (Grand Rapids: William B. Eerdmans, 1987), 402.

13. One translation says, "When Jesus therefore saw her weeping, and the Jews who came with her also weeping, he was *deeply moved in spirit and was troubled*" (v. 33 NASB, emphasis added) and wept with them. Another describes him as "moved with indignation" and "deeply troubled" (NLT). Scholars wrestle with the causes of this mix of anger and sorrow in Jesus. Some suggest he may have been angered by the unbelief reflected in her tears. Others, that he was incensed by the hypocritical wailing of the Jews, knowing some of them would shortly turn on him. Neither explanation holds up when Jesus himself wades into the pathos and weeps in grief along with them.

Many are convinced, and I am inclined to agree, that his anger was directed at the underlying causes of their grief; it is "the revulsion of everything that is in him against the power of death" and its devastation of his friends. Death is the final war zone, and Jesus will soon face it alone for those he loves. "Christ does not come to the sepulchre as an idle spectator, but like a wrestler preparing for the contest. Therefore, no wonder that He groans again, for the violent tyranny of death that He had to overcome stands before His eyes." John Calvin, quoted in Herman Ridderbos, *The Gospel of John: A Theological Commentary*, tr. John Vriend (Grand Rapids: William B. Eerdmans, 1987), 402.

Chapter 6: Battling Our Unbelief

1. A don is a professor of the Oxford University faculty.

2. Some experts say Sudden Infant Death Syndrome, or crib death, is the major cause of death in infants during the first year of life.

3. Franz Julius Delitzsch, *Commentary on the Epistle to the Hebrews*, vol. 2, tr. Thomas L. Kingsbury (Minneapolis: Klock and Klock Christian Publishers, 1978), 298.

4. Hebrews 10:32–34; 12:3–4; 13:3 all allude to their difficulties.

5. "See to it, brothers, that none of you has a sinful, unbelieving heart that turns away from the living God" (3:12).

"Let us hold firmly to the faith we profess" (4:14).

"Let us hold unswervingly to the hope we profess, for he who promised is faithful" (10:23).

"So do not throw away your confidence; it will be richly rewarded. You need to persevere so that when you have done the will of God, you will receive what he has promised. . . . But we are not of those who shrink back and are destroyed, but of those who believe and are saved" (10:35–36, 39).

6. John Owen, *Hebrews: Epistle of Warning* (Grand Rapids: Kregel Publications, 1953), 244.

7. Martyn Lloyd-Jones, *Spiritual Depressions* (Grand Rapids: William B. Eerdmans, 1965), 21.

8. Jerry Bridges, *Trusting God: Even When Life Hurts* (Colorado Springs: NavPress, 1988), 102.

9. Matthew Henry, *Matthew Henry's Commentary on the Whole Bible, Joshua to Esther,* vol. 2 (New York: Fleming H. Revell, n.d.), 253.

10. Chris Ogden, *Maggie: An Intimate Portrait of a Woman in Power* (New York: Simon and Schuster, 1990), 124.

11. Acts 26:31–32.

Chapter 7: Fixing Our Eyes on Jesus

1. Rob Hughes, "The Power and the Glory," *The Sunday Times Magazine,* 16 August 1992, p. 16.

2. Ibid., 24.

3. *Christianity Today* (5 October 1998): 96.

4. Omniscience means God is all-knowing. He knows everything.

5. Omnipresence means God is fully present everywhere at all times.

6. James I. Packer, *Knowing God* (Downers Grove, Ill.: InterVarsity Press, 1973), 37.

7. Elizabeth D. Dodds, *Marriage to a Difficult Man: The Uncommon Union of Jonathan and Sarah Edwards* (Philadelphia: Westminster Press, 1971), 35.

8. Ibid., 204.

9. Ibid., 197.

10. Ibid.

Chapter 8: A Warrior in the Heat of Battle

1. This event is also recorded in Matthew 26:6–13 and Mark 14:3–9.

2. "The idea readily suggests itself that the supper (or 'dinner' if one prefers) was prompted by love for the Lord, specifically by gratitude for the raising of Lazarus and for the healing of Simon, the man who had been a leper, is still called 'Simon the leper,' but had presumably been healed by Jesus." William Hendriksen, *The Gospel of Matthew,* New Testament Commentary (Grand Rapids: Baker Book House, 1973), 898. And Alfred Edersheim writes, "It was the special festive meal of the Sabbath. The words of St. John seem to indicate that the meal was a public one, as if the people of Bethany had combined to do Him this honour, and so share the privilege of sharing the feast. In point of fact, we know from St. Matthew and St. Mark that it took place 'in the house of Simon the Leper'—not, of course, an actual leper—but one who had been such. Perhaps his guest-chamber was the largest in Bethany; perhaps the house was nearest to the Synagogue; or there may have been other reasons for it, unknown to us—least likely is the suggestion that Simon was the husband of Martha, or else her father. Other scholars believe it may have been a more intimate gathering." Alfred Edersheim, *The Life and Times of Jesus the Messiah,* book 4 (Grand Rapids: William B. Eerdmans, 1971), 359.

3. Luke's account connects what Jesus said with the teachings of the prophets and also describes in terms of a spiritual blindness the disciples' inability to comprehend what he was saying.

"Jesus took the Twelve aside and told them, 'We are going up to Jerusalem, and everything that is written by the prophets about the Son of Man will be fulfilled. He will be handed over to the Gentiles. They will mock him, insult him, spit on him, flog him and kill him. On the third day he will rise again.' "The disciples did not understand any of this. Its meaning was hidden from them, and they did not know what he was talking about" (18:31–34).

4. "Then [following the feast in Bethany] one of the Twelve—the one called Judas Iscariot—went to the chief priests and asked, 'What are you willing to give me if I hand him over to you?' So they counted out for him thirty silver coins. From then on Judas watched for an opportunity to hand him over" (Matt. 26:14–16).

5. Philip Yancey, *The Jesus I Never Knew* (Grand Rapids: Zondervan Publishing House, 1995), 195.

6. William Hendriksen writes, "As it was not considered proper for women in public to be reclining along with men, we must assume that the guests were exclusively men. There were at least fifteen of them: Jesus, the Twelve, Lazarus, and a certain Simon, who is mentioned only in the Synoptics (Matt. 26:6; Mark 14:3)." Hendriksen, *The Gospel of John*, New Testament Commentary (Grand Rapids: Baker Book House, 1961), 173.

7. Herman Ridderbos, *The Gospel of John: A Theological Commentary*, tr. John Vriend (Grand Rapids: William B. Eerdmans, 1987), 414.

8. Matthew and Mark report that she poured the perfume on his head; John on his feet. Jesus, in Matthew and Mark, is quoted as saying, "She poured this perfume on my body" (Matt. 26:12; Mark 14:8). In support of the abundance of perfume that she gave, Dr. Hendriksen writes, "Evidently there was enough for the entire body: head, neck, shoulders, and even for the feet . . . but here in John the ointment does not merely flow down, but is actually *poured out* upon the feet." Hendriksen, *Gospel of John*, 176.

9. Herman Ridderbos writes, "Judas will estimate the price of the oil at three hundred denarii." Ridderbos, *Gospel of John*, 414.

10. His hypocrisy is even more appalling, given the fact that he condemned Mary for lavishing three hundred denarii on Jesus when the price he put on Jesus' head was a shabby thirty pieces of silver or shekels, the rough equivalent of four denarii. Bruce M. Metzger and Michael D. Coogan, eds., *The Oxford Companion to the Bible* (Oxford: Oxford University Press, 1993), 523–24. According to William Hendriksen, thirty pieces of silver was "the price of a slave gored by an ox." Hendriksen, *Gospel of Matthew*, 903.

11. B. F. Wescott, *The Gospel according to St. John* (Grand Rapids: William B. Eerdmans, 1973), 177, emphasis added.

12. Ridderbos, *Gospel of John*, 420.

13. Paul K. Jewett writes, "To the 'unliberated' first-century Jewess, this last touch would have been especially painful. For a woman to take down her hair in

the presence of men would have been deemed highly immodest." Paul K. Jewett, *Man as Male and Female* (Grand Rapids: William B. Eerdmans, 1975), 99–100.

14. Ridderbos, *Gospel of John,* 415.

15. "On coming to the house, [the magi] saw the child with his mother Mary, and they bowed down and worshiped him" (Matt. 2:11). "Then those who were in the boat worshiped him, saying, 'Truly you are the Son of God'" (Matt. 14:33).

16. "The angel said to the women, 'Do not be afraid, for I know that you are looking for Jesus, who was crucified. He is not here; he has risen, *just as he said*" (Matt. 28:5–6, emphasis added).

17. According to B. F. Wescott, this was "the first stage in an embalming." Wescott, *Gospel according to St. John,* 178. Raymond E. Brown notes, "... one does not anoint the feet of a living person, but one might anoint the feet of a corpse as part of the ritual of preparing the whole body for burial." Raymond E. Brown, *The Gospel according to John* (New York: Doubleday, 1966), 454.

18. "An angel from heaven appeared to him and strengthened him" (Luke 22:43).

19. "The atonement is the work Christ did in his life and death to earn our salvation." Wayne Grudem, *Systematic Theology: An Introduction to Biblical Doctrine* (Grand Rapids: Zondervan Publishing House, 1994), 568.

20. "The apostles maintained their interest in the hope of seeing the kingdom of God realized in the restoration of Israel's national independence. They had in earlier days been captivated by the idea that in such a restored order they themselves would have positions of authority." F. F. Bruce, *The Book of the Acts,* The New International Commentary on the New Testament (Grand Rapids: William B. Eerdmans, 1976), 38.

21. Yancey, *The Jesus I Never Knew,* 195.

22. Hastings Robinson, ed., *Original Letters Relative to the English Reformation, 1531–1558,* vol. 1 (Cambridge: Cambridge University Press, 1846–47), 97. Edited by Robinson for the Parker Society.

Chapter 9: God Created an Intimate Ally

1. Gen. 2:23.

2. Anthropology, or the doctrine of man (as it has historically been called), focuses on God's "creation of human beings, both male and female, to be more like him than anything else he has made," including God's purposes for us, our natures, sin and disobedience, and God's plan for our salvation and his covenants with his people. Wayne Grudem, *Systematic Theology: An Introduction to Biblical Doctrine* (Grand Rapids: Zondervan Publishing House, 1994), 439ff.

3. C. S. Lewis, *A Grief Observed* (New York: Bantam Books, 1961), 55–56, 70.

4. The narrator creates suspense and "allows us to feel man's loneliness." Gordon J. Wenham, *Genesis 1–15,* David A. Hubbard and Glenn W. Barker, eds., Word Biblical Commentary, vol. 1 (Waco, Tex.: Word, 1987), 68.

5. Ex. 18:4; Deut. 33:7, 26, 29; Ps. 20:2; 33:20; 70:5; 89:19 (translated "strength" in the NIV); 115:9, 10, 11; 121:1, 2; 124:8; 146:5; and Hos. 13:9.

6. Isa. 30:5; Ezek. 12:14; Dan. 11:34.

7. Some have gone so far as to argue that because the same word is most often used for God, the woman must therefore be superior to the man. But as we have already noted, Genesis 1 makes this a moot question. "To help someone does not imply that the helper is stronger than the helped; simply that the latter's strength is inadequate by itself." Wenham, *Genesis*, 68. This notion is backed up by the fact that in Genesis 2 the word *ezer* does not appear alone. It is qualified by the Hebrew word *kenegdo*, which appears only in this passage and literally reads, "I will make him for him a helper as in front of him (or according to what is in front of him)." Victor P. Hamilton, *The Book of Genesis Chapters 1–17*, The International Commentary on the Old Testament, ed. R. K. Harrison (Grand Rapids: Eerdmans, 1990), 175. Dr. Hamilton goes on to explain, "The new creation will be neither a superior nor an inferior, but an equal. The creation of this helper will form one-half of a polarity, and will be to man as the south pole is to the north pole.... Any suggestion that this particular word denotes one who has only an associate or subordinate status to a senior member is refuted by the fact that most frequently this same word describes Yahweh's relationship to Israel. He is Israel's help(er)."

8. R. Laird Harris, Gleason L. Archer Jr., Bruce K. Waltke, eds., *Theological Word Book of the Old Testament*, vol. 2 (Chicago: Moody Bible Institute of Chicago, 1980), 660.

9. Actually, the choice of the word *ezer* to describe the woman is even more striking than we have indicated, for the term *ezer* is "masculine in gender, though here it is a term for woman." At the least, this tells us the choice of wording here deliberately emphasizes the strength and help the woman will offer the man. See Hamilton, *Book of Genesis*, 175–76.

10. Bruce K. Waltke, "The Role of the Valiant Wife in the Marketplace," *Crux* 35 (1999), 23–34.

11. Ibid., 23, 25.

12. Ibid., 25, quoting Erika Moore.

13. Dr. Dan B. Allender and Dr. Tremper Longman III explore the idea of man and woman as intimate allies in their book on marriage, *Intimate Allies: Rediscovering God's Design for Marriage and Becoming Soul Mates for Life* (Wheaton: Tyndale House, 1995). See "Recommended Reading" for more information.

14. "So God created man in his own image, in the image of God he created him; male and female he created them. God blessed them and said to them, 'Be fruitful and increase in number; fill the earth and subdue it. Rule over the fish of the sea and the birds of the air and over every living creature that moves on the ground'" (Gen. 1:27–28).

15. For "a man will leave his father and mother and be united to his wife, and they will become one flesh" (Gen. 2:24).

16. Quoted from John Donne's "Anatomy of the World: The First Anniversary" (1572–1631). John Donne, *Complete English Poems*, ed. C. A. Patrides (London: Everyman, 1994), 252.

17. Raymond C. Ortlund Jr, "Male-Female Equality and Male Headship: Genesis 1–3," in *Recovering Biblical Manhood and Womanhood: A Response to*

Evangelical Feminism, eds. John Piper and Wayne Grudem (Wheaton: Crossway Books, 1991), 107.

18. James M. Boice, *Genesis: An Expositional Commentary,* vol. 1, Genesis 1–11 (Grand Rapids: Baker Book House, 1998), 222.

19. Ortlund, "Male-Female Equality," 110, emphasis added.

20. According to John Piper and Wayne Grudem (who feel strongly that husbands need to listen to their wives' counsel), "Satan's main target was not Eve's peculiar gullibility (if she had one), but rather Adam's headship as the one ordained by God to be responsible for the life of the garden. Satan's subtlety is that he knew the created order God had ordained for the good of the family, and he deliberately defied it by ignoring the man and taking up his dealings with the woman. Satan put her in the position of spokesman, leader and defender. At that moment both the man and the woman slipped from their innocence and let themselves be drawn into a pattern of relating that to this day has proved destructive." John Piper and Wayne Grudem, "An Overview of Central Concerns," in *Recovering Biblical Manhood and Womanhood,* eds. Piper and Grudem, 73.

21. Larry Crabb, *The Silence of Adam* (Grand Rapids: Zondervan Publishing House, 1995), 97.

22. Jerry Bridges, *Trusting God: Even When Life Hurts* (Colorado Springs, NavPress, 1988), 102.

Chapter 10: Body Building in the Church

1. 1 Peter 3:7 exhorts husbands to "live with your wives, and treat them with respect as the *weaker partner* and as heirs with you of the gracious gift of life, so that nothing will hinder your prayers" (emphasis added). Most scholars interpret this as a reference to the *physical* strength of a woman as compared to that of a man. Alan M. Stibbs writes that a husband "should recognize her more limited physical powers as a woman, and should give her corresponding consideration and protection. Only so will he render her due honour and be worthy of her marital confidence and devotion. On the other hand, spiritually, he should also recognize their full equality as fellow-sharers in the grace of God, ... called together to a spiritual fellowship with God and Christ, a sphere in which his wife is not weaker or inferior, but a joint heir." Alan M. Stibbs, *The First Epistle General of Peter,* Tyndale Bible Commentaries, gen. ed. R. V. G. Tasker (Grand Rapids: William B. Eerdmans, 1960), 127.

In his commentary on 1 Peter, Scot McKnight concurs. "This expression [the weaker partner] has given rise to two major interpretations: physical weakness, and spiritual weakness. Inasmuch as the preponderance of evidence in the ancient world uses identical or similar language when describing a woman's physical condition, it is almost certain that Peter has in mind a wife's physical capacities." Scot McKnight, *1 Peter,* The NIV Application Commentary, gen. ed. Terry Muck (Grand Rapids: Zondervan Publishing House, 1996), 186.

2. "Their [apostles, prophets, evangelists, pastors, and teachers] responsibility is to equip God's people to do his work and build up the church, the body of Christ, until we come to such unity in our faith and knowledge of God's Son

that we will be mature and full grown in the Lord, measuring up to the full stature of Christ" (Eph. 4:12–13 NLT).

3. Klyne Snodgrass, *Ephesians,* The NIV Application Commentary, gen. ed. Terry Muck (Grand Rapids: Zondervan Publishing House, 1996), 224.

4. "Aquila and Priscilla greet you warmly in the Lord, and so does the church that meets at their house" (1 Cor. 16:19).

5. Douglas Moo, author of the New International Commentary on Romans, explains the debate over the name Junia. "It is because Paul thus calls Junia(s) an 'apostle' that earlier interpreters tended to argue that Paul must be referring to a man; for they had difficulty imagining that a woman could hold such authority in the early church. Yet it is just for this reason that many contemporary scholars are eager to identify Junia(s) as a woman, for Pauline recognition of a female apostle would support the notion that the NT places no restrictions on the ministry of women."

Ruth A. Tucker and Walter Liefeld write, ". . . since Junia as a Latin female name would be the feminine counterpart of Junius, as Julia is the feminine counterpart of Julius (a masculine name known from Latin literature), there is every reason to assume that Paul refers to a woman. . . . John Chrysostom and Jerome referred to this person as a woman; in fact, it was not until the late thirteenth or early fourteenth century that a commentator referred to her as a man." Ruth A. Tucker and Walter Liefeld, *Daughters of the Church: Women and Ministry from New Testament Times to the Present* (Grand Rapids: Zondervan Publishing House, 1987), 73.

Moo concurs. "Interpreters from the thirteenth to the middle of the twentieth century generally favored the masculine identification. But it appears that commentators before the thirteenth century were unanimous in favor of the feminine identification; and scholars have recently again inclined decisively to this same view. And probably with good reason. For while a contracted form of Junianus would fit quite well in this list of greetings (for Paul uses several other such contractions), we have no evidence elsewhere for this contracted form of the name. On the other hand, the Latin 'Junia' was a very common name. Probably, then, 'Junia' was the wife of Andronicus (note the other husband and wife pairs in this list, Prisca and Aquila [v. 3] and [probably], Philologus and Julia [v. 15])." Douglas Moo, *The Epistle to the Romans,* The New International Commentary on the New Testament, ed. Gorden D. Fee (Grand Rapids: William B. Eerdmans, 1996), 922–23.

6. William Hendriksen writes, "In the New Testament the word *apostle* is used in a looser and in a stricter sense. According to the broader application of the term, such men as Barnabas, Epaphroditus, Apollos, Silvanus, and Timothy are all called 'apostles.' They all evangelize. They can be described as missionaries or itinerant Christian evangelists." William Hendriksen, *Romans Chapters 9–16,* vol. 2 (Grand Rapids: Baker Book House, 1981), 504–5.

7. In addition to Lydia (Acts 16:40), other women are identified as having hosted churches in their homes: Priscilla (Rom. 16:3–5; 1 Cor. 16:19), Nympha (Col. 4:15), and possibly Chloe (1 Cor. 1:11).

Epilogue

1. In John's gospel, six individuals testify that Jesus is the Son of God:

John the Baptist: "I have seen and I testify that this is the Son of God" (1:34).

Nathanael: "Rabbi, you are the Son of God; you are the King of Israel" (1:49).

Peter: "Lord, to whom shall we go? You have the words of eternal life. We believe and know that you are the Holy One of God" (6:68–69).

Martha: "I believe that you are the Christ, the Son of God, who was to come into the world" (11:27).

Thomas: "My Lord and my God!" (20:28).

John the apostle: "Jesus did many other miraculous signs in the presence of his disciples, which are not recorded in this book. But these are written that you may believe that Jesus is the Christ, the Son of God, and that by believing you may have life in his name" (20:30–31).

2. C. S. Lewis, "The Weight of Glory," in *The Weight of Glory and Other Essays* (Grand Rapids: William B. Eerdmans, 1965), 1–2.

Recommended Reading

1. John Calvin, *Institutes of the Christian Religion*, ed. John T. McNeill, tr. Ford Lewis Battles, 2 vols. (Philadelphia: The Westminster Press, 1960), 1 37.

DISCUSSION QUESTIONS

Introduction: "No Great Women Theologians"

Focus: To see that our ability to trust God depends on how well we know him.

Read: John 10:10; 17:3

1. Describe a difficult situation in your life when God didn't do what you were hoping, praying, and expecting he would do.

2. When you were in that situation, what questions were you asking about God?

3. When we ask questions about God, we're already doing theology. According to the definition of theology on page 19, why is *theologian* a good way to describe any Christian, including you?

4. Why do we hesitate to think of ourselves as theologians?

5. If theology is about knowing God, do these hesitations make sense? Why or why not?

6. How does what you believe about God affect your ability to trust him?

7. According to Dr. James I. Packer (p. 23), why are we "cruel to ourselves" when we don't make knowing God better our highest priority?

8. Since theology is your relationship with God, what are some practical reasons for you to know him better?

Chapter 1
In the School of Rabbi Jesus:
Mary Learns at Jesus' Feet

Focus: To discover that Jesus calls women to make knowing God our highest priority.

Read: Luke 10:38–42

1. What's so amazing about Jesus teaching Mary? If Mary's culture was more like Fatemah's culture (p. 37), what strong statement is Rabbi Jesus making through his interaction with Mary?

2. Since the conversation between Jesus and Mary was not recorded, what clues do we find in Jesus' other conversations that indicate he was teaching Mary the same deep truths about himself that he taught his male disciples?

3. Why does Martha object to Jesus? Which sister do you sympathize with more and why?

4. If you didn't know what happened next, what would you expect Jesus to say? Again, considering the culture in Mary's day, how would everyone there—the two sisters, their brother, and the disciples—expect Jesus to respond?

5. Why do we tend to view Mary of Bethany as a "woman who thinks" and her sister Martha as a "woman who serves"? How do these personality types influence our interpretation of Jesus' response to Martha's request?

6. Why does Jesus defend Mary? What impact would his answer to Martha have on Mary? What impact on Martha? What impact should his words have on you?

7. Would Jesus accept the notion that some women are "Marys" and others are "Marthas"? Why or why not?

8. If theology is a *relationship*, what does Jesus want Mary to gain from the time she spends with him? What should your purpose be in reading and studying his Word? What is Jesus calling you to do?

Chapter 2
The Dreaded T-Word and Why Women Avoid It

Focus: To discuss honestly and address the obstacles that prevent us from pursuing a deeper relationship with God.

Read: Ephesians 1:16–19a; 4:14–15; 2 Peter 1:5–8; Romans 12:2

1. List some of the reasons why you or your friends might be inclined to avoid theology.

2. Have you ever felt that because you are a woman, you didn't need or weren't responsible to know as much theology as a man? Why or why not?

3. If we accept the notion that theology is for men and not for women, how well equipped are we to face difficulties, such as breast cancer, dysfunctional and broken relationships, death, loneliness, times of spiritual doubt and discouragement?

4. What limits did women in the Bible place on how much they were willing to know about God or how freely they used that knowledge?

5. How did their knowledge of God affect their relationships, particularly their relationships with men?

6. How have you observed theology being used in hurtful ways? How can you address these abuses honestly without allowing them to interfere with your relationship with God?

7. Why does every Christian—regardless of gender, age, education, or occupation—need to know God better?

8. Why is it important for you to reject these obstacles and freely pursue a deeper knowledge of God? What can you do to know him better?

Chapter 3
Colliding with God

Focus: To understand that God has a plan for each of us—plan A—which he is accomplishing for our good and his glory through everything that happens in our lives.

Read: Daniel 4:28–37

1. Describe a circumstance from your life that has caused you to doubt God's goodness, his care for you, or whether he really is in control.

2. How does disappointment with and anger at God provoke us to ask questions that lead us into a deeper relationship with God?

3. What does King Nebuchadnezzar learn about God's sovereignty from his collision with God?

4. How do Hebrews 12:1–2 and Psalm 139:16 bring God's sovereignty into the everyday moments of our lives?

5. Do you believe God has a plan for your life that he is accomplishing for your good and his glory? Why or why not? Why is it important to admit there is mystery to this teaching? (See p. 73.)

6. If you are troubled by the notion that plan B is a myth, how does the cross of Christ reveal God's heart for you and reassure you that he can be trusted, no matter what happens? Why is it important to connect God's sovereignty with his other attributions—his goodness, justice, and love, for example?

7. Remembering that God is everything that we long for in a father, how is God parenting and maturing us through everything that happens in our lives?

8. How does it affect your view of your life to know he cares for you as though you were his only child?

Chapter 4
Surviving the War Zones of Life

Focus: To help us see that God's good plan for us can never be destroyed, no matter what powerful, destructive forces invade our lives.

Read: Isaiah 46:9–10; Psalm 139:13–16

1. What are the three biggest threats to God's plan for you, and how have you run up against them?

2. What is the difference between God's *revealed* will and God's *hidden* will? How safe is God's plan (hidden will) for you if it collapses under certain pressures, if he rules over some but not all circumstances?

3. What is our greatest concern when we speak of God's ruling over everything in our world? Read the first two paragraphs on page 86, beginning with, "One of my struggles ..." as a reminder that at some level, all of us struggle with God's sovereignty but that the struggle will help us grow deeper in our understanding of and confidence in God.

4. What does Job teach us about Satan's power to destroy God's good plan for our lives? What does Job learn about God through his pain that he would never see through his prosperity?

5. What does Joseph teach us about the power others have to destroy God's good plan for our lives? What does Joseph learn about God's plan through the abuse, injustice, imprisonment, and abandonment he suffered?

6. What does Rahab teach us about our ability to destroy God's plan for us through our sinful choices and foolish mistakes, whether we made them before or after we became a Christian? How does God use our sin to deepen our love for him?

7. How does the mystery of concurrence (p. 94) help us rest in God's plan for our lives while at the same time compelling us to take seriously our responsibility to obey his Word?

8. How does our theology make us strong in the war zones of life?

Chapter 5
Disappointed with Jesus: Mary Weeps at Jesus' Feet

Focus: To help us see that theology is not just facts and ideas. Theology is life and must be lived out in the everyday moments of our lives.

Read: John 11:1–6, 11–14, 17–21, 28–37

1. Describe a situation in your life when you were counting on God and he didn't come through for you. What did you think?

2. What is Mary's theology (what she believed about Jesus) that prompted her to send for him when Lazarus was dying?

3. If you didn't know the story, what would you expect Jesus to do when he receives her message? What would you expect him to do when he finally arrives and encounters the grieving Mary? What does he actually do?

4. How do God's glory and our good intertwine? How does God's passion for his glory guarantee our good in every situation?

5. How does Jesus' weeping with Mary affirm and validate our own suffering? What kind of theology does Jesus model when he weeps?

6. What does Mary learn about Jesus through this crisis?

7. How do the uncertainties and crises of life increase our need to pursue a deeper knowledge of God now?

8. What are some suggestions that will help us pursue a deeper understanding of God? (See pp. 237–40.)

Chapter 6
Battling Our Unbelief

Focus: To brace ourselves for the battle of faith as we live in God's plan for us.

Read: Hebrews 12:1–2; 1:1–3; 3:1

1. Just as Mee-Yan carried a deep burden of grief because of the deaths of her sister and her two babies, what burdens weigh you down and make it hard for you to run the race God has marked out for you?

2. What burdens were impeding the first-century Jewish Christians who received the letter to the Hebrews? What did they seem to be thinking about God?

3. What is the antidote for unbelief? What can you do to throw off your unbelief?

4. Can you relate to Susan's endurance running? What makes you feel you are running an endurance race? What makes you feel like giving up?

5. Why is running such an important metaphor for how you are to live your life? How does running challenge you to invest yourself in your circumstances?

6. How does Paul's example help you see how you are to face your circumstances, whether you like them or not?

7. What kept Elizabeth going when her overwhelming routine was compounded by her husband's academic crisis?

8. How does fixing your eyes on Jesus help you remember that everything you do matters?

Chapter 7
Fixing Our Eyes on Jesus

Focus: To explore practical ways of fixing our eyes on a Jesus we can't see.

Read: John 14:6–10; Philippians 3:7–11; Hebrews 5:11–14

1. Why are a runner's eyes so crucial to successful running? In practical terms, what does it mean to "fix your eyes on Jesus" when you can't physically see him?

2. What often happens to your theology when you hit a new crisis in your life? Where do you tend to focus? What is the result for you personally?

3. Why is Jesus the best person to teach you theology? What does he teach us about God?

4. How can you get personal with what you are learning about God? How do you write your name into the truth you are learning about God from his Word?

5. One of the greatest dangers of loving theology is that we will get caught up in lofty ideas without connecting what we're learning to our everyday lives. What can you do to overcome this problem? How can you learn to use your theology? What difference will it make for you?

6. Why is your theology *not* a private matter? Why does your theology matter to others? How did the apostles expect women to use their theology to teach and strengthen others?

7. What are we doing to ourselves and what are we doing to others when we neglect the study of God and settle for a diet of spiritual baby food? By taking your theology seriously, what do you have to offer others?

8. How can *you* invest more in your relationship with Jesus?

Chapter 8
A Warrior in the Heat of Battle:
Mary Anoints Jesus for His Burial

Focus: To discover the wide door of ministry that Jesus opens to women.

Read: John 12:1–8

1. As the Passover drew near, Jesus' enemies were plotting his death and he knew the cross awaited. Describe what it must have been like for Jesus to attend the feast at Bethany under such conditions. How do his disciples make things worse?

2. Looking back over Mary's first two encounters with Jesus, what is her theology (what she believed about Jesus) now?

3. Why does Jesus defend her? According to Jesus, what was Mary doing?

4. Where did Mary learn the compassion and sympathy she displayed in her ministry to Jesus? Who was her role model and mentor?

5. What can you learn from Mary's ministry to Jesus in a room full of male leaders after Jesus affirmed and defended her actions?

6. How do men depend on the spiritual and pastoral ministries of women? What would Jesus have missed if Mary had held back?

7. How do Mary's actions and Jesus' affirmation of her anointing expand your opportunities for spiritual ministry?

8. What opportunities do you have to enter into the struggles of others and encourage them to trust and obey God?

Chapter 9
God Created an Intimate Ally

Focus: To trace the origins of every woman's calling to be a theologian back to God's blueprint for the creation of the woman.

Read: Genesis 1:26–28; 2:18–25; 3:1–7

1. When you hear the creation story, what comes to mind when you think of the terms *helpmeet* or *helper* with reference to the woman God created to be with Adam?

2. Did Adam need the woman you described? Does your description apply to every woman? If not, who does your definition leave out?

3. In the Old Testament, who does the word *ezer* or "strong helper" refer to most often?

4. What are the four ground rules for understanding what *ezer* means when it refers to women and why are these rules important?

5. Why is the word *ezer* generic? What are the implications for us?

6. How does it change your understanding of your calling as a woman to realize the word *ezer* is a military term? How were the man and the woman warriors together? How did they need each other?

7. How was Eve functioning as an *ezer* when she contemplated eating the fruit? How did she fail as an ezer by eating and then giving the fruit to her husband?

8. What is the most important asset that a woman brings to her marriage? How are you called to be a strong helper in every relationship, and what can you do to equip yourself for ministry to others?

Chapter 10
Body Building in the Church

Focus: To explore God's calling for women to be Body builders in his church.

Read: Ephesians 4:11–16; Romans 16:1–16

1. How do you see yourself (and other women) contributing to the spiritual health of the church?

2. Who needs your ministry in the church? Is your ministry restricted to a specific group, a specific place and time, in content? If yes, in what ways?

3. According to Romans 12:4–5, Colossians 3:16, and Ephesians 4:16—passages addressed to all Christians—what kinds of ministries do you have to offer to your fellow-believers? What ministries do you need from them?

4. What happens to a body when some part isn't functioning? How do we hinder the body of Christ when we withhold our ministries from others?

5. What women are named in Romans 16:1–16 and what kinds of ministries were they doing?

6. How does Paul evaluate the contributions of these women? How did their ministries benefit Paul?

7. How does your theology equip you for deeper ministry within the body of Christ?

8. What can we do to encourage and equip women for greater spiritual ministry in the church?

Epilogue: "Martha, Martha"

Focus: To see that Jesus calls all women—including those who call themselves "Marthas"—to pursue a deep relationship with God.

Read: John 11:17–28, 38–44

1. What is Martha's chief concern when she asks Jesus to send Mary back to the kitchen? (See Luke 10:38–42.)

2. If you had been in Martha's shoes, what would you have done after Jesus said, "Martha, Martha ... you are worried and upset about many things, but only one thing is needed. Mary has chosen what is better, and it will not be taken away from her" (Luke 10:41–42)?

3. What evidence indicates that when Jesus arrives in Bethany after the death of Lazarus, Martha also is a student of Rabbi Jesus?

4. What conflicting information about Jesus is troubling Martha? When have you experienced the same conflict in your own circumstances?

5. How does Jesus help Martha confront her questions and take her deeper in her relationship with him? How should this encourage you to face the hard questions that come up in your life?

6. What kind of faith does Jesus call Martha to exercise in him? How does Martha become a role model for all Christians here?

7. Why do "Marthas" love theology? How do they combine head and heart in their ministries to others?

8. Why is knowing God your highest calling and your most pressing need?

Lost Women of the Bible

The Women We Thought We Knew

Carolyn Custis James

It's easy for Christian women—young and old—to get lost between the opportunities and demands of the present and the biblical teachings of the past. They live in a confusing world, caught in the crossfire between church and culture. Although home and family still remain central, more women than ever, by choice or by necessity are blending home, career, and ministry. They need strong biblical role models to help them meet these challenges.

Building on solid scholarship and a determination to wrestle honestly with perplexing questions, author Carolyn Custis James sheds new light on ancient stories that brings the women of the Bible into the twenty-first century. This fresh look at the women in the Bible unearths surprising new insights and a powerful message that will leave readers feeling challenged, encouraged, and deeply valued. Rediscover and be inspired by these women and others:

- Eve
- Sarah
- Hagar
- Tamar
- Hannah
- Esther
- Mary

Softcover: 978-0-310-28525-0

ZONDERVAN®
.com

The Gospel of Ruth

Loving God Enough to
Break the Rules

Carolyn Custis James

This isn't the Ruth, the Naomi, or the Boaz
we thought we knew. Carolyn James has
unearthed startling new insights from this
well-worn story ... insights that have life-
changing implications for you. Naomi is no longer regarded as a
bitter, complaining woman, but is seen as a courageous overcomer.
A female Job. Ruth turns out to be a gutsy risk-taker and a powerful agent for change among God's people. She lives outside the
box, and her love for Yahweh and Naomi compels her to break the
rules of social and religious convention at nearly every turn. Boaz,
the kinsman-redeemer, is repeatedly caught off-guard by Ruth's
initiatives. His partnership with her models the kind of male-female
relationships the gospel intends for all who follow Jesus.

Carolyn James drills down deeper into the story and uncovers
in the Old Testament the same passionate, counter-cultural, rule-
breaking gospel that Jesus modeled and taught his followers to
pursue. Within this age-old story is a map to radical levels of love
and sacrifice, combined with the message that God is counting on
his daughters to build his kingdom.

The Gospel of Ruth vests every woman's life with kingdom purposes and frees us to embrace wholeheartedly God's calling,
regardless of our circumstances or season of life. This story of two
women who have lost everything contains a profound message: God
created women not to live in the shadowy margins of men or of the
past, but to emerge as courageous activists for his kingdom.

Hardcover, Jacketed: 978-0-310-26391-3

Share Your Thoughts

With the Author: Your comments will be forwarded to the author when you send them to *zauthor@zondervan.com*.

With Zondervan: Submit your review of this book by writing to *zreview@zondervan.com*.

Free Online Resources at

www.zondervan.com/hello

 Zondervan AuthorTracker: Be notified whenever your favorite authors publish new books, go on tour, or post an update about what's happening in their lives.

 Daily Bible Verses and Devotions: Enrich your life with daily Bible verses or devotions that help you start every morning focused on God.

 Free Email Publications: Sign up for newsletters on fiction, Christian living, church ministry, parenting, and more.

 Zondervan Bible Search: Find and compare Bible passages in a variety of translations at www.zondervanbiblesearch.com.

 Other Benefits: Register yourself to receive online benefits like coupons and special offers, or to participate in research.